Herbert Hoover and Stanford University

Herbert Hoover and Stanford University

· GEORGE H. NASH ·

HOOVER INSTITUTION PRESS

Stanford University   Stanford, California

Hoover Press Publication 369

First printing, 1988

Manufactured in the United States of America

05 04 03 02 01 00 99 98   08 07 06 05 04 03 02

Incorporated into this work are chapters 3 and 25 of the author's *The Life of Herbert Hoover: The Engineer, 1874–1914* (New York: W. W. Norton, 1983). Reprinted by permission of the publisher.

Photographs courtesy of the Hoover Institution Archives (HIA) *and the Herbert Hoover Presidential Library* (NLH).

Cover illustration of Herbert Hoover by Barbara Mendelsohn, Stanford University News and Publications Service.

Library of Congress Cataloging in Publication Data
Nash, George H., 1945–
    Herbert Hoover and Stanford University.

    Bibliography: p.
    1. Hoover, Herbert, 1874–1964—Contributions in higher education.   2. Stanford University—History.
I. Title.
E802.N367 1988   378.794′73   87-29716
ISBN 0-8179-8691-X
ISBN 0-8179-8692-8 (pbk.)

To Charles and Miriam Palm

Contents

Foreword

Herbert Hoover was many things at many times—engineer, food relief worker, President, author, and statesman—but through it all there existed a strong relationship between the man and his alma mater. From the time he took a train from Oregon to Palo Alto in 1891 until his death in 1964, Herbert Hoover and Stanford University "grew up together"; on each is the mark of the other. It is most fitting that George Nash, the man who has undertaken the exciting but exhausting task of writing the definitive Hoover biography, has written the story of that relationship.

As strong as it would become, the relationship began humbly. Mr. Hoover, who had failed the entrance exam on his first try and was admitted only on the "condition" that he become proficient in English, was among the youngest students in his class. An orphan, he was neither wealthy nor distinguished. But his "strength of will," as a Stanford mathematics professor termed it, took control of him and of his life. It would not be long before he was off and running in the changing and challenging world of the twentieth century.

Much would change in his life, but whether he was in the outback of Australia, the war-torn countryside of Western Europe, the White House, or the New York hotel suite where he spent many of his later years, Mr. Hoover stayed close to his alma mater. Stanford University, as Dr. Nash points out, had given Herbert Hoover a chance. He never forgot that.

Over the years, Herbert Hoover would bring to Stanford many of the buildings and institutions for which it is today so well known. For the Hoover Institution on War, Revolution and Peace, the Student Union, the Food

Research Institute, the Lou Henry Hoover House, and the Graduate School of Business, he was directly responsible. Through his efforts, the Stanford Medical School remained a part of the university. But perhaps his greatest gift to Stanford was the personal interest Mr. Hoover took in it.

The relationship between Mr. Hoover and his university, however, was not always comfortable. In fact, when Mr. Hoover pled with the international community to rescue German-occupied Europe from famine in the midst of World War II, the same Stanford Food Research Institute that he had persuaded the Carnegie Corporation to create "as a contribution to feeding the hungry" claimed there was no famine. He fought regularly with the Board of Trustees and often found fault in the directions taken and decisions made at the university.

In the end, however, Stanford University was Herbert Hoover's alma mater. It was his parent, his child, and his friend. In that context, criticism and even disappointment could come naturally without threatening the ties that bound them together. In *Herbert Hoover and Stanford University*, Dr. Nash captures that remarkable relationship with skill and grace. As a Stanford alum and a great fan of Mr. Hoover, I am grateful to Dr. Nash for his contribution.

At Mr. Hoover's commencement, Stanford president David Starr Jordan told the graduating class that men and women "are judged by achievement, not by dreams." Shortly after World War I, Mr. Hoover himself wrote to a friend: "There is little importance to men's lives except the accomplishments they leave to posterity." More than anyone except Leland and Jane Stanford themselves, Herbert Hoover helped shape Stanford University into the excellent institution it is today. He did much for his country and indeed for the people of the world throughout his long life, but by his own standard and that of its first president, Stanford University now stands as perhaps the best proof of Mr. Hoover's enduring importance.

Mark O. Hatfield
United States Senator

Preface

In less than five years Stanford University will celebrate the centennial of its opening. As every Stanford graduate knows, among the 400 students who gathered in the California sunshine for the inaugural ceremonies on October 1, 1891 was an unassuming Iowa-born orphan named Herbert Hoover who later became President of the United States. Every Stanford graduate also knows that Hoover subsequently did much for the institution of higher learning that gave him the opportunity to transcend his humble origins and achieve success in life.

But few persons to this day realize the profound, abiding, and often hidden influence that Hoover exerted on the development of his alma mater. Not only was he Stanford's most honored alumnus—an engineer, humanitarian, and statesman who lived a life of prodigious accomplishment—he was also for several decades the most influential alumnus in the shaping of Stanford's own destiny. When Hoover died in 1964 at the age of 90, his life and that of his alma mater had intersected for nearly three-quarters of a century. He left behind a record of service to his university that was exceeded only by that of Leland and Jane Stanford themselves.

This volume tells that story. In some ways it is a classically American story of an impecunious youth who strove for a college education, attained it against the odds, did well in the world, and then resolved to do good. It is also the story of a brilliant and indefatigable institution-builder whose influence on his alma mater far exceeded the generous monetary contributions that he gave or was instrumental in obtaining.

Hoover's institutional legacy to Stanford, in fact, was manifold: the archive, library, and international research center that today bears his name; the Stanford Union of which he was rightly called the father; the Food Research Institute that he founded in 1921; the Business School whose creation he inspired and engineered in 1924; the magnificent house on San Juan Hill that has become the official home of Stanford presidents. Other benefactions were less visible. It is still little known, for instance, that Hoover played a crucial role in saving the Stanford Medical School from an early demise in 1914, that at least twice he rescued the university from a debilitating financial morass, that time and again he lent his enormous prestige to enhancing its coffers and its reputation, and that he as much as any other man was responsible for selecting four of Stanford's first five presidents. In a multitude of ways, then (and this list is not exhaustive), Hoover left an enduring imprint on his alma mater.

The extraordinarily close bond between the university and its most famous graduate at times engendered criticism and controversy. Particularly was this true of the great, autonomous war library that evolved into the Hoover Institution. Then, in Hoover's later years, the university's faculty and administration diverged politically from the man his admiring friends called the Chief. The resultant ideological and institutional contention nearly eclipsed his past accomplishments. This, too, is part of the story.

The Stanford Centennial observances, which have already begun, provide a fitting occasion to re-examine and assess this remarkable record. As the university searches for perspective on its past, perhaps it will find in these pages some keys to its self-understanding. I hope also that my monograph will illuminate a fascinating chapter in the history of American higher education—and in the career of an American Renaissance man.

In preparing this book I have benefited from the interest and cooperation of numerous individuals. It is now my pleasure to acknowledge them. At the Hoover Institution on War, Revolution and Peace, W. Glenn Campbell, Charles Palm, Elena Danielson, and the staff of the Hoover Institution Archives were unfailingly generous with their time and expertise. At the Herbert Hoover Presidential Library in West Branch, Iowa, Robert Wood, John Fawcett, Mildred Mather, Dale Mayer, Dwight Miller, Cora Pedersen, Shirley Sondergard, and Patrick Wildenberg were all helpful, as they always are. The library's retired director, Thomas T. Thalken, cordially answered many questions and illuminated the later phases of the Hoover-Stanford relationship. At the Stanford University archives, Roxanne Nilan, Judy Adams, Robin Chandler, Elizabeth Fischbach, and Linda Long answered numerous queries and maintained a standard of cheerful efficiency to which I (and no doubt others) have most agreeably grown accustomed. In the Special Collections Department of the Stanford University Libraries, Margaret Kimball and her associates did the same. In Palo Alto a Stanford alumnus and old friend of the Hoover family, Edgar McDowell, graciously satisfied my curiosity about a number of points.

In the course of conducting research for this volume—and, in some cases, long before—I became acquainted with several other individuals who at various times shared with me their knowledge of Herbert Hoover and Stanford University: Thomas Bailey, Charles Burdick, Birge Clark, David Packard, C. Easton Rothwell, and J. E. Wallace Sterling. I am pleased to acknowledge here their interest and willingness to reminisce.

Of course, while a book may have many sources, in the end it can have but one author, upon whom falls the responsibility for the "product." In the words of a writer in my acquaintance, "I call them as I see them." The narrative that follows is my own.

This monograph is an outgrowth of a multivolume biography-in-progress that I have been invited to prepare by the Herbert Hoover Presidential Library Association, an Iowa-based, nonprofit educational foundation. My first volume in this series was published in 1983 by W. W. Norton & Company of New York City under the title *The Life of Herbert Hoover: The Engineer, 1874–1914*. Chapters 3 and 25 of that volume have been slightly revised and are here reprinted by permission of the publisher. For permission to quote various materials duly cited in the text and notes, I am grateful to the following: the Herbert Hoover Presidential Library Association; the Huntington Library, San Marino, California; and the Stanford University Archives.

For translating my handwritten manuscript into a form fit for a publisher, I express my thanks to three expert typists: Jean Dunbar, Nadine Loescher, and Crystal Wahl. And for shepherding my typescript to publication, I am pleased to acknowledge the conscientious staff of the Hoover Institution Press.

Finally, but never least in my thoughts, is my family, whose support from the beginning has been unstinting.

George H. Nash
May 22, 1987

Editor's Note

In the interest of authenticity, the original spelling and punctuation in quotations have been retained.

· 1 ·

The Road to Palo Alto

Like so many Americans who set root in California in the early twentieth century, Herbert Hoover was an immigrant from the Middle West. Born of Quaker parents in the tiny village of West Branch, Iowa, on August 10, 1874, he experienced the harsh vicissitudes of life at an early—too early—age. Both his parents—Jesse, a blacksmith and a farm implements dealer, and Hulda, a Quaker minister and evangelist—were dead before he was ten, victims of diseases that darkened the idyll of the American frontier. In 1885, at the age of eleven, the orphaned boy was dispatched by solicitous relatives to Oregon and the family of a maternal uncle, Henry John Minthorn. Here, for nearly six years, he would live.

An educator, country doctor, and missionary, Minthorn in 1885 had become superintendent of the newly established Friends Pacific Academy in the Quaker settlement of Newberg, about 30 miles southwest of Portland. In this little school (now George Fox College), Bert Hoover matriculated until he was almost fourteen, earning the rough equivalent of an eighth-grade education. Then, in 1888, Dr. Minthorn resigned his superintendency and moved his family to the state capital of Salem, where, with some associates, he launched the Oregon Land Company to transform the Willamette Valley into an arcadia of fruit orchards and Quaker towns. His nephew Bert became the company's office assistant—and quickly showed an aptitude for business that impressed his enterprising elders.

As Hoover grew into his teens, his thoughts focused increasingly on education. Virtually a high-school dropout (although not, perhaps, by choice), in the fall of 1889 he attended night classes at a local business college in Salem. Here he learned more about mathematics, a further step in a determined effort to improve himself. At about this time he became acquainted with a Presbyterian Sunday School teacher named Jennie Gray, who took a deep interest in the reticent youth and introduced him to classics like *Ivanhoe* and *David Copperfield*. For Hoover such books revealed a world of the imagination that he had barely glimpsed before. Not long afterward, in the summer of 1890, his older brother Theodore (who had been sent from Iowa to Oregon in 1887) returned east with Uncle John's approval to enter William Penn College.

Brother Tad's decision to seek a college education no doubt encouraged Bert to do the same. So, too, did conversations with an engineer who chanced one day to visit the Oregon Land Company's offices. The visitor impressed upon Hoover the importance of university training as preparation for a profession. The visitor's own field, engineering, prompted Hoover to consider this calling with eagerness. The excellent economic prospects for mining engineers in particular refined his ambition. Already eager to get ahead in life, he told a friend that mining engineers were "very scarce" and "just about set their own price."

And so Hoover began to study the catalogues of various institutions. Some of his relatives were anxious that he attend a Friends college like Theodore. According to Hoover, they obtained the promise of a scholarship for him from Earlham College in Indiana. But Herbert was determined to make his own selection and to attend a college which offered instruction in engineering (which Earlham did not). According to Dr. Minthorn's philosophy of life, two things were especially vital to success: "good opportunities" and readiness "to improve the opportunity." In 1891 opportunity came. A new, ambitious, modern university devoted to the ethic of usefulness was arising in California—the creation of Senator Leland Stanford in memory of his son. When entrance examinations for the university were scheduled in Portland in the spring of 1891, Herbert Hoover resolved to take them.

On the day of the examination Hoover performed satisfactorily in the fields he had previously covered. But his studies at the Friends Pacific Academy and at the business college scarcely constituted a complete high-school level of preparation, and his deficiencies were only too apparent. Judged solely by his examination scores, Hoover was not qualified to enter Stanford.

Yet as he struggled, the examiner—Professor Joseph Swain of Stanford's nascent mathematics department—noticed the "strength of will" of this "quiet and serious" youth who spoke "with monosyllables":

> As Mathematics was my own subject I naturally observed him most when he was working at his Plane Geometry questions. I observed that he put his teeth together with great decision and his whole face and posture showed his

determination to pass the examination at any cost. He was evidently summoning every pound of energy he possessed to answer correctly the questions before him. I was naturally interested in him. On inquiry I learned that he had studied only two books of Plane Geometry and was trying to solve an original problem based on the fourth book.

To Swain, Hoover's "method of work" was more revealing of his potential than his inadequate level of preparation. He interviewed the boy afterward and was convinced that he only required an opportunity in order to succeed. Swain decided to admit him. The opposition of Hoover's relatives to his attending a secular university evidently dissolved when Swain, a prominent Quaker, stopped briefly in Salem and informed Dr. Minthorn that his nephew was the kind of student Stanford wanted.

In order to be assured entrance, however, Hoover would have to master the geometry he had not yet studied; this, Professor Swain required. He also suggested that Hoover come to Stanford early for tutoring before additional entrance examinations and the opening of classes in the autumn. Hoover now plunged intently into geometry, poring over books on a table in the upper story of Dr. Minthorn's barn. This was his opportunity; he would spare no effort to "improve" it.

During his six years in Oregon, Hoover had been technically under the supervision of a guardian appointed by a court in Iowa after he had been orphaned. The guardian, a Quaker named Lawrie Tatum, had carefully managed the modest inheritance that had come to Hoover, his brother, and his sister. By August 1891 Hoover's share amounted to $822.67. In that month Tatum reported to the district court of Cedar County, Iowa, that his ward, "an industrious and faithful boy," proposed to enter Stanford University. Tatum recommended that the court grant Hoover his wish; the court agreed.

The worst thing a man can do, Dr. Minthorn often declared, is to do nothing. There is a story, perhaps apocryphal, that as Hoover prepared to depart for California his Grandmother Minthorn prayed he would do a "conscientious work" and that Hoover promised she would someday be proud of him. Certainly he was determined to succeed; as Swain had discerned, he possessed a "superior will." On August 29, 1891, accompanied by a friend named Fred Williams, Herbert Hoover left Salem for Stanford University. Less than three weeks earlier he had reached his seventeenth birthday.[1]

· 2 ·

A Son of the Stanford Red

I

In 1884 Leland Stanford was a wealthy man. Born on a farm in New York, he migrated to California in the 1850s and became its Republican governor in 1861. As one of the "Big Four" railroad titans of the Golden State, he developed the Central Pacific Railroad and helped to bind the nation with ties of steel. Able, energetic, daring, and farsighted, to his contemporaries he personified the American dream: from humble beginnings to remarkable achievement and spectacular success.

As he grew older, Stanford's thoughts centered increasingly on his only son and heir. But in 1884 Leland Stanford, Jr., died of typhoid on a trip to Europe when he was not quite sixteen. Overcome by anguish, his father fell into a fitful slumber and dreamed that he heard his departed son speak: "Father, do not say you have nothing to live for. . . . Live for humanity." The next morning Stanford awoke with words of purpose implanted on his mind and lips: "The children of California shall be my children." He resolved to dedicate his fortune to creating a worthy memorial for his son.

Seven years later, in the summer of 1891, his "monument" was nearly ready. On his ranch of more than 8,000 acres in the Santa Clara Valley, 30 miles south of San Francisco, Stanford, now a United States senator, had supervised the development of a university. With the same acumen that marked his business ventures, he had selected Doctor David Starr Jordan, the youthful president of Indiana University, to transform the still-unfinished assortment of buildings into "a University of high degree." Early that summer Jordan took up residence; gradually the faculty filtered in. Scores of laborers hastened to complete the structures before the students—no one knew how many—arrived. Housing was scarce; roads through the campus were dusty, primitive, and few. The nearest villages were Menlo Park and Mayfield; the city of Palo Alto did not yet exist. No wonder skeptics scoffed at the thought of a university located amidst the senator's stables and vineyards under the hot California sun.[1]

To alleviate the housing shortage, workmen quickly built ten wooden-frame cottages for the faculty along what Jordan named Alvarado Row; students soon would label it "the Decalogue." At the invitation of Jordan, two Eastern schoolteachers trekked across the continent to establish a preparatory school for girls near the campus. An unoccupied farmhouse, later called Adelante Villa, was the only housing Lucy Fletcher and Eleanor Pearson could find, and they promptly converted it into a boardinghouse for early Stanford arrivals.[2] While construction proceeded and the nascent community awaited opening ceremonies, a few faculty members and students sought temporary quarters there. Among them, at the end of August, were "two raw boys from Oregon," Herbert Hoover and Fred Williams.[3]

When Hoover disembarked from the train at Menlo Park and found his way to Adelante Villa, he was seeking more than a place to stay. If he were to seize the opportunity for education that lay almost within his grasp, he must pass the entrance examinations that he had failed in Oregon. In the short time before school opened, he was tutored by Misses Fletcher and Pearson.[4] In return for his board and their coaching, he took care of the tutors' horses.[5]

When examination day came, Hoover successfully met the entrance requirements in arithmetic, elementary algebra, plane geometry, geography, and American history. Discovering that he needed to elect another subject in which to be tested, he chose physiology, studied for a night, and passed.[6] The English language test, however, was too formidable; in this subject he was "conditioned." But his objective had been attained: he was permitted to enroll, with the stipulation that he remove this "condition" before graduation.[7]

A few days before opening day Hoover and Fred Williams were assigned to the men's dormitory, Encina Hall. They were the first Stanford students to occupy rooms in this building.[8] Years later Doctor Jordan recalled that Hoover in fact was the first student to whom he allocated an Encina room. In this sense, Hoover was the first student to enter Stanford University.[9]

On October 1, 1891 Leland Stanford Junior University formally opened before a large and expectant throng. More than 400 students registered that day; they greeted the arriving benefactor with a yell:

> Wah hoo! Wah hoo!
> L. S. J. U.
> Stanford![10]

The ethos of the infant university was easily discernible from the addresses delivered at the convocation. To Senator Stanford, a self-made man, education was "training for usefulness in life,"[11] and in his speech he expounded his philosophy:

> You, students are the most important factor in the university. It is for your benefit that it has been established. To you our hearts go out especially, and in each individual student we feel a parental interest. All that we can do for you is to place the opportunities within your reach. Remember that life is, above all, practical; that you are here to fit yourselves for a useful career; also, that learning should not only make you wise in the arts and sciences, but should fully develop your moral and religious natures.[12]

But not education for oneself alone. While the instruction of its own students was the university's immediate goal, Senator Stanford hoped his creation would contribute to "the general welfare of humanity."[13]

David Starr Jordan—ebullient and optimistic, Emersonian in his rhetoric—expounded further the uplifting vision. Here, he said, was a university, imbued with grand ideals, "hallowed by no traditions" and "hampered by none." "Its finger posts all point forward." "The Golden Age of California begins when its gold is used for purposes like this."[14] In the audience Herbert Hoover listened and was thrilled.[15]

Five hundred fifty-nine students eventually enrolled at Stanford University during its formative year, thereby rendering it at once the largest academic institution in California.[16] For a few days the nearly 300 male students of Encina had to use candles until electricity could be installed. Hot water was not provided until late October. Since the kitchen at Roble Hall, the women's dormitory, was not yet finished, the coeds (or "angels," as they were called) were obliged to take their meals temporarily in the dining hall at Encina. All was excitement and malleability during these first few months. Not without reason did the Class of '95—the first full four-year class—become known as the Pioneers.[17]

As the days passed the students began to organize clubs, athletic teams, and other manifestations of college life.[18] The faculty, meanwhile, instituted Friday evening "at homes" for their students. It was indeed an exciting world, this nascent, still-forming community on Senator Stanford's ranch.

In his first semester at Stanford, Hoover took courses in solid geometry, algebra, trigonometry, linear drawing, freehand drawing, and mechanical engineering (shop). For these he would be graded, as all students were in those days, simply on a pass/fail basis. Perhaps because the head of the geology department had not yet arrived on campus, Hoover initially declared his major as mechanical engineering.[19] But when Doctor John Caspar Branner came at the beginning of 1892, Hoover dropped the courses in drawing and enrolled in Branner's course in geology.[20]

Although Stanford University did not charge tuition, board at Encina Hall cost twenty dollars per month, a considerable sum at a time when student workers were paid around fifteen cents an hour.[21] Like many other students Hoover had no cushion of parental wealth to support him—only the $822.67 that Lawrie Tatum guarded back in Iowa. With board, books, clothing, and sundry other expenses now piling up, this reserve would not last very long. It would be necessary for Hoover to work his way through college.

With the help of Professor Swain he secured a temporary job as a clerk in the Registrar's office.[22] For much of the ensuing year he continued to care for the horses at Adelante Villa—performing his chores twice daily, efficiently, wordlessly.[23] During his freshman year he also delivered newspapers on campus and served as agent for a nearby laundry, using as transportation a discarded old bicycle that he had repaired. At first he collected the laundry and distributed the clean clothing himself. Later he sublet the business and kept the accounts. From these two activities he derived a small but steady income.[24] Sometime after Professor Branner reached campus, Hoover obtained employment as his office assistant, a position he held for most of his undergraduate career.[25] In the second semester of his freshman year, Hoover's labors were interrupted by a case of measles, the effects of which compelled him to wear glasses during much of his remaining time at college.[26]

During this first year, Hoover, one of the youngest in his class, made relatively little impression on those around him, except for one characteristic repeatedly noticed by acquaintances: his shy, abrupt taciturnity. Years later David Starr Jordan recalled him as "a very quiet and almost retiring youngster."[27] Professor Branner's wife remembered him as "always blunt, almost to the point of utter tactlessness." When students came to the Branners' home for evening receptions, Hoover "usually sat back in the corner and listened. He rarely spoke and always seemed to be a little ill at ease."[28] One of his closest student friends, Lester Hinsdale, who sat with him at meals in Encina in freshman year, recalled that Hoover was "very immature in appearance, probably the youngest looking of us all. He seemed shy to the point of timidity—rarely spoke unless spoken to. It wasn't until later, when we got into politics on the same side and I began to see under his surface, that I realized how much it was possible to like him."[29]

Yet slowly he was emerging from his protective shell. At a meeting of the Geological Club in May 1892 he presented a paper.[30] Sometime in his first year he tried out for the freshman baseball team and briefly served as shortstop. Whether because of an injury to his finger (as his friend Will Irwin later reported) or because of his peers' judgment about his ability (as Hoover himself stated), he soon abandoned his player's uniform for the more congenial role of managing the team's finances and schedule.[31]

By far the most spectacular athletic event of the spring was the first football game between Stanford and the University of California, played in San Francisco on March 19, 1892. Ten thousand vociferous fans gathered on the Haight Street grounds for the "Big Game" between the team from Berkeley and the Stanford "kidlets," as their opponents derisively called the upstart challengers. At first the game was delayed for an hour by the ludicrous fact that no one had remembered to bring a football. When, to general astonishment, the inexperienced "kidlets" actually won the contest, 14–10, bedlam reigned among the Stanford supporters.[32] Hoover was there. But—contrary to legend—he had no role in the arrangements and was not the person who forgot to bring the football.[33]

Later that spring Professor Branner offered Hoover a summer job. One of the most eminent geologists of his day, Branner was still serving as director of the Geological Survey of Arkansas. He arranged for Hoover to work as an assistant on the survey with one of Branner's graduate students, John Fletcher Newsom, at a salary of forty dollars a month. Hoover eagerly accepted; it meant practical experience in the field—and income, too. In the summer of 1892, sometimes alone and sometimes with Newsom, he tramped and rode on horseback through the woods and ravines of northern Arkansas, mapping geological formations on the slopes of the Ozark mountains.[34] It was rugged country, populated by suspicious mountaineers and moonshiners whose cabins were the only available shelter at night. It was also a land of rattlesnakes, which sometimes made life unusually interesting.[35] But Hoover was not deterred. Newsom was impressed by his young associate's energy, efficiency, and capacity for work.[36]

II

When Hoover returned to the university for the fall semester, he changed his major from mechanical engineering to geology.[37] During his sophomore year his studies again focused heavily on science, with courses in mineralogy, paleontology, inorganic chemistry, chemistry laboratory, and geology. He also took (and passed) a year-long course in elementary French, his first venture into the humanities.[38]

Discovering that the cost of room and board at Encina had increased substantially, Hoover and several other friends, including Samuel Collins (class of '95), established a cooperative living arrangement in an off-campus boardinghouse known as Romero Hall. Here Hoover roomed during his second year.[39] It was well that he did so, if he could thereby economize. For despite all his jobs during the preceding school year and summer, he had drawn frequently on Lawrie Tatum's dwindling reserves, which now stood at $418.73, scarcely half the total of the year before.[40]

He told a friend about his plans to go into the "baggage business" when school opened. "Dr. B[ranner] says I can swim it[;] if not he will throw in a cork," Hoover reported. "Am working awful hard. Have considerable buisness [sic] worked up & 300000000000 schemes for making more."[41] During this second year he worked for Professor Branner, serving at least part of the time as his assistant in Arkansas Geological Survey work.[42] He also acted as campus agent for a San Jose laundry. In this capacity he met early in the year a tall, lanky, Iowa-born freshman from Riverside, California. Ray Lyman Wilbur (class of '96) instantly took a liking to this quiet, unassuming sophomore who did not condescend to lowly freshmen. Their acquaintance developed into a lifelong friendship.[43] When Wilbur, anxious to work his way through college, sought Hoover's advice, the experienced sophomore counseled: "Do your work so that they notice it and be on the job all of the time."[44]

When classes ended in the spring of 1893, Hoover helped Dr. Branner complete a massive topographical relief map of Arkansas for display at the Chicago World's Fair.[45] Later that summer he seems to have spent some time in Oregon searching for fossils for Branner. Before going back to college he stopped in Salem to see his brother Theodore, who had left William Penn College and was working in the printing trade. To Tad, Bert was no longer "the chubby, small brother" but "a tall, slender sophomore" who "looked very scholarly with glasses."[46] Hoover also visited an old Oregon chum, Burt Brown Barker, and urged him to enroll at Stanford. But Barker, who had been accepted at the University of Chicago, could not be persuaded. Frustrated and annoyed by his friend's intransigence, Hoover climbed into his buggy and said, "Don't go to the University of Chicago. No one goes there except preachers who eat yellow legged chickens." With this parting shot the ardent Stanford loyalist drove off.[47]

III

Hoover received fifteen hours of academic credit—virtually an entire semester's worth—for his modeling and mapmaking work in the department of geology that summer. In the fall semester, with the permission of the faculty, he registered for a heavy nineteen hours of course work in paleontology, mineralogy, civil engineering (surveying), chemistry, and philosophy. In the spring he took more courses in mineralogy, surveying, and chemistry, as well as calculus and a course in mining engineering (assaying).[48] During his junior year he roomed again on campus in Encina and became the local agent for the

United States Laundry Association of San Francisco.[49] By the start of school in September, Lawrie Tatum's fund had sagged to $110.26.[50]

The dramatic events of Hoover's junior year did not occur in the classroom. In 1893 and 1894 the Stanford campus was in ferment, divided between fraternity and nonfraternity students. In its very first year Stanford University had witnessed the introduction of Greek-letter fraternities, whose domination of student affairs increasingly irritated some of the "barbarians" or "barbs," as the nonfraternity students were called. Furthermore, despite the existence of a student constitution and officers, little system or financial accountability prevailed in the management of student activities. Athletic events in particular, involving substantial receipts and the reputation of the Associated Students, were largely unsupervised. As Ray Lyman Wilbur observed, "Student organizations had been rather loosely set up, with no central treasury. They had a football manager and a baseball manager who sold tickets and were accountable for the most part to no one. The Glee Club had developed a habit of going off on trips and leaving debts that were not paid, although contracted in the name of the Associated Students."[51]

To the restless "barbs" the situation was intolerable, and so a reform movement commenced. The first manifestation of the "barbarian" rebellion was the election of E. R. Zion (class of '94) as president of the student body in September of 1893. Students called him "Sosh" Zion (for "Socialist") because of his frequent battles against the status quo. During the winter Zion and his executive committee labored to devise a new student constitution to replace the ineffectual document adopted in October 1891.[52]

Years later many who reminisced about these exciting days tended to attribute to Hoover unique or pre-eminent leadership of the reformers.[53] Such an allocation of responsibility was exaggerated. It was Zion who chaired the student executive committee that drafted and presented the proposed constitution. Hoover was not a member of this committee, nor were such other "barb" leaders as Lester Hinsdale, Sam Collins, and Herbert Hicks.[54] Nevertheless, in the high councils and behind-the-scenes strategy sessions that preceded and accompanied the executive committee's work, Herbert Hoover undoubtedly played his part. One sign of his emerging status appeared on January 23, 1894, when 140 Pioneers held a class meeting. On nomination by Sam Collins (who had first gotten him interested in politics at Romero Hall), Herbert Hoover was unanimously elected treasurer of the junior class.[55]

On February 28 the proposed new constitution was printed in the student newspaper, the *Daily Palo Alto*.[56] The desire to systematize and centralize control of financial and athletic activities was patent. One of the executive committee's principal objectives was to insure that "the treasurer of the Associated Students be such in fact as well as in name, and have charge of all money collected by the various teams. . . ."[57] Accordingly, the draft constitution provided that the treasurer would "collect and have charge of all funds of the association" and would disburse these funds to groups who presented requisitions, which would be audited. The constitution further stipulated that no football, baseball, or track manager could incur debts exceeding five hundred dollars "without the sanction of the president and treasurer of the association."

Early in March an aroused student body gathered to consider the constitution. As originally drafted, the document provided that the athletic managers should receive a percentage of the net profits derived from their team's contests. Many students from Hoover's faction supported this idea. Hoover himself, at one meeting, unsuccessfully moved that each athletic manager be paid 25 percent of the first $1,000 in profits and 15 percent of the rest. The idea of a "remunerative clause," however, evoked a storm of opposition, and in the end all forms of it were defeated. As finally adopted, the constitution did not provide for the payment of any officers.[58]

The stage was now ready for the final struggle: the election of the first officers. Elections were to be held in April, with the winners to take office in the fall. As the "barb" leaders pondered slots on the ticket, the name of Herbert Hoover came up as a possible candidate for the key position of treasurer. There was logic in the thought. He was already treasurer of the Pioneer Class and was thoroughly experienced in the laundry agency and other enterprises requiring financial and organizational ability.[59] As a close friend of Collins and Hinsdale, he had been active in the "barb push" and had joined in the debate to adopt the constitution. In the eyes of the "barb" politicians, he possessed another asset. Since he was earning his way through college, he might win the voters in the "Camp," four rough barracks originally used to house workmen but now inhabited by undergraduates who could not afford to live in Encina.[60]

Would Hoover agree to run for treasurer? Years later several of his friends recalled that a matter of principle initially made him hesitant. According to one version, before he accepted he insisted that the new constitution include a clause that the treasurer receive no salary until the second year. He did not want to be accused of supporting a salary for the treasurer and then seeking the position; such a stance would smack of self-interest.[61] Another version asserted that he favored a salary but vowed that he would not take it if elected.[62] In fact, however, when the proposed constitution was first published in late February, it contained a reference only to the athletic managers' compensation.[63] The document's silence about the treasurer's salary may have reflected Hoover's opposition. In any case, when the Associated Students of Leland Stanford Junior University assembled on April 11, 1894 to determine officers for the coming election, Hoover was among those nominated for treasurer, Lester Hinsdale for president, and Herbert Hicks (class of '96) for football manager. These three posts were considered the most prestigious.[64]

For the next few days the fury of a political hurricane gripped the campus. Parades, speeches, demonstrations, midnight caucuses, get-out-the-vote drives, even a campaign slogan:

> Rah! Rah! Rix!
> Hinsdale! Hoover! Hicks!
> Barbs on top
> And the frats in a fix![65]

On election day, 686 students—a phenomenal 85 percent of the electorate—cast ballots. The vote was close and, for most of the major offices, inconclusive. For president: Hinsdale, 336; Magee, 330; others 6. Hinsdale had failed by one vote to gain a majority. For treasurer: Hoover, 253; Grosh, 235; White, 180. For football manager, a similar result. No one had attained a majority; a runoff would be necessary.[66]

Another week of frenzy and calculation followed. Hoover and his colleagues methodically compiled lists of voters and delegated their lieutenants to solicit the support of "queeners," coeds, every constituency, every vote.[67] No resource was overlooked. During the tumult President Jordan was heard to wonder aloud whether he was "presiding over a young Tammany Hall."[68] When the votes were cast and counted on April 24, the "Three H" ticket won. Hinsdale, 380; Magee, 274. Hoover, 370; Grosh, 282. Hicks, 375; Kessinger, 285.[69] That night the "three H's" celebrated in the barbs' stronghold. So packed was the room in Encina that the victors, carrying boxes of cigars in each hand, had to be lifted and passed overhead to a spot near the window.[70] As the *Daily Palo Alto* reported, cigars and lemonade were "freely dispensed" to the exultant crowd.[71]

There was one election that Hoover did not win that spring. Early in May he was a candidate for business manager of the *Daily Palo Alto* for the coming year. But when the Board of Control of the newspaper met to consider the five applicants, another student was selected.[72]

By now, no doubt, Hoover's attention was turning to the summer. In mid-April the campus newspaper reported that he had been appointed an assistant on the United States Geological Survey for the coming vacation.[73] Probably through Professor Branner, he obtained a summer job with Doctor Waldemar Lindgren, one of the outstanding geologists in the United States. For some reason Hoover's initial assignment to work in southern Oregon fell through, and when summer arrived his job prospects were indefinite.[74] So in early June, Hoover, Zion, Collins, and some other friends drove a team of horses from Palo Alto to Yosemite Valley, nearly 300 miles away. Along the way they painted and posted advertising signs for the *San Francisco Examiner*, thereby paying for the trip. While vacationing in Yosemite, Hoover received a telegram that he could now join Lindgren after all, in the California Sierras instead of Oregon. Despite the attraction of remaining with his comrades, Hoover immediately seized the opportunity. He set out alone on foot for the river boats at Stockton, more than 80 miles away.[75]

On July 1, 1894, having joined Lindgren in the mountains, Hoover officially became an employee of the U.S. Geological Survey. This was the summer of the great Pullman railroad strike led by Eugene V. Debs, and because of it Hoover was unable to begin work for three weeks. Finally, late in July, Lindgren and his little expedition (consisting of Hoover and the cook) broke camp at Placerville and headed for the High Sierras southwest of Lake Tahoe.[76] Here, in the Pyramid Peak district (30 by 40 miles square), Hoover spent the rest of the summer assisting Lindgren in studying glaciation and in mapping the Pyramid Peak sheet.[77]

It was rugged territory, including (Hoover wrote) "the roughest country that God or man ever saw."[78] And living conditions were not exactly luxurious. At one point he informed Professor Branner:

> Kindly pardon this horrible effort, but remember that I sit astride a log and write on one knee with 63 big black ants pasturing on my epidermis and have to listen to the delightful bellow of the calf who likes our barley.
>
> We use five horses, have a *cook*, the most important man in the party, about 5:30 at night. Have Ham and Boston Baked beans and buckwheat cakes instead of sowbelly and cornbread. Sleep on the ground—away ahead of an Arkansas bed.[79]

But he was learning a great deal—"getting a whole jug full of experience"[80]—and pleasing Dr. Lindgren besides. "Never have I had a more satisfactory assistant," Lindgren later declared. The geologist was struck by Hoover's eagerness to learn, his precision in recording his data, and his "keen instinct" for solving problems in the simplest manner.[81] At first Hoover received twenty dollars a month as the geologist's assistant; later Lindgren raised it to thirty.[82]

Because of Lindgren's delays in getting underway in July, his field work had fallen behind schedule. Hoover therefore wrote to Dr. Branner on September 2 of his decision to remain in the Sierras at Lindgren's invitation until October 1. It would mean, however, that he would miss the first three weeks of the fall semester. Since this apparently violated a university rule requiring complete attendance during the senior year, he boldly asked Branner to "fix it somehow."[83] Later in the month Branner thanked Lindgren for giving Hoover an opportunity to serve as his assistant: "I'm confident that he is as faithful and hardworking a man as one can find."[84] Lindgren enthusiastically agreed: "He is as you say a faithful and hardworking man and has done very well indeed this summer; I have been very glad to have had his assistance for I could not have finished this sheet without efficient help."[85]

As it turned out, Hoover did not return to the campus until October 14, more than five weeks late.[86] But he had ample reason to be happy, as he confided to a friend:

> Learned much and am better morally, physically & financially than 6 months ago. Pleased the cheif [sic] some and am in consequence sceduled [sic] to return to the U S Geol Survey June 1st 1895. The position to be perminent [sic] in all probability. Salary—if perminent [sic]—$1200.00 a year to start.[87]

If Branner was disturbed that his protégé had missed more than a month of classes, the record does not show it. Instead the university awarded Hoover eight hours of academic credit for his summer's labors.[88]

IV

In its first three years Stanford University had grown substantially; in 1894–1895 its enrollment exceeded 1,000.[89] Self-confident and determined, Hoover, now treasurer of the student community, concentrated on his new duties. Instituting a voucher system that he had learned while assisting Dr. Lindgren, he strove to establish efficiency where chaos had previously reigned.[90] According to Lawrie Tatum's 1894 report to the court in Iowa, he was "frugal, industrious, and energetic."[91] These were precisely the qualities he now showed.

Hoover soon let it be known that, from now on, every expenditure must be justified, every disbursement must be documented. The story is told that one day a football player informed Hoover that he needed new football shoes. "Let's see your shoes," the treasurer replied. After examining the pair, Hoover declared, "What you need is a pair of new laces," and authorized them instead.[92] Such a response was unlikely to win many friends. But Hoover was not interested in popularity. He wanted order—and influence.

Not everyone on campus was pleased by his relentless insistence on strict accounting and scrupulous attention to detail.[93] Perhaps this was why in November 1894 the *Daily Palo Alto*, in response to "numerous inquiries," published a lengthy explanation of the new constitution. Among other things, the newspaper pointed out that the treasurer "receives all incomes from games, annual dues, etc., directly, and with the advice of the president advances such sums to managers as exigencies may require." Furthermore, no athletic manager could contract a debt exceeding five hundred dollars without the approval of the treasurer and president of the Associated Students.[94] In other words, the power of the purse now lay with the treasurer, not with the managers of the teams.

If any opposition did manifest itself, Hoover seems not to have noticed. On October 30 he published his first financial report in the student newspaper. It revealed the distressing fact that the student body was more than $1,200 in debt, including $550 still outstanding from the previous three years. No wonder, he remarked, that the student body had "an unenviable reputation for careless financiering."[95] Further research disclosed that the old debts totaled at least six hundred dollars.[96] Throughout the fall and winter months Hoover arranged to pay off these accumulated liabilities and to rationalize student finances. Football "absorbs everything—all my time," he wrote to a friend in November.[97] Frequently he traveled off campus. He accompanied the football team on some of its trips, made arrangements for the fourth "Big Game" against Berkeley at Thanksgiving, and even went to Los Angeles at Christmas for the football contests against the University of Chicago and another club.[98] Often his balance sheets and reports appeared on the front page of the *Daily Palo Alto*.[99]

Before Christmas, Hoover was able to announce that the Associated Students organization was "a solvent body, the first time since its birth," a statement that earned the student newspaper's encomium for the "business acumen of the treasurer."[100] When Hoover produced an elaborate report in January for the football season showing a substantial surplus, another student journal editorialized:

> For the first time in the history of Stanford athletics an itemized account of all receipts and expenditures of the football season has been rendered. It was a pleasant surprise to read Treasurer Hoover's report in the *Daily Palo Alto*. His books have been kept in a businesslike way and are thrown open to the students, something before unheard of . . . . Treasurer Hoover is to be highly commended for the precedent he has established.[101]

The system that Hoover inaugurated remained virtually unchanged for years.[102]

Since Hoover received no salary as treasurer, it was necessary to scrape up an income from other sources. By the beginning of Hoover's senior year Lawrie Tatum's guardianship fund had diminished to a mere $12.74.[103] During his senior year Hoover undoubtedly earned some money as Professor Branner's assistant. A campus lecture and concert bureau that he and some other friends operated also helped to tide him over.[104]

For all his activism Hoover continued to be somewhat introverted, a kind of "impersonal force" with a "surface repression," as a Stanford friend once put it.[105] Years later many Stanford alumni of those pioneer days still retained an image of him as slightly stooped and diffident, with a tendency to avert his gaze. Some noticed his habit of thrusting his hands in his pockets and jingling his change.[106] When Will Irwin was injured playing football, the student treasurer came to his room to determine the cost of the plaster cast. Although Irwin felt that Hoover was sympathetic, Hoover did not at first utter a word of commiseration; demonstrativeness did not come easily. Irwin never forgot how, as he left, Hoover "jerked out" the words "I'm sorry." [107]

Yet Hoover was not all aloofness and reticence. His few surviving letters from this period reveal a good-humored, active personality. If not naturally gregarious, he nevertheless impressed many friends. According to Irwin, Hoover participated willingly in his share of the "rushes," practical jokes, and pranks of the high-spirited student community.[108] Behind the mask, in fact, was a clever mind. One night he and some friends decided to race around the oval track in the darkness to determine who was the fastest. When the contest was over, Hoover had easily won. His friends were amazed. Back in the dorm he cheerfully divulged the secret of his success. At the start he had deliberately dropped behind, crossed the infield, and placidly waited at the finish line. His comrades gleefully rewarded his "victory" by throwing him in the shower.[109]

Early in his senior year an unexpected influence entered Hoover's life: a freshman named Lou Henry enrolled in the geology program at Stanford. It was unusual, if not unprecedented, for a woman to select such a field of study. Hoover became interested in this tall, lithe, athletic young woman who so easily defied the conventions of the time. The more he became acquainted with her in laboratory work, field trips, and social gatherings, the more impressed he became.

It turned out that Lou Henry had been born in Waterloo, Iowa—only 70 miles from West Branch—in March 1874. Ten years later she had migrated to California with her parents and sister, Jean, because it was feared that her mother had tuberculosis. Since 1890 the family had lived in Monterey, where her father was a successful banker. Lacking a son, Charles Henry had raised his daughter Lou to be an outdoor woman, proficient at horseback riding, camping, fishing, and marksmanship. They had taken strenuous hikes together in the hills.

In 1893 Lou graduated from San Jose Normal School (now San Jose State University) in preparation for a career as a teacher. During the following year, she was assistant cashier of her father's bank and then a third-grade school-teacher in Monterey. But then one of those chance events occurred that change the course of a life. She heard Professor Branner deliver an extension lecture on geology; it inspired her enormously. Swiftly she determined to enter Stanford and study with this gifted teacher. By the second semester of her freshman year, she and the student body treasurer were more than casual friends.[110]

Hoover was a big man on campus now and enjoying himself thoroughly. "I have vertually [sic] control of affairs," he wrote a friend in November, "and am making a hard effort to pay of[f] our old indebtedness of $600.00 & conduct the present foot-ball season successfully."[111] He was in the thick of efforts to reform the management of the campus co-op store.[112] In January 1895 he was elected president of the Geological Club for the second semester. In January, also, he left the campus for a few days on a trip to Yuba County to complete some Geological Survey work left undone the summer before.[113] In mid-January he was nominated to be Class of '95 treasurer but declined.[114]

At some point early in his senior year (or possibly at the end of his junior year) Herbert Hoover, "barbarian" leader, was even invited to become a member of the Stanford chapter of the Sigma Alpha Epsilon fraternity. Apparently this offer was momentarily tempting, for he "gave it some consideration" and may have accepted briefly. After thinking it over, however, and possibly at the urging of his friends, Hoover decided not to abandon the ranks of his associates and supporters. And so a "barb" he remained.[115]

But now, at mid-year, crisis loomed—the consequence of too much whirl. Not only had Hoover missed the first five weeks of classes; in November he acknowledged that his time-consuming treasurer's work was "a bigger job than I bargained for." Already Professor Branner had warned him that he "must quit at the end of the semester and go to studying." "You may be able to Graduate all right," said Branner, "but we are not turning out A.B.'s but Geologists."[116] When his first-term grades came in, they were a disaster: Hoover had flunked German outright and had been "conditioned" in his two other courses. In short, he received no credit for an entire semester.[117]

To salvage the situation, Hoover, with faculty approval, registered for eighteen hours of courses in the second semester, including nineteenth-century history, personal hygiene, ethics, and three courses in geology.[118] In addition, he strove to eliminate the conditions that he had just incurred. It no doubt took some buckling down, but in the end he passed.[119]

Only one obstacle—the nemesis of his undergraduate career—remained. Despite several attempts, he had not yet removed his entrance condition in the English language.[120] Professor Anderson of the English department insisted that no student should graduate unless he or she could demonstrate the ability to write accurate English. Unfortunately, Hoover's spelling and punctuation were still noticeably irregular.[121] In the waning days of his senior year, the nagging requirement assumed ominous proportions.

Finally, just a few days before graduation, Professor J. P. Smith, from whom Hoover had taken courses in mineralogy and paleontology, came to his rescue. He handed Hoover a course paper that Hoover had submitted to him some time before, a paper that, in content, was satisfactory. He instructed

Hoover to rewrite it with meticulous attention to spelling, grammar, and punctuation. When Hoover returned, Smith corrected and refined the paper thoroughly, had Hoover recopy it, and then confronted the head of the English department with the finished product. The English professor accepted it as adequate evidence of improvement and Hoover was duly passed in English composition. Without Smith's assistance Hoover probably would not have received his diploma. [122]

Somehow during these last weeks of college Hoover found time for a final burst of extracurricular activities. With Lou Henry at his side he attended the Junior Hop in April. [123] When he ran short of cash for the Senior Ball, he borrowed $7.50 from his brother, Theodore, who had just moved to the Bay Area. [124] Hoover did not miss a single major social event that spring—becoming, in his words, "quite a social swell." And all the while, as student body treasurer, he "ran baseball field athletics and did about as much politics as ever." [125] He helped the "barbs" sweep the campus elections in the spring. [126]

Early in his senior year he privately told a friend that he favored a salary for the treasurer of the Associated Students. [127] Shortly before he graduated, the student body amended the constitution so that the treasurer would henceforth be a postgraduate who would receive a monthly salary. Hoover supported the change. But when he was nominated for another term he declined, probably because he did not plan to be on campus in the coming year. Instead, his friend Lester Hinsdale was elected. [128]

By graduation Hoover had earned a reputation as a student politician, skilled at behind-the-scenes maneuvering and calculation. He found himself humorously memorialized in the class yearbook. Under a picture of Hoover, Zion, and Collins, clad in olive wreaths and togas, appeared these words:

> We are the great triumvirate,
> The awful Trinity of Fate.
> On things scholastic or athletic
> We speak with utterance prophetic.
> This place, we Three, by love inspired,
> Have scientifically wired;
> And so (our motives all the best)
> When an election comes, with zest
> We press the buttons and do the rest. [129]

In four years Stanford University had done much for Herbert Hoover. It had trained him in geology and brought him into rewarding association with several distinguished scientists, particularly John C. Branner and Waldemar

Lindgren. Since Stanford used the pass/fail grading system it is impossible to determine precisely Hoover's record in his major. He was certainly a capable, although probably not a brilliant, student. One of his professors, C. D. Marx, later told an interviewer that, while Hoover was a good student, he was not pre-eminent and was distinguished more for his "first class executive ability" than for intellectual achievement. [130]

But that he was able, resourceful, and ambitious, no one denied. "Do your work so that they notice it and be on the job all of the time." It was this quality that had first impressed Dr. Branner. When he asked Hoover to accomplish something, Hoover did so quickly and quietly, without fuss and bother. [131] "It was characteristic of him," Branner once remarked, "that when a task was set before him he took off his coat, fixed his whole attention on the task in hand, and went at it, and did it." [132] There is a story that one day in the lab Dr. Branner overheard some students grumbling about "Hoover's luck." Branner immediately admonished them, contrasting their behavior with Hoover's ability to get things done. Hoover, he exclaimed, had not enjoyed "luck"; he had received "reward." [133]

Stanford University had done even more for Herbert Hoover. It had inculcated in him an ethos of adventurousness, resourcefulness, and idealism, an ethos that fit well with his determination to succeed. It had reinforced, in secular terms, the lessons of his Quaker relatives: that one should live productively, that life is meant for accomplishment, that one ought to do a "conscientious work." To the assembled Pioneers of the Class of '95 at commencement, President David Starr Jordan invoked such themes. Men and women, he said, "are judged by achievements, not by dreams." "The highest value of tradition lies in the making of it; the noblest wealth is the wealth of promise. . . . In helpfulness alone can wealth or power find consecration." [134] For at least one senior in the audience the message had enduring impact.

Above all, Stanford University had offered the Iowa-born orphan an opportunity—a gift he never forgot. In that self-reliant, pioneering community-in-the-making, created on a ranch by a self-made man and dedicated to the ideal of "direct usefulness in life," Hoover grew and thrived and found warmth. It was an exhilarating environment, and it made an indelible imprint. His alma mater became, in Will Irwin's apt phrase, "a kind of complex" with Hoover. [135] "The children of California shall be my children." For the rest of his life, wherever he roamed or resided, Stanford University was his home.

On May 29, 1895 Hoover received his A.B. in geology. [136] His worldly assets amounted to forty dollars. [137] Around commencement time a Stanford trustee remarked to Dr. Branner, "I wonder if there are many of our boys who will attempt to do anything in return for this education which has been given them?" After a moment's pause Branner said, "I call your attention to *one* young man, Herbert Hoover." Of all his student assistants, he added, Hoover "is the only one who brings me the work *finished*." [138]

Neither man could yet know that Hoover's work for Stanford had only begun.

· 3 ·

The Alumnus
Becomes a Benefactor

I

After working again for the U.S. Geological Survey in the summer of 1895, and then for a short time as an underground laborer in mines near Nevada City, California, Hoover in 1896 joined the staff of Louis Janin, a San Francisco–based mining engineer, one of the ablest of his profession in the West. It did not take Hoover long to impress his eminent employer. Early in 1897, the British firm of Bewick, Moreing & Company sought an experienced American engineer to undertake mine examination and exploration work in the remote gold-mining regions of Western Australia. Contacted for advice, Janin recommended his youthful assistant, even though Hoover was not yet 23 and the British firm wanted a man of at least 35. To conceal his callow appearance, Hoover prudently grew a beard—and headed, via London and the Suez Canal, for the distant continent "down under."

From the spring of 1897 until November 1898 Hoover worked in the rough, forbidding "outback" of Western Australia, a country (he wrote) of "red dust[,] black flies and white heat." It was, he said, "an endless desert, no water no nothing but mines." [1] In so many ways it was a land to make him think of home. Writing to his cousin while on a trip into the desolate "bush," he declared: "Am on my way back to Coolgardie. Am glad to get back within the borders of civilization. Coolgardie is three yards inside of it; Perth is about a mile, and of course San Francisco is the center. Anybody who envies me my salary can just take my next trip with me, and he will then be contented to be a bank clerk at $3 a week the rest of his life, just to live in the United States. Stanford is the best place in the world." [2]

Nevertheless, Hoover persevered and triumphed. Within a year and a half the laconic Yankee engineer had established himself as one of the most respected mining men in the entire colony and as the successful superintendent of the Sons of Gwalia, one of the greatest gold mines in Australian history. "Hail Columbia" Hoover, they called him (after his first and middle initials, H.C.). Hundreds of miners were under his command. His salary was in the vicinity of $10,000 a year.

Then, toward the end of 1898, a new and even larger opportunity beckoned: Bewick, Moreing & Company asked him to go to China to guard its expanding interests in the Celestial Empire and to serve as technical consultant to the Director-General of Mines for two of China's most important provinces. Hoover accepted—and turned his thoughts to a girl back home. During his three years since leaving Stanford, his affection for Lou Henry had not diminished. In mid-1898 she had graduated with a degree in geology—the first woman at Stanford, and possibly the first woman in the history of American higher education, to graduate with a concentration in this subject. Now she was living with her parents in Monterey. Before leaving Australia Hoover dispatched a cable to his Lou: Would she marry him? By cable she replied that she would.

On February 10, 1899, then, Herbert Hoover and Lou Henry took their wedding vows in her parents' living room in Monterey. The next day they sailed from San Francisco for Tientsin, China, where they lived for more than two years. During this time Hoover became engineer-in-chief of the Chinese government's Mining Bureau in Chihli and Jehol and co-manager of the company that operated the vast, almost legendary Kaiping coal mines. Success was following success for the hustling young American engineer.

By 1901 Hoover was reputed to be "the highest salaried man of his years in the world"; so at least a San Francisco newspaper reported after interviewing him upon his return from China.[3] Not yet 28 years old, he now became a full partner in the prestigious Bewick, Moreing & Company, a position from which he retired in 1908. From then until 1914 he was on his own as an international freelance mining engineer and financier. Although London—world hub of mining promotion and finance—was his base of operations from 1901 until World War I, the scope of his endeavors was worldwide: from California to Korea, Siberia to South Africa, Burma to Trinidad, the oil fields of the southern Caucasus to the zinc-lead-silver mines of Broken Hill, New South Wales. It was a restless, peripatetic existence; he later calculated that he spent more than 100 weeks of his life—virtually two years—on ships at sea. Several times his journeys circled the globe. Permeating his career during this period was a determined, unrelenting drive for success. "If a man has not made a fortune by 40 he is not worth much," he said more than once to a friend.[4]

During these "years of adventure" (as he afterwards called them),[5] the United States—and his alma mater—were never far from his thoughts. Perhaps it was during his sojourn around Nevada City in late 1895 that he first heard the tale of a merchant in the California Sierras who once gave away an expensive stock of provisions to an injured prospector living alone in a shack in the hills. The incident had occurred during the Gold Rush days of the early 1850s; Hoover made it the subject of a short story that appeared in a Stanford University magazine in January 1896. This literary effort was his first publication; he entitled it "And Their Deeds Are Remembered After Them." The philanthropic storekeeper, he revealed, was Leland Stanford.[6]

Wherever Hoover traveled, the influence of his alma mater radiated. To Australia and to China he brought Stanford men (including old friends) to be his mining associates. In Tientsin, in the spring of 1900, he and Lou organized an alumni association consisting of the seven Stanford graduates already living in China.[7] In London the Hoovers entertained ceaselessly. Their rambling old villa known as the Red House became a "mecca for Californians," especially traveling Stanford alumni and faculty, including David Starr Jordan himself.[8] It was also home for two little Hoover boys: Herbert (born in 1903) and Allan (born in 1907).

By the summer of 1914 Hoover, just turning 40, was at the pinnacle of his profession. He was a director of eighteen mining and financial companies having an authorized share capital of more that $55 million and interests on nearly every continent. At least 100,000 men were employed in enterprises for which he was partly, even primarily, responsible. As early as 1907 he had told David Starr Jordan that he was earning $100,000 a year.[9] By the month of his 40th birthday his total assets undoubtedly exceeded one million dollars.[10]

Hoover was proud of his success, proud and apparently sensitive. About 1913, on a visit to Stanford, he proposed to a professor of engineering that a few faculty members receive prize professorships with super-salaries. Evidently Hoover felt that such a system would foster and reward individual merit. The professor, however, disagreed. A huge disparity in faculty salaries, he argued, would subvert faculty morale. Furthermore, it might lure "mercenary" individuals to the university. At this remark Hoover angrily clenched his fist and pounded on the window sill. "After all," he replied, "the dollar is the counter of the game—and to have it shows that you have played the game successfully.[11]

Yet like other self-made men of wealth in this era, Hoover yearned to do more. Success had come too hard for him to scorn the counters, but, as he told friends, the counters did not interest him any more. To a Stanford faculty friend in 1908 he divulged his desire to "stop making money" and take up a life of service in the United States.[12] Time and again he repeated this sentiment to callers at the Red House.[13]

Six thousand miles away, the administration of Stanford University was keenly aware of Hoover's spectacular achievements in his profession and of his deepening interest in a new career as an altruist. As early as 1902 David Starr Jordan acclaimed him to Stanford freshmen as the university's pre-eminent graduate, a man whose life of usefulness was just beginning.[14] For many undergraduates he was already the "Ideal Alumnus."[15] Jordan was eager to promote the young university's first great success story. In 1910, after visiting the Hoovers in London, he enthusiastically notified President William Howard Taft of Hoover's availability for "executive service." The American engineer, said Stanford's president, had "no superior in executive work" and would "make himself felt" if he entered public life "in any capacity."[16] Three years later Jordan learned that President Woodrow Wilson was thinking of seeking an independent engineer's assessment of the Panama Canal then being built. Possibly at Hoover's instigation, Jordan wrote a letter in his behalf to the new president.[17]

Nothing came of these particular exertions. But by 1914, and even before, Hoover in a variety of ways had signaled his aspiration for a life of benefaction. In 1912 he told an old friend from college days, Will Irwin, that he was rich—"as rich as any man has much right to be." To Irwin he also confided his dream of retiring from his profession and returning to the United States. But what will you do? Irwin asked. "Get into the big game somewhere," Hoover replied. "Just making money isn't enough."[18]

II

No, the singleminded amassing of a fortune could not suffice. Hoover, to be sure, did not disdain the "game" of making money. He enjoyed the thrill of maneuver, the challenge of conceiving and executing a plan, the joy of constructive accomplishment, the mental exercise of wheeling and dealing in the shark-infested waters of London mining finance. To stand at the pinnacle, to manage men and resources: in Hoover's words, to "co-ordinate and control the best efforts of other people"[19]—this was deeply satisfying, and at it he excelled. But the simple pursuit of wealth no longer encompassed his ambition.

"Get into the big game somewhere." Whence had arisen this budding altruism, this growing restlessness with purely financial success? Was it a legacy of his childhood Quakerism, of his relatives' teaching that he should accomplish something useful in the world? Was it an expression of his engineering professionalism, with its ethic of disinterested achievement? Probably these influences had some effect. But there was another.

"Get into the game." The words were David Starr Jordan's when he addressed the graduating seniors of Stanford University in 1905, while Hoover visited the campus for his tenth class reunion. Get into the game. "Whatever you have acquired," said Jordan, "should be an impulse for action."

> If you have planned somewhat, then carry out your plans. If you have learned the nature of something, then turn your knowledge into execution. If you have gained higher aspirations, these count for nothing except as you try to make them good . . . .
> Get into the game, somehow, somewhere. Carry your thoughts over into action. Do your part, and the greatest surprise of your life will come the day when you find out how great that part may be.[20]

Jordan's message was not new. He had expounded it before—to Herbert Hoover, among others, during the pioneer days of Stanford University. It was, in fact, the "Stanford spirit" that Jordan in his ebullient way was extolling, a spirit of idealism mixed with practicality, of doing good fused with doing well.

And now this spirit—so deeply imbued in Hoover in his impressionable undergraduate days—was drawing him toward a second career. By his mid-thirties Hoover's urge to do well financially was yielding to a yearning to do good. As he groped towards a new vocation of useful service, his first efforts focused on the place he now considered home: Stanford University, the principal positive experience of his early life; Stanford University, "the best place in the world."

III

Hoover's benefactions to his alma mater began early. While in Australia in 1897–1898 he constituted himself a veritable one-man scholarship fund, discreetly funneling a large portion of his income through Lester Hinsdale to relatives and friends who were now striving to complete their educations—relatives like his brother Theodore, who had entered Stanford and was to graduate in 1900.[21] Several intimate friends from his undergraduate days also received assistance at various times. As Hoover told Hinsdale, a fledgling attorney in San Francisco, "I want to give any of my old pards who are struggling along a lift now that I am making something. . . ."[22]

Characteristically, however, he concealed his acts of generosity. He instructed Hinsdale to be "a sphinx about matters of mine."[23] Not even his beneficiaries always realized the source of their good fortune. Ray Lyman Wilbur, one of his closest friends, did not discover until years later that Hoover had sent money from Australia to finance Wilbur's way through medical school. And then he only learned this fact from Hinsdale; Hoover himself never mentioned it.[24] "Doing good deeds by stealth," one friend called it.[25] It was a trait that was to find repeated expression in the decades ahead.

Having embarked upon the path of philanthropic giving, Hoover never paused or deviated. Starting in 1902 he quietly paid the salary of one of the university's librarians, a practice that continued for several years.[26] After the 1906 San Francisco earthquake, he offered Professor Branner $1,000 to publish an earthquake investigation as a Stanford University publication.[27] In 1910 he offered another $1,000 to finance Branner's geology expedition to Brazil.[28] By World War I, he had helped several relatives obtain an education—and would assist still others in the decades ahead.[29]

An ardent bibliophile, Hoover contributed generously toward the enrichment of the university's book collections. Early in 1907 a young Stanford history instructor, Payson J. Treat, crossed Hoover's path in Colombo during a trip to get acquainted with his area of specialty, the Far East. When Hoover learned of Treat's purpose, he replied, "Well, you'll get nowhere without books. As you travel, buy $1,000 worth of books and send the bill to me."[30] A little later Hoover and another Stanford alumnus jointly donated £250 more (about $1,200) for further book purchases by Treat in the same field.[31] All of Treat's acquisitions went to the Stanford University Library, with the result that by 1908 Stanford had the best collection of Australian books of any library in the United States.[32] In 1913 Hoover donated to the university his own collection of 500–600 volumes on China alone, including a rare complete set of early Jesuit publications on China. He estimated his collection to be worth between $4,000 and $5,000.[33]

Such acts of liberality—most of them unpublicized—would have been enough for most alumni, but Hoover wished to do more. In one of his earliest known statements about his future, he confided his ambition in November 1906 to Treat, who was visiting him in London. "The plan," Treat later recalled,

> was, in a few years he would be able to retire from the engineering firm and he wanted to go back to California, make a home on the Stanford campus and spend the rest of his life doing something for the University. He thought he could probably be helpful in the organization and development of their financial resources and also perhaps in their instruction in mining.[34]

Treat was profoundly impressed: here was Hoover, only 32 years old, with an objective like this! Hoover's idealism was not the only quality that struck his visitor. "After being with him for a whole day," Treat later stated, "I wrote in my journal . . . that Mr. Hoover had the best stored and most accurate, and most accessible mind of any man I'd ever met."[35]

One opportunity for Hoover to be of service to Stanford arose in 1908. Late that summer he learned that the university's board of trustees was seeking to fill a prospective vacancy with a younger man living near the university and able to participate actively in its affairs. Having heard of Hoover's desire to return to California, his undergraduate mentor, Professor Branner, was eager to get his protégé on the board.[36] So, too, was President Jordan, who told one trustee that Hoover would be "ideal" if he lived near San Francisco. Jordan pointed out that "few men in the world" had displayed "greater skill in bringing about financial results" than Hoover.[37] Responding to Branner's inquiries, Hoover was uncertain what to say: " . . . ultimately I hope to make my headquarters in the West, and to be of some service to the University; but certainly for the next 12 months I shall very largely [be] tied to London."[38] Probably in part because he was not yet a resident of the Bay Area, Hoover's name was passed over.

Branner was more successful in another direction. Early in 1907 he invited Hoover to deliver a series of lectures to Stanford's geology and mining students when he next visited the campus. Branner pointed out that Hoover could then revise and publish the lectures as a book.[39] In due course Hoover agreed, and in September 1908 the university's trustees appointed him lecturer in mining engineering for the academic year without pay.[40] Hoover arrived on campus in mid-January 1909 and remained over three weeks.[41] His lectures became *Principles of Mining*, published that spring.

It was during this brief visit that Hoover's larger service to Stanford really commenced. His stay on campus occurred during the aftermath of a bitter episode in Stanford history. For a number of years student drinking had been increasing and with it the problem of public drunkenness and disorder on campus. Early in 1908, following faculty pressure and new provocations, the university authorities cracked down, initiating a prohibition policy and making drunkenness a ground for suspension. An angry student demonstration one evening led to massive disciplinary proceedings, including the suspension of 41 seniors for the remainder of their final semester. That summer the trustees further tightened the rules. By the time Hoover arrived in 1909 Stanford was quiet but sullen; the gulf between students and faculty persisted.[42]

During his few weeks on campus Hoover discussed the university's malaise with fully 200 persons. In a speech evidently prepared for a faculty gathering just before he left, he presented his findings:

My sympathy is on the side of government always. Rebellions sometimes must be put down by volleys in the streets and then some innocent allways [sic] get hit. But all rebellions have causes and disturbance is a symptom of disease. In any event when a rebellion is over military government should give place to a civil government which devotes itself to elimination from the community of the vicious individual and its my impression that the time for a change of front has arrived here.

To Hoover, Stanford was suffering from a "profound change" in spirit since its early days, a change that was "the root of [its] trouble." This change, he said, was "the lack of solidarity of feeling and purpose."

Evidence of this deficiency was everywhere. On one side, said Hoover, were the students, generally satisfied with their departmental professors but extremely distrustful of the rest. In the eyes of the students the faculty committee on scholarship, responsible for enforcing academic standards, "acts without consideration of the worth of the men and leaves loafers in college," while the faculty committee on student affairs, responsible for social decorum, repeatedly suspended "good men on outbreak of animal spirits on misinformation and spies." To the students the faculty committees were "not in touch with student values." Hoover did not agree with this perspective, but he felt it must be faced.

On the other side, Hoover reported, was a faculty divided into three factions. One group, the advocates of "military government," believed "that students are inherently wicked[,] that all are liars and 50% are cheats[,] that there is no difference between animal spirits and inherent viciousness," that force was essential to preservation of order, and that constant effort was necessary to "keep the lid on." Those on the other extreme, according to Hoover, held "that moral conduct is no concern of the faculty, that this is a great educational institution where police duties have no place[,] where if the student does his work it is no concern of the faculty what else he does." Somewhere in between was the majority of the faculty, the "intermediates."

Hoover forcefully dissociated himself from the two extremes. He denounced the view that "the lid needs a constant weight on it." Very few men, he had found, will lie when appealed to on their honor. If the student body really contained as many "scoundrels" as some alleged, Hoover said, "you can have my degree back," for in that case the university had failed. But Hoover did not believe it. Stanford, he said, has "a fine body of students," virtually untainted by the "insensate luxury and idleness common enough in the east." Hoover also attacked the other extreme—"that the professor has no obligation to look after the moral rectitude of students." Yes, he does, Hoover countered:

These boys come immature in mind and character and it is the function of the university to build the latter as much as the former. It is true this is not a place of moral reformation but it is a place of moral inspiration. Students lend themselves easily enough to that more than any other class of humanity.

Aligning himself with the faculty "intermediates," Hoover confessed that he was an "amateur in academic matters." But "managing the human side of men" has been "my business for many years," he observed, and students were human beings, too. As an experienced executive, therefore, he offered an "amateur panacea" for Stanford's faculty-student friction.

First, he denied that academic standards could be justly enforced by a faculty committee unfamiliar with the student being judged. He criticized reliance on impersonal criteria like "minute divisions of the alphabet" (grades) as a true measure of student merit. Grades might be useful in a preliminary way, as a means of testing the "loafer." But if grades alone were "the final court of appeal," the faculty would "not only lose much good material but discourage others and do an injustice to some." Every case of academic delinquency, Hoover argued, must be treated individually. He therefore proposed that every decision of the committee on scholarship be subject to a veto by the student's department. The department should know best the student's true circumstances, and it should be responsible for retaining any "laggards." Hoover was blunt: " . . . no professor in the university has a right to do the so-called productive scholarship until he knows the human units which the university pays him to instruct."

Similarly for matters of discipline: the crux of the system should be the department, not a distant committee that could not possibly know every student in the whole university. Here also the departments should have a veto, in this case over any punishment voted by the committee on student affairs. Not only would this encourage the departments to know their students and "compel the rescued defaulter to make good"; it would increase student confidence in the likelihood of justice because of students' faith in their respective departments.

In effect, Hoover was saying that circumstances alter cases and that the best judge of the students' circumstances was or ought to be the faculty members closest to them. He was applying to university administration one of his fundamental convictions as an executive. "To my mind," he declared in his speech, "decentralization is the soul of administration."[43]

Hoover may never have delivered this blunt but thoughtful address. But while still on campus in early February, he did make at least one public attempt to restore Stanford's lost "solidarity of feeling and purpose." Even before he arrived on campus a scheme was maturing in his active mind. Upon reaching New York from London on January 1, he told a waiting friend that he planned to propose the construction of a student union building at Stanford. He thereupon promptly went up to Cambridge, Massachusetts, and inspected the Harvard Union, reputed to be the best in the country.[44] As always, he intended to be thorough.

A month later, before a student assembly at his alma mater, Hoover unveiled an ambitious plan for a $50,000 men's clubhouse on the campus. This facility, he explained, should be constructed and maintained by students and alumni and should be "entirely independent of the University authori-ties." Pointing to the success of student unions in eastern universities, Hoover asserted that the proposed building "would serve as the rallying point for student spirit" and as a common meeting place for students, faculty, and alumni. It would "restore the solidarity that existed between students and faculty in the old days." It would foster the "Stanford Spirit."[45]

Hoover's proposal won immediate enthusiastic support. The idea of estab-lishing such a clubhouse had been much bruited about for some time, but it took Hoover to galvanize talk into action.[46] In short order an organization called the Stanford Union sprang into being with Hoover as its president, and a pledge canvas of alumni commenced.[47] To handle initial expenses, Hoover personally put up $1,000 but barred any initial publicity of this fact.[48] As usual, he was concealing his benefactions.

Hoover left the campus in early February with the Stanford Union move-ment still in an embryonic stage. But even in this short period he had begun to instill a new sense of possibility on the campus. A year later his good friend E. D. Adams of the history department reported that, thanks in considerable measure to Hoover's 1909 visit, the conciliatory wing of the faculty was still in control and that a year without major turmoil had passed.[49]

From early 1909 to late 1912 Hoover did not visit Stanford University. In his absence the $50,000 fund drive for the Stanford Union proceeded slowly and seemed to lose momentum. Initially Hoover thought that ground-breaking could begin in early 1910, but he was unwilling to proceed until a substantial portion of the $50,000 was in hand.[50] By late 1912 the Union's treasury held only $21,000.[51]

At one point in 1909 it was announced that Hoover himself had pledged $11,000—44 times more than anyone else.[52] Hoover objected to this word-ing. The $10,000 he pledged beyond his initial $1,000 payment, he said, was the joint subscription of himself and certain friends.[53] From time to time over the next several years, Hoover paid his installments when requested until the $10,000 total was reached. No names of his friends were mentioned, however. More likely than not, he paid the whole amount himself.[54]

With the project he had initiated at a standstill, another infusion of Hooverian energy was clearly needed. Returning to the campus in September 1912, the resourceful alumnus launched a spirited "final" campaign for the Union. On the campus, fund-raising projects sprouted. Hoover sent a personal appeal to every living member of his Pioneer Class. Mrs. Hoover, too, became involved, as chairman of the drive to raise money for the women's clubhouse that would be built near that for the men. To this effort she contributed several thousand dollars.[55] When it appeared that the Union might be unable to withdraw when needed an $11,000 deposit from a shaky local bank, Hoover personally guaranteed to provide this amount as desired.[56] For him the Union was more than a worthy project; it had become a crusade.

In an address to an undergraduate assembly in September 1912 he explained why. The Union, Hoover asserted, "will allow us to inoculate against the bacillus of social inequality." The distinctive feature of Stanford's student body, he said, was its "democracy"; the Union would help to maintain it. "The undemocratic social stratification which has been so much discussed of late in our eastern neighbors, has not yet entered Stanford to any alarming extent. Nor do we want it." In that season of surging Progressivism, as Woodrow Wilson and Theodore Roosevelt battled for the presidency, Hoover the Bull Moose Progressive exhorted the students of Stanford to maintain their democratic ideals:

> There has been a great growth of class feeling in this country during the past few years and we have seen with dismay the transplanting of privilege into the social life of some of our universities . . . . Certainly the older [European] universities are not cradles of democracy.
>
> In this country, however, with the ideals upon which our government is founded, we have a right to expect or even demand that the universities should be in the forefront of the fight for equality of opportunity and not a playground for childish institutions. The ideals of a university are made by its members and yours are right so far. You must see that you keep them.[57]

The father of the Stanford Union, however, could not accomplish instant miracles. Not everyone, apparently, was as enthusiastic or as generous as he. To keep within its resources, the Union was forced to scale down its plans in 1913. Even then, construction of the two clubhouses did not begin until December 1913 and was not completed until February 1915.[58] It was not until after World War I that the Union in its full conception reached fruition, and once again Herbert Hoover would be the catalyst. Without his push and persistence, one of the favorite structures on the Stanford campus might never have been built.

IV

By the autumn of 1912 the Stanford Union was actually a secondary concern for Hoover. During his three-and-a-half-year absence, an abortive faculty reform effort had dissipated and his beloved university had stagnated.[59] Stanford's most accomplished alumnus was determined to change all this. After visiting Hoover in London in mid-summer 1912, a Stanford classics professor reported to a colleague that Hoover was coming back to launch a campaign to get himself elected to the board of trustees.[60] In late summer he came.[61]

Hoover's return to the Bay Area coincided with his financial labors in behalf of the California-based General Petroleum Company. As it happened, two men soon to be directors of this company—J. D. Grant and Leon Sloss—were also Stanford trustees. Through them Hoover seems to have worked. To find room for him on the Stanford board, it was necessary to create a vacancy. As it happened, two trustees were just completing their ten-year terms, the first trustees to have done so. The board accordingly decided that it was "inadvisable" to re-elect ten-year members upon the expiration of their terms.[62] On October 29 the vice president of General Petroleum confidentially informed Hoover that Grant and Sloss had arranged Hoover's nomination to fill one of the vacancies being created.[63] A few weeks later, Hoover was formally elected a trustee.[64] He was only the second Stanford alumnus so honored and the first to be selected by the trustees themselves.[65] For virtually the next half century he was to sit on the board.

In announcing Hoover's election, the *Stanford Alumnus* stated, "He has recently returned from London, where he has lived for several years, and taken up his residence in San Francisco."[66] This hint of permanency was premature; Hoover still had too many global interests to permit him to sit still. But between late August 1912 and early January 1913, he did manage to stay mostly in California.[67] It was his longest continuous sojourn in the United States since 1897.

With characteristic zeal he used the time to investigate the problems of Stanford University. He asked his friend Professor Adams to send him titles of certain publications on educational administration—"in fact anything which will educate the budding trustee to university management!"[68] From President Jordan he received a report that Stanford's academic standing was slipping, mainly because of failure to maintain a competitive pay scale.[69] Early in January 1913, Hoover told a fellow trustee that he had spent "a large portion of the last three months" studying Stanford's situation.[70]

What he found was disturbing. In a lengthy memorandum dated January 2, 1913 on Stanford's "present position," Hoover asserted that the university was generally failing to do work of an outstanding character and was lagging behind other institutions. The problem, as he saw it, was that the university did not have enough "pre-eminent" professors, a fact he attributed to Stanford's inferior pay scale. It was becoming more and more difficult to hire and retain superior professors because of better job offers elsewhere. Hoover was also distressed by the fact that many junior faculty were no better paid than "fully employed mechanics in San Francisco." With salaries low and not keeping pace with the rising cost of living, more than half the faculty could not hire a servant, and wives of lower-paid faculty were being forced to do all the "domestic work" themselves. Such salaries, said Hoover, made it difficult for many faculty to "maintain some position," buy books, travel during sabbaticals, and "above all . . . maintain social relations" with students—all essential to their "service to the University." The fundamental academic problem of Stanford, in other words, was a lack of money.

Hoover strenuously rejected all proposals to "prune down the scope" of the university, as many had advocated. Instead, he proposed the "more progressive" approach of strengthening existing departments and weakening none. Specifically, he recommended an increase in the salaries of all faculty by 10–15 percent and an increase in the number of highly paid pre-eminent professorships "so as to be able to hold and attract . . . exceptional men." Hoover estimated that his plan would cost $125,000 a year. But only such expenditure, he maintained, would "raise this institution to the level of the very best."[71]

Hoover considered his plan a "progressive" one, but where was he to find the money? Since its founding in 1891, the university had been crimped for funds, a chronic predicament exacerbated by damage to campus buildings in the 1906 earthquake. If the pre-eminent professor was Hoover's first concern as a trustee, his second was the university's finances. Almost at once he began to agitate for revision and publication of the institution's heretofore secret accounts. He was appalled to discover that the trustees were annually deducting $100,000 from university income for depreciation—a quite unnecessary action, he thought, in view of its repairs budget and new construction program. He was also aghast to find that the budget-conscious trustees did not even expend all their general funds in 1911–1912, instead adding the leftover amount to a "surplus of income not expended" account that now totaled over $384,000. "It does seem to me," Hoover commented tartly, "that it is the primary function of this Institution to spend its income, not to save it."[72]

Meanwhile, Hoover was exerting himself in other directions. In January 1913 he was appointed to a committee of trustees established to study the needs of the university's young medical school, administered by his intimate friend of twenty years, Ray Lyman Wilbur.[73] He served on a trustee committee to build a new gymnasium.[74] In April he was appointed to a special four-man trustee committee to examine the academic and financial position of the university and to recommend "a general policy of academic management and development during the next two or three years."[75] The pot was beginning to boil, and Hoover was stirring it.

In asserting that Stanford's fundamental need was more money, Hoover was closely in accord with the views of President Jordan. "Money is the basis of reputation," Jordan told him in 1912. "The strong men make the institution. . . . A growing university must grow at the top."[76] Such an analysis was no doubt congenial to an engineer-executive like Hoover, who liked to encourage initiative.

At some point in early 1913, however, Hoover evidently became convinced that at least one of Stanford's problems was not monetary at all. It was David Starr Jordan himself. By 1913 Jordan, now in his early sixties, had been president of Stanford University for more than twenty years—in fact, had been the only president the university had known. Particularly after the "rebellion" of 1908, signs appeared that his period of greatest usefulness to Stanford was over.[77] Jordan, too, seems to have felt the same way; in 1911 he seriously considered resigning to devote himself to one of his principal causes, the promotion of world peace. But by late 1912 he had decided to remain at Stanford until he reached retirement age in just a few years.[78]

If Hoover knew of Jordan's decision he was not inclined to accept it as final. Yet if, as seems clear, he wanted Jordan removed, the engineering of such an objective would be a delicate mission. An internationally famous scientist, educator, and reformer, Jordan could not be unceremoniously dumped from office. Hoover, though, had a fertile brain in such matters and a tenacity of purpose that could rarely be deflected. He soon proved equal to the challenge.

In a series of deft negotiations in April and May 1913, Hoover arranged for Jordan to give up the presidency and all its administrative responsibilities for a new position: chancellor of the university. Hoover broached the subject to Jordan on April 27; finding Jordan at least open to the idea, he speedily contacted fellow trustees.[79] On May 9 Hoover reported to Jordan that the trustees shared Hoover's view that Jordan's greatest future service to the university and the public lay outside the administrative realm, in the peace movement and other social concerns. Hoover also disclosed that the vice president of the university, John C. Branner, was willing to assume the presidency under the proposed new scheme.[80]

While the inspiration and initiative came from Hoover, Jordan was eagerly receptive. "If the Trustees really believe in the value of my services under the title of Chancellor, and that it is worthwhile," he told Hoover, then he would accept "with very great pleasure."[81] To his daughter, Jordan even confided that it was "at my request" that the trustees were relieving him of "the details of the University business and management," evidently forgetting that it was Hoover, in fact, who instigated the transition.[82] Jordan regarded the chancellorship both as a "quite unexpected" honor and as a "promotion" that would enhance "my power of carrying out the work for peace."[83]

It now remained for Hoover to formalize the understandings for ratification by the trustees. His own desire was abundantly clear. He told Jordan that administration of the university "should be in Dr. Branner's hands entirely" and that Jordan's involvement would be confined to topics of the trustees' and

Branner's choosing. Branner would more or less be the "general manager," Jordan the "consulting engineer."[84] Jordan, however, was anxious that the chancellorship be "a position both of dignity and of real service," not a merely titular one like president emeritus.[85] Branner, for his part, was willing to take the presidency only upon trustee acceptance of seven conditions, including an increase in faculty salaries and Branner's retirement in just two years, when he would be 65.[86]

In mid-May, Hoover completed the negotiations and drew up various resolutions for the trustees to adopt that accommodated Jordan's desires, Branner's requests, and Hoover's aims. Branner's conditions were acceded to, except for silence on the question of his retirement. As for Jordan, Hoover's resolution acknowledged what it called Jordan's "expressed desire" to be "relieved from administrative demands," and it expressed the trustees' wish "to afford him both freedom to represent the university in its functions towards the public, and the relations of the university to educational agencies outside the university itself." But the chancellorship as Hoover's resolution defined it seemed suspiciously honorific and had, in fact, less power than Jordan originally wanted. Although the chancellor was to have the right to attend meetings of the board of trustees and one of their key committees, his only prescribed duties were to "represent the university at public functions" when present and to "advise and cooperate on such matters as may be proposed by the Trustees or the President."[87]

In colloquial parlance, Jordan had been "kicked upstairs." But the deed had been accomplished with his hearty concurrence, and if he regretted his "elevation" he did not show it. "To me," he told Branner, "it seems a great honor as well as a great opportunity."[88] In 1916, at the termination of his chancellorship, Jordan expressed to the Hoovers his feeling of obligation for the opportunities that the 1913 arrangement had given him to see the world.[89] In 1920 and 1928 he ardently supported Hoover for president. Hoover's action in May 1913 was, in fact, a graceful, mutually advantageous maneuver. Jordan, at no diminution of his high salary, retained the dignity of a Stanford connection, escaped the administrative chores that he already found burdensome, and gained the liberty to turn to the public issues where his heart now lay. It was an attractive package for him. Hoover and his fellow trustees, anxious to rejuvenate a university adrift, were able to make a much-desired change of administration three years ahead of schedule and without a public spectacle or bitterness.

But not, perhaps, without a moment of embarrassment. Apparently fearful of adverse publicity, Hoover initially proposed (and Jordan agreed) that public announcement of the change be delayed until summer, when both Jordan and Branner would be traveling abroad, beyond the range of inquisitive newspaper reporters.[90] As it turned out, however, Jordan himself made the announcement at Stanford's commencement on May 19. At first the unprepared audience sat in stunned silence; then it burst into applause.[91] But when a few moments later Hoover rose and requested "three cheers for the chancellor," the response from the assembly was feeble. As Jordan wrote afterward, few could see a reason to celebrate the sudden, bewildering, seemingly painful news.[92]

Selecting a new university president was only one of Hoover's initiatives that spring. Jordan was amazed at the momentum Hoover was building. "It is marvellous," he told Branner, "how Hoover is handling our Board. Almost every reform we have dreamed of has slipped through as if oiled."[93] The president of the board of trustees told Jordan that Hoover had given the trustees more ideas in ten days than they had had in ten years.[94]

The climax of Hoover's reform movement occurred at a trustees' meeting on May 23, 1913. Most of the key resolutions were drafted by Hoover personally.[95] The trustees approved the Jordan/Branner transition arrangement. As requested by Branner, they approved a significant increase in the faculty salary budget. In a dramatic reversal of the parsimonious policy of the previous few years, they boldly authorized construction of a new library, a new gymnasium and a stadium, and several facilities at the medical school, all at the urging of committees on which Hoover served actively.[96] To help free funds for this ambitious program, the trustees revised their accounting methods on lines advocated by Hoover. They also created a Grounds Committee with a mandate to devise a plan for improving the university's grounds and housing facilities. Predictably, Hoover was named to this committee.[97]

Finally, on the recommendation (prepared by Hoover) of the special committee on future academic policy created the month before, the trustees announced several changes in the university's direction. Until the university's financial situation improved markedly, there would be no expansion in the male enrollment or the "educational range" of the institution. The current academic budget would be increased substantially each year, but this new expenditure would be devoted to strengthening "certain selected departments," particularly "in the direction of securing further prominent educational leaders" (Hoover's pre-eminent professors).[98] Nothing was said about eliminating any existing department. In an optimistic press release possibly drafted by Hoover and issued after the meeting, the trustees declared that Stanford University did have the resources to increase its academic budget, resources sufficient to "extend and improve" the "most important" of the existing departments until they became "pre-eminent among such departments in the United States." In a fateful ambiguity, the trustees did not specify which departments they considered "most important" and planned to favor with their resources.[99]

This portent of future controversy was overlooked in the general optimism that greeted the reforms which Hoover, more than any other person, had wrought. Jordan declared that the trustees' meeting of May 23 had been a "perfect love feast":

> It would seem that Mr. Hoover devoted his entire time to working up these things in the month that he was here, and persuaded everybody that it was his duty to stand for these radical improvements and to convert all conservatists, so everybody was busy converting everybody else. All these matters in the aggregate are a great jump forward. . . .[100]

Many people in the Bay Area were astonished at Stanford's sudden forward motion; Hoover's faculty friend, E. D. Adams, called him a wonder-worker.[101]

Hoover now returned to England for the summer and autumn; Jordan set out on a lengthy world tour. Originally Jordan had intended to return to campus in late January 1914, which happened to be when the university's next budget would be prepared. But at Hoover's and then the board's urging, Jordan agreed to extend his sojourn abroad in order to visit (and cultivate) Leland Stanford's wealthy brother in Melbourne, Australia. As a result Jordan was absent from the university an entire year—conveniently absent, no doubt, from the perspective of Hoover and his fellow reformers.[102]

Hoover returned to Stanford University on Christmas Eve, 1913, and remained in California more than two months.[103] Once again his presence catalyzed a burst of accomplishment by the board of trustees. Under Hoover's prodding, the trustees further reorganized their accounting system and in February 1914, for the first time ever, made a public disclosure of the university's finances, thereby ending a much-criticized policy of secrecy that had hampered efforts to attract outside financial support. (Hoover wrote the resolutions instituting the change.)[104] On another front, the board approved a new leasing system proposed by its Grounds Committee, thereby making it easier for faculty to build housing on campus.[105]

Meanwhile, the board was proceeding with its expensive construction program—apparently with some second thoughts, for on February 24 Hoover felt obliged to send a blunt defense of the scheme to the board's president. The new library, gymnasium, and hospital approved last spring, he declared, were "absolutely necessary if the Institution is to go forward. . . ."[106] The trustees continued with their building plan.

Hoover's principal achievement in the winter of 1913–1914, however, lay in another area. From the beginning he had been particularly concerned about faculty salaries, a concern not allayed by the modest increase in the salary budget voted by the trustees in May 1913. During the following summer he told incoming President Branner that he wished to raise substantially the salaries of Stanford's "pre-eminent professors." [107] At the request of the chairman of the trustees' influential University Committee (to which Hoover belonged), Hoover, on his return to the campus, prepared a comprehensive report on faculty pay.

Hoover's report reiterated themes he had enunciated a year before. On the one hand, he argued, faculty salaries were failing to keep up with the rising cost of living, and lower-paid faculty were "absolutely unable" to meet "even the barest necessities" of their positions. Hoover was particularly concerned that assistant professors were unable to maintain the level of dignity and affluence needed to entertain and otherwise exert proper influence over students. This level, to Hoover's mind, required at least one household servant per faculty family. Instead, Hoover found that many assistant professors were being forced to do menial work on the side and to take in boarders, while their wives were doing all the domestic work. (Hoover evidently felt it demeaning for faculty wives to do housework.) All this, said Hoover, had produced "absolute demoralization" and a "spirit of rebellion" among the assistant professors. Such a spirit would lead to "improper influence" on students. The situation at the top was no better. Stanford's salaries for its outstanding professors were inferior to the salaries offered by eastern universities, and the prospect of losing such distinguished men was increasing.

Hoover therefore proposed a comprehensive restructuring of the helter-skelter salary roll and a substantial immediate increase in the pay of most faculty. Two considerations governed his thinking (and said much about his social as well as educational philosophy): the desires to establish a fair, livable salary base at the bottom and to reward excellence at the top. Not a man to overlook crucial details, Hoover listed in his report the current salary of each of the 160 or so members of the Stanford faculty. Beside each name he listed the amount of a raise, if any, that the individual, in his judgment, should receive. He also proposed the creation of a new category of pre-eminent professors, and he carefully recorded who among the faculty should be placed in it (and how much they should get). It is interesting to note that Hoover recommended only three professors for the largest raise, $1,000. Two— Adams and Wilbur—were his close friends. The third, Vernon Kellogg, became a key associate in World War I. [108]

It was surely remarkable for a university trustee to be so immersed in the details of individual professors' salaries. Quite possibly Hoover, in preparing his report, received the input of men like President Branner. Nevertheless, Hoover's document mentioned no associates and was signed by himself alone. It was dated January 27, 1914. Three days later the board of trustees adopted both Hoover's proposed new salary classification and the individual salary revisions that he recommended. [109] In large measure one man, Herbert Hoover, had just set the salaries of the entire Stanford faculty!

As an engineer and executive, Hoover was accustomed to promoting the able and to firing the incompetent. This was the way things worked in the business world, where the discipline of the free market prevailed. It was only to be expected, then, that a man accustomed to such procedures should chafe at the tenure system that governed academe. In his quest to attract brilliant professors to Stanford, he confronted the fact that the university, like all universities, had its share of "dead wood" and that tenure protected them.[110]

Hoover was not one to be intimidated by hallowed tradition if it stood in the way of his objectives. By his calculations, half of the full professors at Stanford were either "humdrum" or "weak," and the university was second-rate because of it.[111] Why not, he proposed to Adams one evening, get rid of the faculty who were no longer valuable? Specifically, he evidently suggested that such unwanted professors (even long-serving ones) be given a year's leave of absence on full pay and then dismissed. Adams was appalled at such a drastic proposal and debated the matter with Hoover until three o'clock in the morning. A few days later Adams wrote to Hoover that such an assault on the entrenched tenure principle would devastate Stanford's academic reputation. Furthermore, if long-established faculty did not have security of tenure, no pre-eminent professor would ever come to Stanford.[112] Hoover's response was quick:

> I quite recognize the justice of criticism in regard to any sudden scattering of staff, and such has never been any view of my own. On the other hand, though I am not prepared to say at the moment what the solution is, there has got to be some remedy for the Professor who will not or cannot do his work. It is to me an outrage on the whole sanctity of higher education to think that a man can deliberately rob students and endowment in such positions. I do not know of any other profession, or calling, in this whole wide world where laziness and incapacity are wrapped up in the sacred garment of perpetual tenure.[113]

Hoover eventually altered his views. He later told Adams that his original idea had been a "theorist's dream" and that he now recognized that tenure was a necessary device to recruit worthy people into an underpaid calling.[114] But Hoover was scarcely enthusiastic. In his report of January 1914 he opposed an automatic annual salary increase for professors, regardless of qualifications; such a system would reward the "dead wood" and be "wasteful." Accordingly, he structured the new salary plan so that a professor might not receive a step increase for five years and then only with the consent of the university president.[115] Perhaps he hoped that by withholding pay increases from the "dead wood," he could induce them eventually to leave.

By the end of 1913, on a variety of fronts, Stanford was undergoing a renewal. Then, suddenly, a tempest arose for Hoover and his fellow trustees from a most unexpected direction: the new university president, John Caspar Branner.

V

In many ways Branner's appointment in 1913 was a fitting and logical one. A distinguished scholar and teacher, he had served as vice president of the university under Jordan since the 1890s. But in one respect the appointment seems odd: Branner was actually a year older than Jordan and planned to retire in just two years. Such a man could only be a transitional figure as Stanford entered its new era.

Was there perhaps more than met the eye in Branner's appointment? At least one faculty member suspected that Hoover placed his mentor in the presidency in the expectation that he would dutifully implement the reforms Hoover wished to effect.[116] The two men had long been cordial friends. It was to Branner, in fact, that Hoover and his wife dedicated their highly acclaimed translation of the Latin mining classic *De Re Metallica*, which appeared early in 1913.

Some even suspected other motives. In 1915 Branner would presumably retire; in 1915 Hoover, the university's most successful alumnus and now its dominant trustee, would be 41 years old. Was Hoover himself contemplating the Stanford presidency? According to one former mining associate, this had indeed been Hoover's ambition for years.[117] On the Stanford faculty the story circulated that when Branner retired, Hoover would become chancellor and his friend Wilbur, currently dean of the medical school, would become president.[118]

Whatever Hoover's personal goals, it was Branner, a rugged native of Tennessee, who was president for the moment. And if the board of trustees thought it could easily control him, it soon learned otherwise.

On August 29, 1913, during Hoover's absence, the university's trustees made a critical decision:

> It was resolved that in the opinion of this Board the university funds and income will be insufficient to adequately extend and develop all departments of the university, and that it will therefore be necessary to select such courses of education as may be so developed to the highest point, abandoning or reducing other courses; and that the President is requested to submit to the University Committee of this Board his recommendations relative to such action by the Board.[119]

In one respect the policy here enunciated was not new. For ten years the trustees had been attempting to eliminate certain departments in the university.[120]

And at the May 23, 1913 meeting just a few months before, the trustees had signaled their intent to build up "certain selected departments" only. From this perspective the August resolution was merely another step on a path already taken.

Yet in another respect the August resolution seemed contrary to the trustees' decision in May—and contrary to the views of Trustee Hoover. In his January 1913 report on "The Present Position," Hoover had favored retaining "practically all" the existing departments and had sharply rejected any "pruning" or policy of retrenchment. The trustees' actions in May 1913 had embodied Hoover's optimistic thinking. Their May resolutions had indicated that existing departments would be retained but that some among them would henceforth be favored. Now, however, in their August resolution, the trustees said that some departments would be favored *at the direct expense of others*. The May resolutions—Hoover's resolutions—with their authorization of a bigger academic budget, promised survival for all and prosperity for some. The August resolution promised prosperity for some but only by weakening or extinguishing others. In Hoover's absence the trustees had issued a call for retrenchment.

Incoming president Branner now confronted the unpleasant task of re-arranging the size of the slices of Stanford's economic pie. In short order he found his target. Just a few years before, Stanford had acquired a medical college in San Francisco. It had done so, however, on the understanding that its new medical department would be largely self-sufficient and need no more than $25,000 from the university's budget per year.[121] But when Branner examined the books in 1913 he found that the medical school was already absorbing far more than this amount and that its requirements were inexorably increasing.[122]

Not a man to mince his words, Branner bluntly informed Hoover in November that "as we now go this university is rapidly approaching a collapse as a university." The reason was the enormous and spiraling cost of the medical school. Either the medical school "must be endowed," Branner stated, "or we must expect to see it swamp the university." Branner was determined to rid the university of this growing financial incubus. He cared little for some trustees' ideas of consolidating and eliminating various departments; this, he claimed, would only drive out some of Stanford's best professors.[123] The trustees, he told a friend, "think it possible for me to so overhaul things here at the university that a lot of what they regard as purely ornamental departments can be done away with, and that this will release funds enough to keep the medical school going." In Branner's judgment this could not be done.[124]

On December 20, 1913 Branner replied formally to the trustees' economy resolution of August 29. He told the board that "no considerable economies are possible" and that most of the existing departments were "half-starved."

Instead, he boldly took aim at the young and expensive medical school up in San Francisco. Not only was it "by far the most expensive part of the university," but it was also the newest and least essential. Branner therefore proposed that Stanford University terminate all financial support to its medical school after July 31, 1914 and take measures to turn the entire facility over to the University of California (which also had a medical school in San Francisco). [125]

Branner's proposal (which commanded overwhelming faculty support)[126] was totally unexpected, and the trustees' University Committee (now including Hoover, back from London) was stunned. [127] But Branner was determined to force the issue. The medical school, he believed, must be eliminated "at once and for all." [128]

At its meeting on January 30, 1914 the board of trustees made its first response. It created a committee, including Hoover, to confer with any similar committee from the University of California about possible "joint action" by the medical schools of the two universities. [129] From Branner's perspective it was not an auspicious beginning. Of the three trustees selected, one, in Branner's opinion, was amenable to reason, and one was vehemently in favor of Stanford's keeping its medical school. The third, Hoover, was a close friend of the medical school's dean, Ray Lyman Wilbur, and "will probably do what Wilbur wants." In Branner's view "personal interests" were now "sadly mixed in the matter." [130]

It soon became evident that Branner's bombshell was greatly discomfiting the trustees. On February 16, in a confidential letter, Hoover told Branner frankly that the time had come for Branner to reconsider his position. Hoover declared that Branner "had been allowed to secure a mis-impression" that nothing could be done for the university's Palo Alto branch "without drastic reduction in some quarter." The fact that the trustees had just raised the university's budget, said Hoover, belied Branner's belief. It was not yet possible, Hoover asserted, to determine whether the university could support the medical school or not. Furthermore, the public impression "that we wish to jettison the Medical Department at any cost has absolutely destroyed any hope of a proper negotiation." And many of the trustees were now "so disturbed" that consideration of the medical school issue was "doubly difficult." Hoover strenuously urged Branner to withdraw his recommendation of December 20 "and state that the matter can probably be better re-considered at a later date." Why withdraw? Because, said Hoover, the "immediate necessities" of the Palo Alto branch of the university had been met and there was now no need to ponder the fate of the medical school. [131]

President Branner, however, was not about to capitulate. On February 19 he bluntly informed Hoover that he would *not* withdraw his recommendations of December 20; they had been made in response to the trustees' own resolution of the previous August. This resolution, Branner reminded Hoover, stated explicitly that the trustees believed that the university's resources were "insufficient" to develop all departments of the university and that some courses would have to be abandoned or curtailed. Branner's conclusions had followed inevitably from that. Branner resented Hoover's suggestion that he had misconstrued the university's difficulties and should now back down. "If the problem was not properly stated by the board," Branner retorted, "then it rests with the board, and not with me, to set the matter right." [132]

If Stanford's president was in an unyielding mood, so, too, was Hoover. In a long emphatic letter to a fellow trustee on February 23, just days after receiving Branner's letter, he declared that the situation was now an "emergency" and unleashed a salvo of arguments for retaining the medical school. Among other things, Hoover asserted that "our institution can meet all present outlays out of its income." [133]

Four days later, at their monthly meeting, the board of trustees adopted a sharply worded resolution prepared by Hoover explicitly rejecting Branner's recommendations of December 20, 1913. Hoover's resolution declared that Branner was "evidently acting under a misapprehension of the university's resources" and that, on the contrary, the university's financial state "does not now require, and may never require, such drastic action as the abandonment of medical education." Furthermore, no "important department" should be abolished on one semester's notice; the "dignity and reputation of the university" mandated "much longer preparation and notice." The trustees did agree to explore some appropriate kind of "joint action" with the University of California's medical school. But they opposed any wholesale abandonment of Stanford's medical facilities to its rival. [134] Upon Branner's objection, the trustees consented to modify a few parts of the resolution and to eliminate a paragraph that Branner found offensive. [135]

By late February 1914, then, Stanford's trustees had voted to retain the medical school (in some form), had approved a new budget that increased aid to the medical school for the next year, and had rebuffed Branner's effort to surrender the facility outright to the University of California. Still, Branner detected a silver lining. As he interpreted the trustees' action of February 27, the trustees had withdrawn their retrenchment resolution of the previous August. For the board in effect was now saying that its resources were not as slender as it had intimated in August. "Drastic action" like elimination of "important departments" might never be required, it now declared. [136]

Early in March, Hoover returned to England. [137] But the medical school controversy was by no means over. To Branner, the trustees' actions had merely postponed the day of reckoning. Although the new budget increase of $62,000 (drawn up by Hoover) was welcome, Branner noted with displeasure that much of it went to the medical school. He also questioned the trustees' new confidence that "we have money enough to care for all departments, medicine included." To Branner this was based on nothing but hope. In his opinion there remained only one chance of preventing the medical school from "swamping the university later on": a combination with the University of California's medical school that might reduce Stanford's expense. [138] But Branner was pessimistic. The trustees' negotiating committee—Hoover and two others—was not, in his opinion, "open-minded." One member was already opposed to amalgamation, and Hoover essentially concurred with him. [139]

Efforts to resolve the issue now proceeded on two fronts. During the spring, various representatives of the two universities explored the possibility of a medical school merger. The negotiations soon foundered: Stanford wanted equal representation on the proposed governing board; the University of California insisted on majority control. On May 29, following a new initiative from the California regents, the Stanford trustees terminated the discussions—convinced, they said, that "no basis of merger" did or could exist and that no savings would be effected thereby. The trustees resolved to maintain an independent Stanford medical school. [140]

Meanwhile Branner had been following another tack. From the beginning he had urged the trustees to bring in disinterested outside experts for assistance, originally to settle the terms of the transfer of Stanford's medical school to California. [141] One such expert, a friend and supporter of Branner's, came in March and met with the trustees' committee of three, minus Hoover. Neither side persuaded the other. [142] Late in March, the trustees authorized Branner to select a medical expert to visit the University of California and advise about the feasibility of merger, and on this Branner pinned his final hopes. [143] Branner also felt relieved: " . . . whatever is done now, we must all agree that we have sought unbiased advice." [144]

Hoover, in London, was uneasy about this turn of events. On April 7, before learning of the board's action, he confidently predicted that "the Medical School agitation will gradually die out." [145] A week later, however, he confided to Wilbur: "I cannot say I am very keen about continuing this agitation on the subject of amalgamating the Medical Schools, and should be very sorry if, as the result of [Branner's designated expert's] visit, we should have him advise that anything of the kind be done." [146]

As it happened, Hoover's apprehension proved groundless. On May 29, 1914, the very day that Branner's chosen expert—the dean of the University of Michigan's medical school—arrived on the Stanford campus, the Stanford trustees voted to reject the merger idea. The purpose of the consultant's visit had thus been eliminated before he could begin his investigation. [147] Nevertheless, the Michigan dean stayed on for a few days and studied the issue while Branner, outmaneuvered, hoped against hope for the best. "Medical matters are still stewing," he told a friend on June 2, "and no good odors come from the mess." [148] When a week later the Michigan dean submitted his report,

Branner could only have been disappointed. The dean enthusiastically lauded the Stanford medical school and urged that it be expanded. Amalgamation with the University of California's medical school (already a dead issue) would not, he said, be wise. And on the crucial question of finances the dean was optimistic: Stanford, from what he learned, could afford to develop its medical school without impairing the growth of its other departments. [149]

The medical school battle was finally over. [150] Branner had lost. On the crucial issue of finances, the trustees had insisted that Stanford did have the money, and Branner's designated expert had agreed with them. Still, the embattled president took consolation from the feeling that he had done his duty. The matter was settled, he informed Jordan, and he felt "bound to accept" the Michigan dean's report as "a justification of the course and action of our board of trustees." [151] Branner felt that he could "accept the situation with a clear conscience. I do feel that I was put in a false position by the trustees at the outset when they called upon me to cut down things here in the university, but so long as the university can grow and I don't really have to cut down on the campus, I shall not have any grounds for complaint." [152]

Branner, however, had not suffered a total defeat. If unable to sever the medical school's ties with the university, he had at least helped to scuttle the trustees' retrenchment plans of August 1913. It was one thing to build up certain selected departments out of increased appropriations (as Hoover favored); it was quite another to eliminate departments altogether. Thanks in some measure to Branner, the trustees reverted to their more optimistic attitude of May 1913.

Hoover was in England when the medical school controversy reached its denouement. The absent trustee was gratified that the issue was "finally buried, once and for all." [153] He told Chancellor Jordan that the trustees were "absolutely unanimous" in their intention to preserve the medical school. [154] To one of his trustee allies, Hoover later expressed guilt that he had not been "on the decks" to assist in the battle. [155]

Hoover did not appear to be angry at Branner. Early in June he told Jordan: "Dr. Branner has been a complete success, in spite of all he has to say himself. He has had only one difference with the Trustees, and that is in the matter of the Medical School, where I was myself strongly against his views that it should be abolished. This matter has now been finally dropped." Pointing to the reorganizing of the faculty payroll, Hoover added that he thought Stanford "has made very distinct progress this year." [156] Eight days later, in a letter to a closer friend than Jordan, Hoover was less cheerful and probably more confiding. The medical school dispute, he said, had retarded "solid constructive work during the period of discussion." [157] The momentum of Hoover's reform campaign had been slowed.

Still, Hoover could properly regard 1912–1914 as years of accomplishment at Stanford, and himself as the prime catalyst. In less than two years he had established himself as the university's most energetic and innovative trustee. Not for the last time, he had rescued his beloved alma mater from a slow descent into stagnancy.

Looking back on this period five years later, Ray Lyman Wilbur credited Hoover with effecting two major achievements for his alma mater: a much-needed construction program and the new faculty salary schedule, which was now fully in place.[158] He might have added Hoover's role in saving the medical school as a part of Stanford University.

The experience of being a trustee and philanthropist was important for Hoover as well. It had given him a further taste of the pleasures of constructive accomplishment and the possibilities of service beyond his profession. Forceful and resourceful, the executive-turned-benefactor had been able to achieve results, to "coordinate and control the best efforts of other people." Having succeeded thus with Stanford's trustees, might he not succeed in wider realms?

· 4 ·

The Benefactor
Becomes a Hero

I

In the summer of 1914 a wider realm of public service unexpectedly opened
for Herbert Hoover and transformed the course of his life.

When World War I engulfed Europe that August, Hoover and his family
were in London. As a leading American resident in the city, he quickly
organized a committee to assist American travelers who were fleeing the war
zone on the continent and desperately seeking passage home. Many were
penniless and frantic; all were inconvenienced and distressed. By early autumn
the local American community, led by Hoover and his wife, had helped
thousands of their stranded countrymen find temporary shelter as well as
tickets for sailing back to the United States. The efficient labors of Hoover's
committee had replaced wild confusion with order and had earned the gratitude of the U.S. ambassador to Great Britain.

Then, as the European war bogged down in the trenches, a tragedy of
immense proportions loomed. In their bid for a quick, decisive victory, the
German armed forces had invaded and conquered virtually all of the neutral
nation of Belgium, a densely populated, industrialized country that imported
up to 80 percent of its food. Caught now between a German army of occupation that refused to feed it and an Allied naval blockade, the population of
Belgium, in the fall of 1914, suddenly faced the threat of famine and death
by starvation.

With the approval of the belligerent governments and the U.S. ambassador in London, Herbert Hoover—fresh from his successful repatriation of the
American travelers—was asked to create a private humanitarian relief agency
to deliver food to the beleaguered Belgian civil population. He called it the

Commission for Relief in Belgium (CRB). To finance his massive food purchases abroad, he depended on charitable contributions, particularly in the
United States, and, a little later, on indirect subsidies from the British and
French governments. The Germans, for their part, promised not to seize the
imported supplies for themselves. Soon American volunteers under Hoover's
direction were on their way to Belgium to supervise food distribution in
cooperation with an elaborate network of Belgian committees extending to
every city, village, and town.

What began as an emergency operation in late 1914 did not soon end.
Instead, as the Great War intensified, the CRB's responsibilities burgeoned.
Food—tens of thousands of tons of it every month—had to be purchased all
over the world, transported in specially marked vessels through dangerous
waters, unloaded in neutral Holland, forwarded by canal into Belgium, stored
in warehouses, guarded from unauthorized requisition, and rationed daily to
more than nine million men, women, and children in Belgium and the
German-held portions of northern France. All phases of the enormous enterprise had to be meticulously managed and regulated, lest the ever-suspicious
belligerents find cause to terminate its mission of mercy. "A piratical state
organized for benevolence," a British diplomat called the CRB. Indeed, it was
an undertaking unprecedented in world history.

Hoover's prodigious efforts ultimately entailed the expenditure of nearly a
billion dollars and earned him international acclaim. They also evoked new
pride from his alma mater. Stanford faculty, students, and alumni participated
enthusiastically in American fund-raising for the Belgian relief; some—
notably Ben S. Allen ('07) and Professor Vernon Kellogg—played important
roles in the CRB's work in Europe.[1] Mrs. Hoover, during visits to California
in 1914 and 1915, made pleas on campus for the cause; support was immediate
and sustained. The Commission for Relief in Belgium: here, par excellence,
was an example of the "direct usefulness in life" that Leland Stanford had
declared to be the object of his university.

Hoover's duties took him frequently to Brussels, Rotterdam, Paris, and
Berlin, as well as to his base of operations in London. From 1914 to 1917 he
was probably the only U.S. citizen permitted to travel freely through enemy
lines. As familiar with the corridors of the British Foreign Office as with the
German General Staff headquarters in northern France, personally acquainted
with the presidents and prime ministers of at least four belligerent countries,
he was one of the best-informed men in Europe on the social consequences of
the war. "I saw that war in the raw," he later observed, ". . . probably more
intimately than any other American."[2]

This awareness of being a privileged witness to events of epochal significance led Hoover in early 1915 to one of the most far-reaching decisions of his
life. On a journey across the English Channel on CRB business in December

1914 or January 1915, he carried with him a copy of the autobiography of Andrew D. White, the distinguished historian, diplomat, and first president of Cornell University. In it White described how, as a student in France in the 1850s, and for years thereafter, he had assembled a vast collection of documents on the history of the French Revolution, including books, pamphlets, manuscripts, cartoons, reports, and other "fugitive publications." His library eventually helped a friend prepare one of the best accounts of the French Revolution written in the English language.[3]

Reading this passage, Hoover realized (he later remarked) that he was "in a unique position to collect fugitive literature" about another revolution: the titanic global cataclysm that he himself was witnessing. With the eagerness of a lifelong bibliophile, the decisiveness of an executive, and the assurance of a man of means, he resolved to undertake an audacious project similar to White's: the systematic collecting of contemporary documents on the Great War before they were lost to history.[4]

Hoover was therefore probably in a receptive mood when, early in March 1915, he received a letter from Professor E. D. Adams of Stanford. Between these men were two deep bonds of interest: the course of modern history and the development of the university in Palo Alto. Less than a year before, Hoover had given his friend $400 to acquire transcripts of crucial British documents for a book Adams was preparing on Great Britain and the American Civil War.[5] But it was not money that the historian was seeking now.

Instead, in his letter Adams called attention to the extraordinary historical importance of the records of the Commission for Relief in Belgium. The CRB, he wrote, was "an absolutely new thing in History" and would seem even more unique in 50 years than it did now. It was "the one great bright spot" in the war and would "reflect greatly upon Stanford such as nothing else has done" in the years to come. He therefore strongly urged Hoover to deposit the CRB's records someday at his alma mater.[6]

Hoover quickly replied that he found Adams's suggestion to be of "extreme value." He agreed that the CRB's records should be preserved (as in fact was being done already), "if for no other purpose than to prove our innocence in the inevitable persecution which we are bound to receive from one quarter or another." "[E]very atom of material," he promised Adams, would be saved. It would be a "fine idea," he added, "to store them at Stanford University."[7] Curiously, though, he said nothing about his plan to collect "fugitive literature," a plan he later said antedated Adams's letter.

Adams was delighted by Hoover's response, and from time to time in the next three years he reminded Hoover of his commitment.[8] President Woodrow Wilson's confidential adviser, Colonel Edward House, also urged Hoover to preserve the CRB's files during a visit to London in the winter of 1915.[9] The commission's chairman needed little prodding. At the moment, as the battles and economic strife raged on, there was relatively little Hoover could do to fulfill his ambition of assembling a personal archive on the Great War. But in his reading of Andrew D. White's autobiography and his correspondence with E. D. Adams lay the germ of an enterprise that was to become the world's largest private repository of documents on twentieth-century political history. [10]

The placing of the CRB's archive at Stanford was not the only university-related topic on Hoover's mind in the early months of the war. By late 1914 President Branner's anticipated term of office was more than half over, and Hoover was increasingly anxious to find a proper successor. On October 25, 1914, only three days after formally launching the CRB, Hoover took time to write a four-page letter about the university presidency to the chairman of Stanford's board of trustees. It was a matter, he said, "very near to my heart."

Hoover's opinion on this subject was emphatic. Stanford, he declared, was "essentially a Western institution, with ideals entirely different from those which obtain on the Atlantic seaboard." Its development policies of the previous two years (policies largely conceived by himself, he might have added) were "practically unique." Indeed, the university's "whole internal academic structure" was "essentially different from that of any other institution." To Hoover it was therefore evident that Stanford's next president should be "a Western man," and "a man from the present University body." He should also be pre-eminently an administrator. "The old-line President who was able to preside at Sunday School Conventions and make choicely classical orations on public occasions is not the type of man that Stanford needs," he argued. "Nothing would be more disastrous than to choose some classical Professor from the East." For Hoover only one man fit his criteria: the current dean of Stanford's medical school, Ray Lyman Wilbur. [11]

Hoover's reasoning was extremely revealing of his educational philosophy and self-image. He wanted Stanford to be led by a Westerner, not an Easterner; an executive, not an orator; a man of practical education, not a classically trained academic. A man, in short, like himself. If Wilbur was "deficient on the side of flowered and classical oratory," he remarked crisply, that deficiency could be supplied by Chancellor David Starr Jordan. Hoover also admired Wilbur's aggressiveness on behalf of his department. If Stanford had "another ten Wilburs" in its other departments, he argued, "they would have been much further forward than they are today." [12] Hoover's choice was significant for another reason. Ray Lyman Wilbur was one of his oldest and closest friends.

Having circulated his views to key trustees, Hoover now awaited developments. At the beginning of 1915 President Branner duly announced his intention to retire on August 1, and the search for his successor began in earnest. [13] It quickly developed that opposition to Hoover's candidate was strong. During 1914 Wilbur had been embroiled in the bitter battle over the future status of his San Francisco—based department, a battle that he had won and Branner had lost. Apparently embittered by this defeat, Branner seemed determined not to let Wilbur succeed him.[14] He was not alone in his opposition. Many members of the Stanford faculty feared that Wilbur, as president, would place the interests of the medical school ahead of those of other departments.[15]

Well aware of these sentiments, Hoover tried to neutralize them by proposing to his fellow trustees that his friend be appointed acting president for a trial period of one year. Hoover was certain that Wilbur would introduce so much administrative "steam and push" to the campus that he would "galvanize the whole place within twelve months."[16] But if he should not meet expectations, he could then return "with dignity" to the medical school and another person could be chosen president.[17] It would be far better to handle matters in this way, Hoover thought, than to embark on what he called the "experiment" of hiring an educator from the East.[18]

Hoover's suggestion went nowhere. It soon transpired that the faculty's apprehensions about Wilbur were shared by certain trustees, some of whom, including W. Mayo Newhall and J. Leroy Nickel, wished to look outside the faculty—to the East, in fact—for a successor.[19] Hoover, in London, was angry at this turn of events. "I am . . . appalled at the idea of Nickel and Newhall dominating the appointment of a President for Stanford University," he told a friend. "Neither of these men has the university instinct, nor have they the remotest idea as to what constitutes such an institution."[20]

Meanwhile Stanford's newest trustee, Ralph Arnold ('98), was pursuing an idea of his own. A petroleum geologist and businessman (as well as Ray Lyman Wilbur's second cousin), Arnold had known the Hoover brothers for years. In January 1915 he asked Hoover whether *he* would accept an offer of the Stanford presidency. Arnold was convinced that the university would be "making no mistake" if it installed Hoover as president for a long enough term to "thoroughly organize the faculty" and establish "a definite policy of administration."[21]

Hoover's reply was swift and clear: Ray Lyman Wilbur, he said, should be chosen. But then he added:

> If it was not for the intervention of all these international troubles, I would have been quite prepared to take on the job for a couple of years, simply as acting president or acting trustee in charge of the University, in order to hold the position open for Ray. I have no intention to become a University President as a permanent occupation.

Hoover pointed out he could not "desert the Belgians until peace has been signed" and that he would then need three or four months to arrange his "private affairs" before he could "take on the job." How soon he might even be available was therefore impossible to determine. Nevertheless, he seemed willing, at least in principle, to accept the position if offered it.[22]

Arnold was extremely pleased. He immediately replied that if certain circumstances materialized, he would nominate Hoover as a compromise candidate for acting president or acting trustee in charge of the university.[23] Hoover, significantly, did not object.

Then, in the winter of 1915, an unexpected event threw the selection process into turmoil. David Starr Jordan, who as chancellor had been attending trustees' meetings, announced publicly that Wilbur would probably be selected as president. Not long afterward, Jordan, a strong advocate of Wilbur, compounded his indiscretion by practically demanding that the board come to a decision in April—a move interpreted by some as an attempt to stampede the board toward Wilbur. Jordan's behavior incensed the trustees, fortified the anti-Wilbur faction among them, and obliged the rest to defer a choice for some time. As a result, the spring of 1915 passed without result, and Branner was induced to remain as president for as much as another year.[24]

Reporting all this to London, Ralph Arnold again expressed his wish that Hoover could step in for two or three years as president and reorganize the entire university. Not only would the institution benefit, he argued; the interim period would enable Wilbur to solidify his credentials as Hoover's successor. Arnold yearned for Hoover's presence at the showdown meeting of the trustees; at such a meeting, he knew, Hoover's influence would be "dominant."[25]

Far from the environs of Stanford, Hoover was disgusted at the course events were taking. He told Arnold that it was a source of "humour" to think that "a narrow-minded farmer like Newell [Newhall] or an extremely avricious [sic], egotistical banker like [trustee Frank B.] Anderson are either one or the other at all capable in choosing a President for Stanford." As for Branner, who was about to head east on a search for candidates:

> You and I have known for years that Branner is capable of the most violent and consistent prejudices and that with all his admirable qualities these prejudices absolutely blind him to the merits or demerits of individuals. I should consider that he above all men associated with Stanford University is the least qualified to nominate a new President; but when I think of Jordan's judgment I am equally appalled. As to myself, if it does not work out in the next six months that Ray is possible, until the above gentlemen have been completely removed from the scenery and their influence entirely excised, I might manage to take the job and hold it for two or three years, provided I had a clear six months to get prepared in. Much depends upon how long this War lasts and a hundred other contingencies, but rather than see some

loudmouthed Princetown [sic] professor put in the position, I would be
willing to take three years out of my life and throw them away.[26]

Hoover's worries about a "loudmouthed Princetown professor" proved
apposite. After a trip east late in the spring to investigate presidential possibilities, Branner and Newhall returned with an enthusiastic endorsement of
Edwin Capps, professor of classics at Princeton—the very epitome of all that
Hoover found objectionable.[27] Thoroughly alarmed, Arnold cabled London
that Wilbur's "only chance" depended on Hoover's attending the next trustees'
meeting.[28] Only Hoover, he said, could win over Trustee Anderson and sufficiently isolate the opposition to prevail. Once again Arnold held out the
prospect of Hoover's becoming president if Wilbur's bid should fail, and he
disclosed that two other trustees seemed amenable to this possibility.[29]

Hoover's reaction to the Capps candidacy was scorching. The Princeton
professor, he cabled, was a "social fop" and "sycophant to [the] Wall Street
bunch." He was the "absolute negation of [the] type required for president."
But for all his vehemence, Hoover had to record that he had "no hope" of
visiting California until the war was over. Millions of people were dependent
on his venture in humanitarian relief. The CRB, he said, would collapse into
"absolute chaos" without him.[30]

By now the Stanford board of trustees was deeply divided between the
pro- and anti-Wilbur factions.[31] Chancellor Jordan agreed with Arnold that
only Hoover, appearing in person, could persuade the board to select his
nominee.[32] To Jordan, Leland Stanford would "turn over in his grave" if he
knew that "a Professor of classics from the most reactionary university in
America" were to become president.[33] Alas, the one man who seemed capable
of resolving the impasse in Wilbur's favor was thousands of miles away.

At its August meeting the board of trustees decided to interview several
candidates; clearly a decision was some time away. Arnold immediately informed Hoover that he might yet be "the victim of circumstances" if Wilbur
were blocked and that "[trustees] Hopkins and Eells are strong for you in case
Wilbur cannot get it."[34] Lou Henry Hoover, cabling to her husband from
California, was more succinct. "Presidential campaign at deadlock," she said.
"May insist on you."[35]

Immersed in Belgian relief problems six thousand miles away, Hoover
could do little to influence the outcome. As it turned out, his personal presence
was not required. During the autumn, a majority of the trustees voted for
Wilbur, the minority acquiesced, and the board tendered its offer.[36] Wilbur
accepted—in order that (he later wrote) "medicine would not be destroyed as
a part of the University." To Wilbur the time had arrived for Stanford to fulfill
its early promise and become in full measure a university, not simply a small

college with a large endowment. The acquisition of the medical school, in his view, was the first great step in this transition.[37] In all these aspirations his friend Herbert Hoover agreed with him. Now, thanks in considerable part to Hoover's own "steam and push," Wilbur was to have his opportunity.

Shortly after the board made its decision, Hoover sent the president-elect a seven-page letter of advice and felicitation. For "the first time in its history," he predicted, Stanford University under Wilbur would "take absolutely first rank." Hoover urged Wilbur to reorganize Stanford's system of "faculty control" in order that the "leaders of the University" might emerge instead of "secondary men." Specifically, Hoover suggested that Wilbur bring related faculty departments together into "groups," administered by committees of department heads, who in turn would elect representatives to a small "legislative body" to be known as the University Executive Committee or University Senate. In this way, he argued, the "best brains" could prevail in university governance, and the influence of assistant professors and instructors could be reduced. With such a body drawn from the "pre-eminent professors," Wilbur might even be able to abolish "the well-known Debating Society called the 'Academic Council.' " Returning to a theme he had expounded often before the war, Hoover also advocated that Stanford hire more "illustrious men." These select few were the key, he asserted, to the university's success and to its standing in the academic world.

Hoover offered his friend one other self-revealing suggestion:

> There is one bit of advice that I will hazard you on the whole question of the administration of any institution and that is never to be afraid of the ability of one's lieutenants but to bear in mind that the more able the men with whom one surrounds oneself the more certainty one has of ultimate success.[38]

Not long after Wilbur assumed the Stanford presidency, Hoover received a letter from the U.S. minister to Belgium, Brand Whitlock, with whom he had worked closely on Belgian relief for more than a year. Whitlock had journeyed on leave to the United States in late 1915. Upon his return to Brussels, he informed Hoover that everywhere in America people had expressed their regard for the chairman of the CRB. "[I]f you don't look out," Whitlock added, "they will try to run you for Vice President. . . ."[39] A few days later Hoover responded:

> As to your remark about Vice-Presidents, nothing could be more abhorrent to me in the wide world than to go into politics in any shape or form. The one chance which had been my life ambition has come and gone as Stanford University, which offered me its presidency, could not wait on my

intangible arrival pending the completion of the Belgian job, and therefore they accepted my suggestion and elected Dr. Wilbur to that position, so that I shall go back to the lead mines with a sufficient amount of experience in public affairs to know that it is an evil connection if one values contentment or even constructive results.[40]

Hoover's reply was not quite accurate. As far as is known, Stanford University never formally or informally offered him its presidency. But during the long behind-the-scenes struggle to select a successor to John C. Branner, at least three of the university's fifteen trustees had been ready to support Hoover as a "compromise" candidate, and he almost certainly could have obtained the position had he sought it. By then, of course, he had other, far larger commitments—and perhaps larger ambitions as well.

In any case, with Wilbur's accession to the university's presidency in January 1916, Hoover believed that his "usefulness in the institution" was "more or less at an end," except insofar as he could "deliver the goods" on the board in behalf of his friend's policies.[41] This feeling of a service completed, combined with his recognition that the European war—and hence his absence from America—would probably last another year, led him on May 30, 1916 to submit his resignation from Stanford's board of trustees. It did not seem "fair," he wrote, to remain a trustee "as I am of no service in executive work."[42]

Hoover's action disturbed Ray Lyman Wilbur. "You must not get an attack of conscience," he wrote his friend and patron. "We need you from time to time and we need you badly."[43] Hoover's colleagues on the board agreed. Instead of accepting his resignation, they merely laid his letter on the table, where the matter quietly died.[44] More than one of them stated that if Hoover insisted on withdrawing now, they would resign later, if necessary, to make way for his return.[45] Such was the esteem with which the 41-year-old trustee was held by his associates. Still, it was now clear that Hoover's next contribution to his alma mater would have to await the end of the war.

II

When the United States entered the European conflict in April 1917, Hoover returned home at last, a humanitarian hero whose talents were now required by his own country. For the remainder of the war he served President Wilson as head of the U.S. Food Administration, a government agency created in 1917 to stimulate food production, eliminate waste, reduce domestic consumption, and stabilize soaring prices. At his right hand, as chief of the Food Administration's conservation division, was Ray Lyman Wilbur, who journeyed east frequently from Stanford by train to pursue his wartime duties in

Washington and elsewhere.[46] Another intimate was Ben S. Allen, who directed Hoover's "educational division" and served as a liaison to the press.[47]

As a senior government official, Hoover resided in Washington during his wartime service. But his long-deferred return from Europe obliged him now to confront a question: where would he make his permanent abode on American soil? For those who knew his sentiments there could be no doubt of the answer. Long before August 1914, he and his wife had acquired the habit, during visits to California, of temporarily leasing homes from faculty friends on or near the Stanford campus.[48] When Lou and the boys returned from England for good in early 1917 they had promptly resumed this practice, renting first the house of Professor Henry David Gray and then (during the academic year 1917–1918) the house of Professor Charles A. Huston.[49] The next step was logical, almost inevitable. Herbert Hoover, who had circled the world several times before World War I, was about to come full circle and stop—on the campus he had long considered his spiritual home.[50]

On May 14, 1917 Lou in Palo Alto telegraphed her husband in Washington: "Do you think it advisable build fifty thousand dollars house or five thousand or none at all."[51] Hoover immediately telegraphed back: "You can build any sort of house you wish but if it is to be the ultimate family headquarters it should be substantial and roomy. The cost is secondary."[52]

The Hoovers soon hired Louis C. Mullgardt, a distinguished San Francisco architect who had recently designed the first official residence for the presidents of Stanford University—the building known today as the Knoll. (President Wilbur and his family moved into that structure in 1918.)[53] The Hoovers' plans called for a two-story, 21-room, $50,000 house on San Juan Hill, overlooking the campus and San Francisco Bay. But when Mullgardt indiscreetly announced their intentions (and his own selection as architect) in the press,[54] his clients were mortified and angry. Ever protective of their privacy, the Hoovers hated uncontrolled publicity; they particularly disliked it now. Here was the U.S. Food Administrator, daily exhorting his countrymen to tighten their belts and eat less, yet preparing (or so it seemed) to build a magnificent edifice for himself in wartime. Furthermore, Mullgardt's preliminary design was in the same Portuguese Gothic style as the university president's house then going up—a structure the Hoovers found distinctly pretentious. The result came swiftly: Mullgardt was paid off and dismissed.[55]

Clearly for political reasons (if no other), the Hoovers could not build their "dream house" as long as the Great War raged. In mid-1918, therefore, Mrs. Hoover purchased the nearby campus home of Professor Albert C. Whittaker for $10,000. Into it she and her sons moved, pending construction on the lot on San Juan Hill.[56]

At the close of the war, in November 1918, Hoover returned to Europe for ten months as director-general of the American Relief Administration

(ARA), organizing the supply of food for starving millions, facilitating the emergence of stable economies, and helping thereby to check the spread of bolshevik revolution in central Europe. As a member of the Supreme Economic Council and as an adviser to President Wilson at the Paris peace conference, Hoover's contribution to the reconstruction of the exhausted continent was enormous. Under his generalship millions of tons of food, clothing, and other supplies flowed to the needy inhabitants of more than twenty nations. Railroads were restored, communication facilities established, and waterways cleared. It was, he later put it, an "American epic."[57] Thanks in substantial measure to the labors of himself and his staff, as much as one-third of the population of Europe was saved from famine and death.

Even as he worked feverishly in Paris, Hoover's thoughts turned at times to Palo Alto. On January 6, 1919 he cabled to his wife at Stanford: "Hope you start building University house at once."[58] Hoover's stipulations were few, notably that the structure must be fireproof.[59] Otherwise its creation was to be his wife's responsibility—a task she accepted with enthusiasm.

Lou immediately approached a neighbor and old friend, Professor Arthur Clark of the university's art department. Clark, who had designed a number of faculty homes, agreed to serve as a general supervisor and consultant, provided that Mrs. Hoover (as he put it) "act as the architect." Lou readily agreed, and, with the help of the professor, his architect son Birge ('14), and an expert draftsman, she began.[60]

Apparently before she proceeded very far she sought her husband's reassurance, for on April 23 another cable went from Paris to Palo Alto. "Build you[r] house as you planned it," Hoover said, and then added: "Probably won't use it much for fifteen years but want it right then."[61] His prescience was almost uncanny.

The home's foundation was laid on June 19, 1919, at what is today 623 Mirada Road, the highest building lot on San Juan Hill.[62] As was obligatory under Stanford's founding grant, the land itself was leased (not purchased) from the university. From the beginning Mrs. Hoover, outgoing and unaffected, immersed herself in every detail—even climbing up on chairs placed precariously on ten-foot-high scaffoldings in order to test the view. Artistic tradition and precedent did not faze her; when told that something was "not done," she would reply, "Well, it's time someone did."[63] Again and again the plans were modified to accommodate her individualistic preferences.

From the first, also, the de facto architect and her associates struggled to keep the structure unpretentious and suitable for a neighborhood of college professors, yet sufficiently capacious for the many guests and entertainments she envisaged.[64] Slowly, inexorably, the undertaking grew. To avoid ostentation, the projected tile roofs were eliminated in favor of less imposing flat roofs (which doubled as terraces), guest rooms were moved to the ground floor, and the building was set as much as possible into the hillside. As Birge Clark put it long afterward, "The house was hammered down and made to flow out to hug the site more and more. . . . The house simply was hammered out and forged as we went along."[65]

By the time it was ready for occupancy in mid-1920, the Hoovers' new residence had evolved from two stories to three, contained 57 rooms (counting large closets, hallways, and bathrooms), and stretched 192 feet by 65 feet at its maximum length.[66] Partly as a result of the immediate postwar inflation, the cost of the project had skyrocketed to at least $137,000 (and possibly as much as $170,000) in 1919–1920 dollars.[67] The large, "irregularly shaped"[68] building reflected the eclecticism, even unconventionality, of its designer. Finished in off-white "California stucco," and distinctly modern in external appearance, the home on the inside resembled a "Tudoresque" English country house, with such features as dark oak paneling, an oak spiral staircase, and nine fireplaces. Every room had leaded glass windows that Lou so loved—every one, that is, except Hoover's study, which at his insistence contained windows made of plate glass. "The Chief" (as his friends called him) wanted *his* view unobstructed.[69]

Over the years the home's architecture has been variously labeled Algerian, North African, Pueblo, Hopi, and "early International." In truth, the Hoovers had no architectural grand design.[70] Commented Hoover on one occasion: "It should look as if a child had piled up blocks."[71] Said he to Birge Clark as the building was being erected: "I really don't care what it looks like just so it doesn't look like that insane asylum of Wilbur's over there."[72]

Hoover emphatically did care, however, about criticism of the dwelling's size. When a political foe in 1919 accused him of building a "palace," he publicly retorted that the "palace" contained "seven rooms and a basement, a kitchen, and a garage"—a figure he obtained by omitting the servants' quarters, guest rooms, and various minor rooms from his count.[73] Perhaps he reasoned that his immediate family would not use these other rooms; hence there was no need to take note of them. In any case, for years to come Lou Henry Hoover, sensitive like her husband to such slings and arrows, was loathe to let the house be photographed for magazines. To the future First Lady the size of her home was no one's business but her family's.[74]

Such irritations were minor compared to the pleasure the Hoovers felt as their home took shape on their beloved campus. The identification of the university with its most accomplished alumnus was taking dramatically visible form. Late in 1919, in a further gesture toward rootedness, the Hoovers bought a nearby house on the hill from the dean of men, J. E. McDowell.[75] At first Mrs. Hoover evidently intended it to be a home for her aging parents in Monterey;[76] later she used it as a guest house and eventually rented it to Professor Walter Miles.[77] (The Hoovers sold this house to another faculty member in the late 1920s.)[78] When, in 1920, the Hoovers' own home was finally ready for habitation, they sold the Whittaker House in which they had been living to Professor Adams, who thus became a close neighbor as well as a close friend.[79]

The house on San Juan Hill was not the only university-related matter to concern Hoover in early 1919. On January 14 Professor Edgar Eugene Robinson of the history department wrote Hoover that the Stanford War History Committee was collecting materials on the roles of alumni in the war—documents to be deposited in the California Room of the new library. The young professor boldly asked Hoover to give his personal Food Administration records to the committee.[80] The next day Robinson's colleague, the indefatigable Professor Adams, wrote still another in his series of letters urging Hoover to preserve and donate the papers of the CRB.[81]

It is not known when these two communications reached their destination, or what impact, if any, they may have had.[82] Then, on April 23, 1919, Lou Henry Hoover received a cablegram from her husband across the sea. The message was terse and unexpected: "Advise Wilbur [and] Adams that if they keep it entirely confidential we can find cost of their sending at once suitable mission to Europe to collect historical material on war provided it does not exceed fifty thousand without further consideration."[83]

Mrs. Hoover was puzzled by this sudden communication; so, too, were President Wilbur and Professor Adams. What, they wondered, did it actually mean? Did Hoover merely want someone to come to Europe to gather up his CRB files and other relief documents? Or did the Chief contemplate something more? Why also was Hoover in such a hurry? Embroiled in his teaching responsibilities, Adams particularly needed to know whether his personal presence in Europe was instantly required or whether he could dispatch someone else. Through Hoover's close associate in New York, Edgar Rickard, the trio in Palo Alto therefore attempted to obtain clarification. What would be the mission's scope and duties? Would it embrace just the CRB, Adams asked, or the Great War generally?[84]

From Hoover on May 15 came a second cable, even shorter than the one before: "My idea is simply collect library material on war generally."[85] To Adams this message was enough. A historical collection on the entire war! For years the distinguished historian had had to get by on an annual university library allocation of just a few hundred dollars for books in his discipline. Now he savored the prospect of spending thousands—and on a pioneering field besides.[86] On May 22, only one week after Hoover's second cable, Professor Adams and his wife left for Europe.[87]

Arriving in Paris (via London) in mid-June, Adams immediately interviewed the Chief. The professor discovered that Hoover had no elaborate scheme for launching his project. Instead, as Adams wrote shortly afterward to President Wilbur, "His general idea is simply a collection of suitable library material on the war for Stanford University, and the fund needed for this is provided by him personally." [88] Hoover did have two suggestions. He thought the collectors should endeavor to acquire all available documents on food conditions and food administration in the various belligerent countries and that they should not particularly emphasize the military aspects of the war. [89] As always, he was primarily interested in the deeper socioeconomic currents of modern history. According to Adams, Hoover laid down one other stipulation in this first conversation: the resultant collection must remain (in Adams's words) a "separate physical entity at Stanford University." [90]

A few days later Hoover formally ratified his understanding with Professor Adams:

> This is to confirm the offer which I made to Dr. Wilbur to find $50,000 at his demand or the demand of anyone he appointed to undertake the work for the purpose of sending a representative to Europe for the collection of historical material for the Stanford University Library. This fund to be entirely at the disposal of Dr. Wilbur or his agent for any purpose of expense for purchase of documents or otherwise that will contribute to the library's strength with regard to a documentary history bearing on the war. This fund is available at any time on demand. [91]

Absorbed in the protean tasks of feeding and rebuilding war-torn Europe, Hoover himself had no time to devote to the impending acquisitions campaign. He even told Adams not to bother him with an expense account but instead to report to President Wilbur. [92]

Nevertheless, the Chief was able to help in other ways than provision of the indispensable funds. He wrote out a letter of introduction on Supreme Economic Council stationery urging readers to assist Adams in his collecting of "historical data on the war for the records" of Stanford University. [93] He asked his farflung network of ARA personnel all over Europe to render Adams "every facility in his work," including the securing of visas and transportation. [94] Even more important, Hoover persuaded the U.S. Army to detach two of Adams's former students who were then stationed in western Europe: Private Robert C. Binkley ('22) and Lieutenant Ralph Lutz ('06). [95] Officially both men were detailed from the military to Hoover's ARA. In the case of Lutz, a professor of history on leave from the University of Washington, Hoover informed the army that the ARA was compiling its final historical report for Congress and that Lutz's services were needed for this task. [96] In fact, both men joined Hoover's private collecting effort. [97]

Hoover's principal contribution, however, was less tangible. In the summer of 1919 his name (in Adams's words) was "the most powerful one in Europe." [98] As "the food regulator for the world," [99] he held the fate of millions in his hands. Where others had fought and left a residue of tears and destruction, Hoover and his colleagues were restoring life and hope. As a result, said Adams, individuals and governments across the continent were "eager to contribute anything they had for us." [100] Such was the prestige of the head of the American Relief Administration.

The Stanford professor recognized that Hoover's name was "the one greatest asset in our enterprise." [101] Ray Lyman Wilbur, too, appreciated the crucial link between Hoover's humanitarian relief work and his success as a collector of documents. "Hoover," he said, "is the greatest packrat of all time because, whenever he leaves a ton of food, he picks up a pound of history." [102] Still, the unique opportunity presented in 1919 would have been an opportunity lost had it not been for a single farsighted man. The world does not usually think of engineers as possessing acute historical consciousness. Hoover, the engineer-turned-public-servant, did. Alone among the statesmen at the peace conference, Herbert Hoover had the vision, generosity, and will to preserve the raw materials of history for a curious and grateful posterity.

During the summer and autumn of 1919 the talented team of Adams, Binkley, and Lutz began to build what they called the Hoover War History Collection. Adams, for the most part, stayed in Paris, acquiring government documents, propaganda pamphlets, and other "fugitive literature" from the 70 delegations to the peace conference. [103] Lutz eventually ventured into the states of eastern and central Europe, armed with a letter of introduction from Hoover and an expense account drawn from Hoover's fund. [104] In late August a snag nearly threw their plans awry: Lutz, about to be discharged from the army, was due to return to his teaching position at the University of Washington. Without clearing the matter with Hoover (who was away from Paris at the time), Adams sent a cable in Hoover's name to the university's president, Henry Suzzallo ('99): "Request permission use Ralph Lutz until December, important work Poland answer." Suzzallo promptly replied—to Hoover— that he would acquiesce "for your greater need." When Hoover learned about the cable from Seattle, he exclaimed, "Who in Hell is Suzzallo?" [105]

If Hoover was affronted by Adams's audacity, the record does not show it. In all likelihood, he was merely amused. Hoover in fact admired men who displayed initiative, men of energy and brains, men who got things done and explained themselves later. These were just the qualities that were needed in his quest for a notable archive on the war and its aftermath. Soon the results were apparent—in a broadening torrent of invaluable documents flowing to his alma mater in California. Adams was justifiably ecstatic. "We were absolutely the first university to attack the problem in Europe of a War Collection," he told President Wilbur in 1920. Furthermore, he now expected that not just printed materials but the papers of Hoover's numerous relief organizations would eventually come to the Stanford library. Said Adams with confidence:

"The historian of the future or the student of food questions who wishes to understand what was accomplished by America and Americans in International European Relief, will have to come to this university to study his subject." [106]

In September 1919, after nearly a year of herculean labor in Europe, a weary Hoover sailed home. Sickened by the inveterate jealousies, power struggles, and ethnic hatreds that had flared during the first months of "peace," he told an interviewer that he never cared to see Europe again. [107] But in this much, at least, he could take comfort: his vast, ambitious war history collection, destined for deposit at his alma mater, was securely underway. It was to be far from the least of his contributions to restoring a riven civilization.

III

Shortly after his return to America, Hoover was hailed by the *Stanford Illustrated Review* as "the most useful man in the world today." [108] To the campus, in fact, he now hastened, for the first time in five and a half years. In a way it was a family reunion. Not only were Hoover, his wife, and two sons together for the first time since the war, but earlier in the year Herbert's brother Theodore, a mining engineer, author, and expert on the flotation process for ore concentration, had also been appointed professor of mining and metallurgy at Stanford. He was to remain on the faculty for the rest of his career. [109]

Hoover arrived to find a university in crisis, [110] its development stunted by the recent world war. Both students and faculty, he discovered, were "woefully underhoused"; in many cases three students were living in one room. [111] Especially pernicious had been the effect of wartime inflation on the faculty. Because of the tremendous rise in the cost of living since 1914, said Hoover, "wholesome life" among "the lower grades of the teaching staff" was now "impossible." [112] He told the press that the 150 instructors and assistant professors at Stanford were earning far less per day than the skilled laborers who were building his home. [113] More ominously still, thanks to the "increasing premiums" now being offered by the universities and the private sector for "intelligence and intellectual skill," Stanford stood in danger of losing its ablest professors. [114] Without immediate action, the aspiring "university of high degree" faced stagnation.

Yet what could be done? To Hoover there was only one solution. At a meeting on September 26, the board of trustees, upon his motion, established a special committee of three "to consider the matter of charging tuition fees at the University." Hoover, predictably, became a member of this committee. [115] It did not take long to energize his fellow trustees. Barely two weeks later, at a special meeting on October 11, the board voted unanimously to institute a tuition fee of $40 per quarter for all students, effective January 1, 1920.[116] For the first time in its history, Stanford would impose general charges upon its students for their instruction.[117]

To cushion the shock, the trustees created a number of fellowships and scholarships for graduate students. At the urging of Hoover's committee, they also agreed to accept seven-year interest-bearing promissory notes from undergraduates whose chance for an education would be "jeopardized by the requirement of these fees." In other words, needy students would not be required actually to pay their tuition until they were out in the world, and presumably earning a living, some years later.[118] With an additional income in excess of $100,000 thus assured, the trustees immediately voted an aggregate $75,000 across-the-board pay increase for the Stanford University faculty.[119]

The trustees' decision angered the student body and evoked regret in other quarters as well.[120] For more than a generation, the institution had adhered to the egalitarian ideal of a tuition-free education. As Leland Stanford's wife Jane had declared in 1902, the university had been endowed "with a view of offering instruction free, or nearly free, that it may resist the tendency to the stratification of society, by keeping open an avenue whereby the deserving and exceptional may rise through their own efforts from the lowest to the highest stations in life."[121] Suddenly this cherished ideal seemed threatened. On a more practical level, many students were incensed that the fees would take effect in the very next academic quarter. After all, they argued, they had registered for classes with the understanding that tuition would not be charged.[122]

Apparently stung by the furor, Hoover replied on October 16 with a public letter assuming "sole responsibility" for the trustees' action. "I have been its advocate for the past six years," he declared, "and President Wilbur has been able to agree only in the last extremity." Hoover pointed out that the university's income from its essentially fixed endowment had attained a "practical maximum," while its expenditures continued to soar, exceeding income continuously during the past five years. To balance its budget, increase salaries, and meet other needs the institution simply had to obtain an additional $200,000 per annum at once.

Hoover rejected the facile suggestion that the university seek more gifts from alumni. The Stanford alumni were still too young and too few to contribute much, he said, and some of them, "like some of the students, appear impregnated with the idea that education in this particular institution imposes no obligation of return support." Nor did Hoover approve of admitting fewer students or eliminating freshman and sophomore year instruction; such measures, he said, would only deprive more people of an opportunity for an education. Still less did he countenance a general reduction of expenditure; that, he remarked scornfully, was "the usual suggestion of the uninformed mind." (Perhaps he was thinking of President Branner's fight against the medical school.) This left only one alternative—tuition, an alternative that had been considered for years, said Hoover, and one that Mrs. Stanford herself had authorized the trustees to charge when they deemed it necessary. [123]

Hoover was convinced that most Stanford students could well afford to pay tuition amounting to $120 per year. The number of automobiles belonging to students and "the receipts of the ice cream parlors in this neighborhood," he remarked pointedly, "would go a long way toward the needed increase in income." As for those students who could not pay such a bill, Hoover, who said he knew "by bitter experience" what it meant to work one's way through college, argued that the promissory note plan would suffice.

The combative Hoover rejected the argument that it would somehow be demeaning or undemocratic for certain students to sign such a note:

> I had the notion that the undertaking of such a liability for future payment would be a matter of pride and a far more self-respecting measure than free tuition to a specially designated portion of the student body. I am able to see no infringement of democracy in such a plan. . . . It is my belief that every man and woman lays here the foundation of an association that is the most valuable of this entire life, and the maintenance of the quality of the association, of its repute, and the extension of its opportunities to others, is the vital interest of everyone in the association. Those who do not value this participation to the extent that makes them willing to pledge themselves to an obligation to come to its assistance and thus to the assistance of others, at a period long enough after graduation, appear to me to cumber the institution with material not worth its exertion or worthy of admission to this association.

As for the students' claim that it was unfair to impose tuition during the present academic year, Hoover was equally unyielding. Legally, he rejoined, students did not register by the year but by the quarter, and no tuition was being charged for the current (autumn) quarter. Nor did the university have any moral obligation to wait. The university up to now had been giving its students an education, and "it is a new doctrine to me that there is any implied obligation in any gift, except repayment with all the return in one's power." [124]

Faced with inexorable economic necessity (and the trustees' determination to proceed), the opposition to the tuition scheme soon dissipated, and Stanford, with Hoover in the vanguard, entered a new era. Never again could the university rely solely upon its original endowment from the Stanford family. From now on, as Ray Lyman Wilbur recognized, it would be dependent on the world beyond the campus for its financial sustenance. [125]

As the man who primarily effected this transition, Hoover faced up to its implications. Within weeks of the trustees' announcement, he addressed an alumni group in New York on the need to increase the university's endowment.[126] Shortly thereafter he contributed $5,000 to a loan fund for students who could not pay their tuition.[127] Early in 1920 he took his alma mater in another pioneering direction: on behalf of the trustees he asked the General Education Board of the Rockefeller Foundation for a substantial grant toward deficits that, even with tuition, exceeded $100,000 per year. Hoover pointed out that the university still suffered from public perception of it as a "personal memorial," a perception that seemed to "drive charitable contribution away" and had thwarted efforts to gain significant outside financial support. He argued, too, that Stanford was "the principal independent endowed institution of the Pacific Slope," an institution "free from all political influence" and government subsidy, and that it had a mission to maintain standards of excellence in higher education "throughout the West."[128]

As Hoover searched for new sources of university revenue, no one could accuse him of personal niggardliness. In 1919 alone he gave his alma mater $41,250, including $25,000 (the first half of his pledge) for his war history collection, $5,000 for the student aid fund, $10,000 for the Stanford Home for Convalescent Children, and $1,250 for support of the Student Union.[129] He also pledged $10,000 to the building fund for a campus memorial to Stanford's war dead.[130] In all likelihood no other alumnus remotely approached this level of benefaction.

In early 1920, having secured the new tuition system and a substantial faculty salary increase, Hoover turned to the university's other pressing difficulty: a chronic housing shortage now rendered acute by a growing faculty and student body. As usual he was prepared to act boldly. On February 28 he formally offered his alma mater $100,000 to expand the Student Union, provided 1) that the trustees supply a similar amount, 2) that Hoover approve the plans, and 3) that his donation be kept anonymous.[131] Hoover specified that the sum be spent on an additional building comprising "eating clubs" and dormitory space.[132] The trustees quickly accepted, appropriating a sum of $100,000 (later raised to at least $176,000) in the form of a loan to be repaid eventually out of student fees.[133] No doubt with Hoover's approval, the board retained the eminent San Francisco architectural firm of Bakewell and Brown,[134] architects to the university since 1913 (an appointment for which Hoover seems to have been responsible). Thanks in part to his enthusiastic patronage, the firm remained Stanford's official architects until the 1940s.[135]

When completed in 1922, the Mission-style, Hoover-approved[136] structure contained rooms for over one hundred students and dining facilities for more than three hundred.[137] It was connected to the men's and women's clubhouses of 1915 by arcades supported by arches, thus making an integrated unit of three buildings. This complex is known today as the Old Union.

Faithful to Hoover's request, the university for many years did not disclose the name of the donor of $100,000, but there was little doubt in Palo Alto who he was. Once again, without his catalytic vigor a much-loved feature of the Stanford landscape might never have been erected.

The enlarged Stanford Union was only one of several Hoover initiatives to resolve the university's housing crisis in 1920. In late August, and undoubtedly under his prodding, the trustees finally allocated $450,000 to build a home for nurses at the Stanford School of Nursing in San Francisco—a commitment made in 1913 but never consummated.[138] At least one nurse thanked Hoover for rousing the board to action.[139] That same month the full board directed its campus committee (of which Hoover was a member) to prepare a comprehensive plan for student and faculty housing on campus.[140] It was scarcely a moment too soon. So severe was the overcrowding that the university was obliged in the autumn of 1920 to ask the residents of Palo Alto to take students into their homes.[141]

At a board meeting on November 5 the campus committee, led by Hoover, submitted its much-awaited report. Upon his motion the trustees swiftly approved an audacious five-year construction program costing $1,470,000, over and above the more than $600,000 already authorized for the Student Union and the nurses' home. The break with past conservatism was staggering; only the year before, the university's disposable income for *all* purposes had been about $1,100,000.[142] The Hooverian building scheme included expenditures for new men's and women's dormitories, dining and other facilities in Encina Hall, and a $250,000 Faculty Housing Fund that would loan professors 90 percent of the cost of constructing new homes on campus. The loans would be interest free and repayable over twenty years. Upon Hoover's motion the trustees also voted to reorganize the faculty pension plan.[143]

The breathtaking decisions of the trustees' meeting, of course, had to be financed. On Hoover's motion tuition was nearly doubled, from $40 to $75 per quarter. But this in itself could not begin to cover the anticipated outlay. Much of the allotted expenditure, therefore, consisted of long-term loans from the endowment funds to the building accounts—funds to be repaid at 5 percent interest, apparently out of future student fees.[144]

Not everyone was happy with the dramatic results of the November 1920 meeting. At least one trustee strenuously opposed the building package and fought unsuccessfully to have it reconsidered.[145] Still, despite this dissent, the university's lost momentum had been restored, and one man more than any other was responsible for it. Early in 1921, a grateful Ray Lyman Wilbur told Hoover that it was his donation of $100,000 for the Stanford Union that had broken the logjam: "I know of no bigger service that has been rendered here," wrote Wilbur, "than that that has followed in the wake of this gift, because it started the whole machine leading towards the handling of our future housing problem." [146] In the next few years the fruits of Hoover's activism became manifest: Encina Commons (1923), Toyon Hall (1923), Branner Hall (1924), and 30 new faculty homes on campus by 1927. [147]

Meanwhile Hoover had begun to confront the challenge of organizing his war history collection. Upon his return to Palo Alto in late 1919, he discussed its future status with Ray Lyman Wilbur, who on January 6, 1920 formally contacted the trustees:

> Mr. Hoover has asked me to notify the Board that he is presenting to the University a collection of books, pamphlets, and other material on the Great War and that he will spend up to $50,000 in making this collection. A large number of volumes have already reached the University Library and others are on the way . . . .
>
> Mr. Hoover makes this gift upon the conditions that it shall be maintained and kept as a separate collection, kept upon separate stacks and with a separate room for its use, also that other books in the Library closely related to the same subject shall be assembled with this collection. This is particularly important since a considerable part of the collection is made up of confidential documents. [148]

The trustees accepted Hoover's gift—and his conditions. [149]

The year 1920 was a rewarding one for the burgeoning Hoover War Collection (as it was now generally called). The Chief himself assisted in soliciting relevant items; at one point he asked the U.S. State Department to donate a complete copy of its daily press summaries. [150] It was increasingly evident that the quest Hoover had initiated in 1919 would not end suddenly or soon. During the year, E. D. Adams succeeded in hiring Ralph Lutz away from the University of Washington; the prospect of working with, and building upon, the Hoover war documents was for Lutz a decisive consideration. [151] In the years to come Lutz was to make seven trips to Europe to obtain further items for the collection. In his letter to the trustees back in January, President Wilbur had predicted that the remarkable collection would "attract graduate students to our departments." [152] Already it was luring professors.

During 1920, too, Adams and Lutz persuaded a visiting young historian from Washington State University, Frank Golder, to remain at Stanford; again Hoover's archive proved an enticement. Before the end of the year, the Russian-born Golder was on his way to the land of his birth in search of materials on its recent social upheaval. He was to be spectacularly successful, eventually acquiring 25,000 books and more than 60,000 pamphlets, newspapers, journals, and government publications. Largely as a result of Golder's Hoover-financed trips to eastern Europe and Russia in the 1920s, the archive in Palo Alto became the greatest repository of documents on the Russian Revolution in the entire noncommunist world.[153]

The rapidly developing war library was not the only war-related institution that Hoover brought into being on the Stanford campus in 1920–1921. As head of the CRB and the U.S. Food Administration, and as coordinator of the relief of Europe in 1919, he had become aware, as perhaps no other living person, of the need for systematic scientific research on contemporary food problems, particularly those involving processing, distribution, and nutrition. Time and again, in devising and implementing policies he had been frustrated by a dearth of pertinent information on these subjects. Furthermore, it now occurred to him that in his own enormous accumulated files lay a unique data base for just such investigations. And so the idea arose: why not establish a permanent food research facility to explore these very issues—and on the Stanford University campus itself?[154]

In drawing up a plan for organization and funding, Hoover worked closely with Dr. Alonzo E. Taylor, a nationally known scientist from the University of Pennsylvania who had been his principal expert adviser on food questions during and immediately after the war.[155] Before long their campaign was in high gear. In July 1920 Hoover informally approached Henry S. Pritchett, a Carnegie Corporation trustee, during the Bohemian Club's annual encampment north of San Francisco.[156] (Hoover had joined in 1913.) A few days later, Stanford's board of trustees authorized its most enterprising member to negotiate with the Carnegie people for an endowment.[157]

During the autumn Hoover consulted Elihu Root of the corporation's board of directors and, later on, the corporation's president, James R. Angell. At one point Hoover feared that his ally Taylor had failed to convey to Angell the institute's immense potential. To the corporation executive, therefore, Hoover addressed a crucial letter:

> Lest you feel that Dr. Taylor, in enumerating only five specimen problems, is not covering the entire possibilities of this proposed Institute, I would like to add that I can enumerate at least fifty important matters that are really vital to the economic and health development of the United States.

The Labor Department's cost of living index, for example: Hoover was convinced that it was "wrongly founded," with profound consequences for the nation. The nature of commodity futures trading was a second subject deserving scholarly attention, said Hoover; the economics of cooperative marketing another. Still another was the American diet: "Our increasing population can be fed more cheaply and better upon more cereals and less animal products.

This is a matter that can be spread only by education through the whole school system, not by crank notions of vegetarians."

Hoover also tried to allay the Carnegie Corporation's worry that a food research center on campus might find its mission subverted by the demands of classroom teaching:

> My own conviction is that there is an extreme value for every man engaged in original research of a certain minimum contact with students. Moreover, I have the feeling that it is through the immediate product of the university that a large part of the drudgery of investigation must be carried out.

Moreover, he asserted, the proposed institute "would have the backing of a great educational institution in the extension of its propaganda work." [158] When it came to finding arguments in support of his objectives, Hoover could be very resourceful.

Hoover's forceful appeal—and the proximity of his food records—proved persuasive. Early in 1921 the Carnegie Corporation agreed to give his undertaking $704,000 over ten years upon certain conditions, including corporation approval of the directors and the appointment of these directors as Stanford professors. [159] The university accepted these and other requirements, and the Food Research Institute at Stanford was born. [160] It was one of the first university-affiliated research institutions in America. [161] By prearrangement, Hoover was named to its advisory committee; according to one newspaper report, the corporation expressed its desire that the new center eventually be named the Hoover Institute. [162] According to Hoover's recollection many years later, he personally selected the institute's first three co-directors, including Dr. Taylor as chairman. [163]

On February 28, 1921 the *Daily Palo Alto* reported that the Carnegie Corporation's massive grant to the Food Research Institute was "the first financial support" that Stanford had ever received "from the outside." [164] One man above all was responsible; no one else, at that time, could have achieved as much. Success on this scale was doubly sweet, for it held out the prospect that Stanford, now certified as a major university, would be able to elicit similar awards from other foundations. In the postwar race of institutions of higher learning for external income, Stanford—led by Hoover—had made its long-sought breakthrough.

The Carnegie grant was significant in another respect: it ushered in the era at Stanford in which centers for advanced study would be conspicuous features of the university's landscape, the era in which pure and applied research would be increasingly integral to its perceived mission. To Ray Lyman Wilbur, who believed that the university should be an "active living organism in direct contact with the whole world," [165] this development was cause for celebration. The Food Research Institute, he declared in 1921, "constitutes one of the most notable opportunities for research of a wide scope that has come to any university in America within recent years." [166] For this, and so much else, he had his best friend to thank.

In the spring of 1921 Hoover could look back on eighteen months of achievement, months in which he had thrust his alma mater forward to a more secure status of excellence. Such accomplishment would have been enough for ordinary men. But Herbert Hoover was not ordinary. The renewal of Stanford University, in fact, absorbed but a small fraction of his time in this period. Larger issues and concerns—the debate over the League of Nations, relief for the children of Europe, reform and reconstruction at home, the presidential campaign of 1920—clamored for his thought and attention. He was one of the leading figures in America now, the only man (in John Maynard Keynes's estimation) who had "emerged from the ordeal" of the peace conference "with an enhanced reputation." [167]

Then, in early 1921, came something more: President-elect Warren Harding invited Hoover to join his cabinet as secretary of commerce.

· 5 ·

"On the Map Again"

I

From 1921 to 1928, Hoover served Presidents Harding and Coolidge as secretary of commerce. From this hitherto lowly cabinet office the energetic engineer-turned-public-servant quickly established himself as one of the three or four most important men in American public life. So pervasive was his influence that it was said he was secretary of commerce—and undersecretary of every other department.

Although Hoover's governmental duties in the 1920s obliged him to reside in Washington, D.C., he returned home to California whenever possible—usually for short intervals during the summers, when he relaxed at the Bohemian Grove and took fishing trips to the remote streams of northern California. His lengthy absences from his alma mater brought no diminution of his interest in its welfare. In 1923, for instance, he and Lou gave approximately 275 books from their private library on geology and mining to the university.[1] It was but one more of countless small benefactions that betokened their love of learning—and of the institution of learning they called their home.

The Hoovers' connection with Stanford, in fact, was deepening. In 1925 their son Herbert, Jr. received his diploma from the university; in 1929 son Allan did the same. In 1925 brother Theodore became dean of the school of engineering—a position he held until his retirement.[2] In 1925 the secretary of commerce himself delivered the address at Stanford's commencement.[3]

This occasion was not the first time in the 1920s that the financially pressed university availed itself of the prestige of its most famous graduate. Early in 1921 the General Education Board of the Rockefeller Foundation—which Hoover had solicited for funds the year before—came through on a scale he had scarcely envisioned. The board offered Stanford $300,000 if the university would itself endeavor to raise another $700,000, all to be allocated to improving professors' salaries. This grant proved the catalyst for something Stanford had never before attempted: a systematic canvas of its alumni.[4]

Early in 1922 "The First Million for Stanford" campaign was launched, with a letter from Herbert Hoover conspicuous in the fund-raising brochure. "Our University must now depend for its greatness upon its alumni," he wrote. "It will go ahead just so fast as we take the burden of support." Stanford, he asserted, was "the only great University in the West," its standards a model for the entire region.[5] Soon the unprecedented drive was supplemented by appeals for a second and third million for other specific purposes. Eventually, in 1928, the "First Million" was attained, with generous assistance from Hoover and many others.[6] Never again would the university's alumni be unorganized—or neglected in the ceaseless hunt for more endowment.

Hoover's willingness to solicit money did not mean that he was content with trends on campus. For several years his friend Wilbur had been striving to restore the "spirit of equality" that had prevailed at the institution during its pioneer days. Back in 1916 the new president had bluntly warned against displays of "excessive expenditure" and "extravagance" by students— behavior exemplified by the increasing presence of automobiles. "A student's principal business is his studies," he declared. "The student who cannot be content to lead the simple, clean, industrious life expected on the Stanford campus should go elsewhere."[7]

Wilbur's strictures were unavailing. With the advent of the Roaring Twenties, the number of undergraduate-owned cars proliferated, along with a lifestyle many deplored as undemocratic. Reckless driving along Palm Drive became commonplace, as did laments at the baneful effect of the automobile on student activities and alarm at "social distinctions" based on wealth. In 1923 the *Daily Palo Alto*, with faculty and administration backing, led a drive to prohibit car ownership by undergraduates. The proposal lost in a student referendum, 721–476.[8]

The new ethos was well entrenched, then, when Herbert Hoover— Pioneer, alumnus, parent—returned home to vote in 1924. He did not enjoy what he saw. At the end of his visit he made his views emphatically known to President Wilbur:

> 1. Its time this university followed her better sisters and prohibited student autos of more cost than $250.00 (i.e second hands.) I have personal experience in it now. I have held Herbert to a second hand Ford for three years on

the ground that the auto of more lavish type was a class distinction and a luxury unwarranted to persons who have not earned it for themselves. He has come of age; has a little accumulated money; proceeds to get a flashy car and justifies it on the ground that many others have them [and] that the University does not discourage it. If the standard is wrong the University would have established it as such. He has about as much business doing this as I as Secretary of Commerce would have traveling by a private car.

Nor was this all. Prohibition was the law of the land, and yet, said Hoover:

2. You have a very considerable amount of drinking in your fraternity houses. Its violation of the law; and its about time the U.S. Atty. raided a place or two and gave you a chance to cancel some Fraternity chapters. The D.K.E. [and] Z Psi might do to start on.

So deeply did he feel about these matters, wrote Hoover, that he hesitated to keep his son Allan at the university.

The secretary of commerce was also disturbed by what he called the "outbreak of Lafolletism on the campus"—a reference to the recent presidential candidacy of Senator Robert La Follette of Wisconsin. Running on the Progressive ticket, La Follette had outspokenly advocated such measures as government ownership of water power and nationalization of the railroads. To Hoover the public statements of La Follette's partisans on the Stanford faculty had retarded the planned creation of a business school on campus. "I am not complaining of this aspect," Hoover told Wilbur:

What I do complain of is that these men—who are experts and *should* know the *truth*, Have flooded this community with untruthful statements on matters of common knowledge to them. [Professor] Guido Marx is an Engineer; he knows that he is not stating the truth about the Ontario Power System; if he dont he is incompetent as an engineer. Some of your economics men are the same course, i.e. either they are deliberately untruthful or they are incompetent in *their* professions.

Now I am perfectly aware of that well established form of blackmail on Universities called Academic Freedom. I am in favor of academic freedom in truthful statements, honest opinion and to competent men: But all the negitives of these freeze into our Universities under this form of blackmail. You will have to pay the price but you dont have to promote and advance this type of people.

Hoover asserted that his remarks did not spring from "political resentment." There were certain faculty supporters of President Coolidge, he claimed, who had "the same penchant for untruth." [9]

Hoover's handwritten complaint was a passionate one; it also revealed, at points, why he had had problems with the English composition requirement as an undergraduate. Yet despite this expression of ire, his zeal for his university's advancement did not abate. In 1924 and 1925, in fact, he found still another outlet for his energies.

For some years the idea of forming a graduate school of business administration at Stanford had been bruited about without result. It took Hoover to convert dreams into deeds. To the Bohemian Club's 1924 encampment he called a select group of San Francisco business leaders. Theoretically, the club's environs were supposed to be exempt from the intrusions of worldly cares. "Weaving spiders come not here" was its motto. Nevertheless, and not for the first time, Hoover used its secluded grove as a "branch office." To the expectant business leaders he disclosed that in the previous year, 40 California students had graduated from the Harvard Business School and had then taken jobs in the East. "California needs those brains," he exclaimed. It was time for a similar institution on the Pacific coast.[10]

The secretary of commerce was always most persuasive when addressing small gatherings of men of affairs. Such was the case on August 2, 1924. Moved by his proposal, the assembled business elite agreed to raise the necessary money, which Hoover estimated at $50,000 per year. During the ensuing months a committee that included several Stanford trustees extracted pledges from California's business community.[11] Hoover himself, in a letter requested by the committee, explained that a business school was needed on the west coast to "teach business as a profession upon a parity with Engineering, Law, and Medicine." "The induction of professional ideals, professional standing, and professional skill into the largest of our occupations," he argued, "is a primary necessity." Such a school could conduct research on commercial problems of the Pacific region, develop "sane economic understanding in the community," attract the "many good brains" that were being drained away to the east, and educate men for leadership in the unique "business empire" that was California. He pointed out that there was no such department in any university west of Chicago.[12]

"Lafolletism" at the university notwithstanding, by June 1925—less than eleven months after Hoover's pivotal conference in "Bohemia"—the university had received sufficient pledges to finance the proposed facility for five years. This was security enough to proceed. On June 18 the board of trustees therefore voted to inaugurate Stanford's Graduate School of Business later that year.[13] When it opened, it was only the second such graduate-level institution in the United States.[14] To his lengthening list of accolades Hoover could now justifiably add another: founding father of what would one day become perhaps the pre-eminent business school in the country.[15]

It was not long before the needs of modern business—and Stanford's potential for responding to those needs—again engaged Hoover's interest.

One of his best friends on the faculty was Professor Robert E. Swain of the chemistry department. In 1925 Swain conceived the idea of establishing some kind of "interdisciplinary research institute" on campus. In 1926 and 1927 he discussed the possibility with Hoover; on each occasion the Bohemian Grove was the setting. At first Swain thought largely in terms of "pure" research in physics, chemistry, and biology. Slowly, under Hoover's prodding, he discerned a need for studies of more immediate application. Ever the exponent of efficiency and the elimination of waste, Hoover hoped that a new institute would be industry-oriented and dedicated to enhancing American productivity. Eager to promote action, he interceded with President Wilbur, who promptly authorized Swain to forge ahead.

As it happened, the Great Depression and World War II overtook and obstructed the professor's quest. It was not until 1946 that the industrial research facility known as the Stanford Research Institute (SRI) was created. A milestone had been reached in the development of what was to be called Silicon Valley. It was Swain, of course, who in Hoover's words "was the first man to visualize the concept of SRI." Still, to Hoover must be awarded credit for giving focus to Swain's vision and for repeatedly encouraging him to actualize his dream. In the twenty-year drama that preceded the founding of SRI, Hoover, particularly in the earlier years, was a significant supporting actor. [16]

II

And still the university's patron did not rest. Of all the campus institutions, facilities, and policies that bore Hoover's imprint by 1928, the one that mattered to him most was the enterprise he had launched with his $50,000 pledge in 1919. Stimulated by his generosity and by the continuing forays into Europe of Professors Adams, Golder, and Lutz, Hoover's historical collection at Stanford developed rapidly in the early 1920s—sometimes by as much as 50 or 60 boxes per week. [17] Not without reason did a university publication in 1925 judge it "comparable in importance to the archives of a great state." [18] By 1926 Hoover could legitimately describe it as "the largest library dealing with the Great War in the world." [19]

Although the eager historians in Palo Alto conducted most of the never-ending search for documents, Hoover himself pitched in whenever possible—by writing personal solicitation letters, for example, to noted acquaintances. [20] Beginning in 1922 he used U.S. Department of Commerce attachés stationed abroad to obtain foreign newspapers, government publications, and books for his library at Stanford. The secretary of commerce paid for these acquisitions with his own money. [21] His agents shipped the materials home at no charge in the American diplomatic pouch available at the various embassies. So clogged did this conduit become that in 1927 the State Department indignantly demanded that the Commerce Department pay it $25,000 for this service. Hoover's men were forced to curb their use of the government pouch and instead send some of the documents to California by regular channels. [22]

The war collection's phenomenal growth was matched by an ever-expanding reputation. In 1922 Professor Adams informed President Wilbur that Hoover's library was "one of the great historical assets of the University." [23] Returning a few months later from the annual meeting of the American Historical Association, Adams reported: "Everybody now recognizes that there is only one American war collection of note and that that is at Stanford." Other institutions had given up, he noted with satisfaction; they could not keep up with us. [24] To Hoover he happily repeated a distinguished Harvard historian's remark that (because of its war library) Stanford was "on the map again." [25] To Hoover also Adams expressed his gratitude in 1924 for the "liberal and unhampered gifts of money" that had made the whole undertaking possible:

> . . . it was no joke when I told you in 1919 that the H.W.L. [Hoover War Library], more than anything else, would stand, when we're all gone, as your monument. Historians erect the monuments of mankind and they will see to it that the name of the creator of the H.W.L. lives. [26]

As the collection that carried his name grew, Hoover and his faculty associates endeavored to secure its niche at his alma mater. From the start of his acquisition campaign of mid-1919, Hoover had stipulated that the collection must be preserved as a separate entity. He told Adams that he wanted it to become a distinct library like the impressive assemblage of railroadiana donated to the university in 1891 by his fellow trustee, Timothy Hopkins. [27]

Hoover's insistence on separateness was not an act of egotism. He believed deeply that his archive could best flourish if it were physically set apart—and known by potential donors to be so segregated. A distinct and well-defined holding, in other words, would be a better magnet for further acquisitions than an impersonal and amorphous university library.

The founder's thinking was probably influenced by an incident involving the very collection he regarded as his model. In 1919 the magnificent Hopkins Railroad Library of at least 10,000 volumes, hitherto maintained on campus as a unit, was broken up and dispersed in the stacks of Stanford's new library—evidently without the prior knowledge of the donor. Some of the books were even discarded in the process. Outraged by these actions (for which the university's librarian, George T. Clark, was held responsible), the Hopkins family evidently withheld financial support from the university—a loss the institution could ill afford. Even more embarrassing for Stanford, the episode evoked publicity in the press.[28] The contretemps apparently fortified Hoover's determination to maintain *his* collection intact, and it may well explain the conditions that he formally attached to his gift. The materials he proffered were to be *in* the university library but not unreservedly *of* it.

As the first wave of documents arrived in Palo Alto in late 1919, the need to devise an administrative framework for it became apparent. In 1920 President Wilbur appointed Professors Adams and Lutz co-directors of the Hoover War Collection. It soon transpired that their conception of its place in the university's library system conflicted with that of George T. Clark. A strong-willed and prickly personality with a well-honed sense of his own status, Clark openly resented the autonomy and initiative of the "Hoover men," as he somewhat derisively called them. A professional trained in the prewar era, Clark believed that libraries were for published books and journals. He had little appreciation for the mélange of hard-to-classify leaflets, manuscripts, placards, and other "fugitive" literature in foreign languages that Hoover's agents were ceaselessly acquiring.[29] As the torrent of such materials relentlessly invaded the hallways and basement of the new main library building, Clark perceived an administrative nightmare. *He* was the librarian of the university, and he meant to take control.

And so began, in the very first months of the war collection's existence, a bitter struggle to define its relationship to Stanford University. On one side was Hoover, supported to the hilt by his allies in the history department. As the collection's farsighted founder, and as its sole source of revenue during its critical formative years, Hoover felt proprietary solicitude for his creation—and a benefactor's keen desire to see it grow. It was, he told a reporter in 1926, his "hobby."[30] Having amassed an internationally acclaimed archive at his alma mater, he was not inclined to let go. Deeply interested in history, acutely conscious of his own recent role in it, he was also Stanford's foremost alumnus, and the campus was literally his home. For all these reasons, the Chief (as Adams and Lutz joined in calling him) could not be expected to fade away. The Hoover War Collection was a gift to the university, but its donor remained its overseer.

To Clark these considerations were secondary, if he even recognized them at all. Apparently unaware of Hoover's agreed-upon "predetermination"[31] that his war collection be kept distinct from the main library, Clark in 1920 launched a long campaign of bureaucratic harassment—deliberately delaying mail deliveries to Adams and Lutz, challenging their requests for space, quarreling continually over their expenditures and expense accounts.[32] To the librarian's understandable concern for unified management was probably added a large dose of professional envy. In 1919 Clark's entire library budget was $25,000; in one stroke Hoover's pledge had dwarfed it. For years the Stanford library had subsisted on meager funding. Now (in Clark's eyes) appeared these aggressive history professors, backed by a well-to-do patron—all intent upon developing a facility that might well overwhelm his own.[33]

Not all the disagreements were so personal. As a professional librarian, Clark naturally placed a priority on cataloging materials for use by professors and students. How, after all, could scholars study library acquisitions unless these were speedily and systematically processed? As the Hoover war collection expanded (reaching an estimated 100,000 items by 1924), Clark grew increasingly anxious to divert limited financial and administrative resources to the task of assimilating this mass.[34] To Hoover and his faculty lieutenants, however, the need for cataloging was subordinate to the imperative of collecting *more* documents *now*, before it was too late. As Hoover put it to Ray Lyman Wilbur in 1924, "There will be a thousand years to catalogue this library but only ten years in which to acquire the most valuable of material."[35] For the rest of his life Hoover held to this preference.

He also resisted every attempt to dilute his collection's singularity. When, for instance, in 1921 Alonzo Taylor proposed its partial merger with the general library (a step Taylor believed would save considerable expense),[36] the Chief replied quickly and firmly:

> I do not want to be arbitrary about the War Collection at Stanford and am willing to abide by the judgment of Wilbur, Adams and yourself as to any working arrangement with regard to minor parts of the collection.
>
> I do feel strongly, however, that in upbuilding a collection of this kind we must have the psychology of a separate body of material. Its mere exhibition and the knowledge of it in its physical situation attracts to itself valuable additions.
>
> I think the Hopkins Railway Library died largely because it was practically merged in the other collections.[37]

In this position he had the wholehearted support of Professor Adams.[38]

Caught between the Hoover/Adams/Lutz desire for autonomy and Clark's unbending wish for control, President Wilbur sought to find a via media. In late 1921, after consultation with various parties, he issued a directive to the university librarian: in compliance with the 1920 agreement between Hoover and the board of trustees, the library would now take over Hoover's collection but preserve it as a "distinct entity." Adams and Lutz (the president ruled) would continue to make all acquisitions for the collection and would have sole control over expenditures from Hoover's fund. Only after they delivered materials to the general library for cataloging would these come under the administrative supervision of Clark and his staff.[39]

Shortly thereafter, with Hoover's approval, the collection was officially renamed the Hoover War Library.[40] In January 1922 its designated reading room was opened on the ground floor of the new main library building, and Clark's assistants assumed the daunting burden of cataloging.[41]

Wilbur's allotment of responsibility did not end the friction. Within months Clark was pressing for increased control over the war collection, including a role in determining just what materials were acquired—an aggrandizement that Lutz and Adams were just as determined to deny him.[42] To the two professors, the never-ending search for documents required imagination, initiative, and flexibility—not qualities for which the university librarian was distinguished. The last thing the historians wanted was to be entwined in the red tape of an old-fashioned petty bureaucrat.[43]

Meanwhile Hoover, nearly three thousand miles away, had conceived a method of strengthening his collection's independence. In 1920 the Commission for Relief in Belgium had completed its remarkable wartime service with a surplus. By 1922 it had given away most of this sum to various Belgian and French institutions as well as a newly created CRB Educational Foundation headed by Hoover and his associates in America.[44] Now the CRB was in the throes of liquidation, with a substantial cash balance yet to be disposed of.

In mid-1922, at Hoover's request, the CRB's directors voted to give Stanford University a trust fund of $200,000, the income from which was to be used to store and preserve the commission's records.[45] In his letter urging this decision, Hoover pointed out that the commission's papers had "great historical value" and that America had no national archives in which to deposit this "national asset."[46]

The CRB's chairman and founder had more in mind, however, than the simple safekeeping and cataloging of his organization's files. At his initiative the CRB's directors imposed a condition on their offer: if any income remained after providing the necessary care for their records, the university must use it to obtain more CRB-related materials and to subsidize scholarship and publications on the years 1914–1920 in Belgian history.[47] In other words, the proposed endowment was intended in part to provide a permanent acquisitions budget for the Hoover War Library. In addition, Hoover revealed, apparently for the first time, his deepening vision of a library that would function not just as a warehouse of books and manuscripts but as a center for advanced research on contemporary history.

The legal documents governing the bequest did not explicitly mention Hoover's war library. Lest there be any doubt of the transaction's purport, Hoover informed Wilbur separately that he had deliberately tried to make the terms of the grant "wide enough so that it will be a perpetually useful income to the historical side of the University and the War Collection" yet also "permit the advancement of knowledge of Belgium amongst our people." The secretary of commerce warned that the gift must not be publicized until he permitted it. There were already many groups "clamoring for something out of the CRB funds," he disclosed, and he did not "want to be bothered with demands which I have no means of gratifying."[48]

One of these supplicants, in fact, was the Belgian government, which wished to use the CRB's leftover charitable funds to build an embassy building in Washington. Only three days after he conveyed the CRB's $200,000 offer to Wilbur, Hoover rejected the Belgian government's request as legally inconsistent with the purpose for which the money had originally been raised. The charitable sums in question, he said, had been turned over to the CRB Educational Foundation for child welfare work inside Belgium. Perhaps fearful of adverse criticism, he did not mention the CRB's impending gift to his alma mater.[49]

The Stanford trustees enthusiastically signed a contract containing the terms that the CRB set.[50] At the same time Hoover continued to provide support out of his own pocket. By the end of 1922 his recorded contribution to his war library had reached $58,629.17—a figure well in excess of his original commitment.[51]

Alas, these manifestations of generosity did not resolve the power struggle on campus. Early in 1923, Adams confessed to a colleague that the relationship between the two libraries was "most delicate." Clark, he reported, was still sensitive about Hoover's unwavering determination to keep his war collection distinct and its budget in Adams's hands alone.[52] At this juncture, in fact, the Hoover War Library had *two* budgets: one for acquisition and accessioning of materials, the other for cataloging, binding, and supervising them. Hoover's fund covered the first set of expenditures, university funds the second.[53] Adams, of course, controlled the former disbursements, Clark the latter.

At this point Adams notified President Wilbur of the suggestion by Hoover's close associate, Edgar Rickard, that an external board be established for the war library.[54] Rickard was joint liquidator of the CRB, and he may have had in mind forming an advisory board like the one the Carnegie Corporation had stipulated in 1921 for the Food Research Institute. Whatever his intent, Ray Lyman Wilbur would have none of it, as he told Adams with some force on January 27: "The present status of the Library is quite clear and I see no way in which we can be helped by an outside Board except in further purchases. As you know my inclination is to get that over into Mr. Clark's hands as soon as possible."[55] Nor was the president receptive when Adams urged creation of a new directorate system for the war library—a mode of governance that would further accentuate its autonomy.[56]

It seems evident that, left to himself, Wilbur would have placed the

Hoover War Library squarely under the control of the university librarian.[57] Neither Hoover nor Adams, however, were about to let this happen. In a conference with Adams in Palo Alto in June 1923, Hoover—without consulting Wilbur or Clark—decided upon a momentous broadening of his library's mission: henceforth it would encompass not just the Great War and its immediate aftermath but the period of reconstruction since the war as well. The collecting of documents, he agreed, should continue indefinitely. He also divulged to Adams that he planned to double his library's endowment—and in such a way that all income from it (including that from the CRB bequest) would go for acquisitions only. As for the costs of staffing his library, the university, he told Adams, should henceforth bear these itself.[58]

Hoover did not immediately disclose his decision to Wilbur, and Adams realized that the president would be shocked by the new burden on the university budget. "But for the life of me," the professor declared, "I don't see how the trustees can longer postpone taking up their share and showing some appreciation" to their benefactor.[59]

Hoover estimated that the income from his projected combined endowment fund would amount to at least $20,000 a year.[60] Eager to strike while this unexpected iron was hot, Adams drew up an annual accessions budget of $19,060, which he submitted to Hoover and Wilbur. Noting the war library's newly enlarged scope, Adams stressed the urgency of at once using "every penny" available for acquisitions, with "large discrimination as to use of money."[61] In other words, the money should be free from the incubus of George T. Clark.

Where, however, was this new endowment to come from? As it happened, in 1923 Hoover and his associates were liquidating another portion of his farflung philanthropic empire: the American Relief Administration. Although originally a government agency funded by a $100 million Congressional appropriation, the ARA had been private since mid-1919. Since then it had engaged in commercial transactions (at a small profit) as part of its humanitarian work and had received the unrecompensed services of Hoover and his principal aides. As a result, wrote Hoover to his fellow ARA trustees, their organization had accumulated a modest surplus. This Hoover now prepared to expend in part for the maintenance of the ARA's files.[62]

In September 1923, therefore, the ARA offered Stanford University its records and $250,000 for their care under fireproof conditions. As with the CRB's gift the year before, only the interest from this gift was to be available for purposes of preservation. But once again Hoover was looking beyond the mere protection and indexing of the ARA's voluminous papers. The contract with Stanford therefore stipulated that the university must use any residual income from the trust for acquisition of further materials relating to the ARA *and* to the period of the world war *and* to the era of reconstruction *and* to "allied subjects" *and* for subsidies of relevant research and publications. Furthermore, the university must maintain all such records and increments *in Hoover's war collection* and "shall not confuse such collection with its general library." This point, for Hoover, was crucial. Unless the "identity" of his "special collection" (as a "center point of interest") was maintained, he wrote to Wilbur, "we can be sure that the whole of these excursions into history will ultimately be side tracked by some future librarian or destroyed in their value just as the Hopkins Railway Library has been effectually extinguished as a center point around which a competent railway collection could have been built."[63]

In another letter to Wilbur, Hoover drove the point home. The CRB and ARA bequests, he said, should yield $20,000–$22,000 annually for "support of the records" and for "acquisition of material to maintain and complete these two national collections." He had already spent "upwards of $100,000" on his war library, Hoover reported, and he intended to spend $1,000–$1,500 per year more for two or three years (for acquisitions) *provided* that his gifts, and the ARA and CRB funds, were "devoted only to new acquisitions and the payment of staff generally, with the library on the same basis as hitherto."[64]

In one respect the ARA's proposed contract did not go as far as Hoover desired. To Adams, earlier in the summer, he had stated his view that Stanford should assume the cost of administering his library. To the ARA a few weeks later, however, he expressed doubt that the university's trustees would be "inclined to find the necessary money" for "clerical staff."[65] Perhaps in recognition of this fact, the ARA's memorandum of agreement permitted the use of its trust fund income to pay for indexing its documents and rendering them accessible to scholars—in other words, for cataloging and administration. Only after these needs were satisfied could the balance, if any, be devoted to acquisitions.[66] It is possible that Wilbur or some of the trustees induced Hoover to accept this compromise.

With a total endowment of $450,000 in the offing, Hoover now attempted to actualize his sweeping vision for his creation. "I do not believe even you appreciate the importance of this collection and the results that will flow from it," he told Wilbur in September 1923.

> It is not often that the University has an opportunity to make a tremendous contribution to original cultural research or cultural stimulation. Through this collection Stanford University has an opportunity to become the actual center of and authority in historic research among many social, political and economic problems of the war and reconstruction periods, and into many vital incidents in our national history and their relationship, for here is the only material that exists in certain matters.
>
> You have, in fact, a chance to establish a history department that will be

of positive national and international importance. I do not see that all this can be developed from the point of view of the library. . . .

He therefore proposed that the Stanford history department be reorganized to permit Frank Golder and Ralph Lutz to concentrate on organizing and conducting research in "this raw material." The ARA's historian and curator, Harold H. Fisher, should be brought from New York and given a professorship in the department. These three men, said Hoover, should be given minimal teaching duties and devote most of their time to "the energetic research organization and building up of this collection." In effect, he was proposing the founding of a War Research Institute similar to the Food Research Institute nearby.[67]

The university's board of trustees gladly accepted the ARA's $250,000 and the formal contract that went with it.[68] But Wilbur firmly rejected the idea of a "separate and distinct" War Research Institute.[69] He told Hoover that it was "unwise" to create "strictly research professorships"; such arrangements took men "out of the student current." Nor, he argued, was it prudent to import outsiders at disproportionate incomes or status; he was willing enough to take Fisher, but evidently not quite at the rank or salary Hoover wished. "Personally," the Stanford University president said to his friend, "my feeling is that the library should be closely coordinated" with the history, political science, and economics departments and the Food Research Institute.[70] In this oblique way he indicated his desire to absorb Hoover's creation into its larger institutional setting.

When the ARA's bequest became certain, Wilbur recognized that the time had come to devise "a more definite organization" for the Hoover War Library—or, as he put it to Hoover, "a stable formulation as to its control and use."[71] Its "Pioneering period" was over, Wilbur told Adams; from now on the enterprise should be organized as a de facto department of the university. At the president's request, a number of individuals on campus (including Adams and Clark) now endeavored to frame a "constitution."[72]

Early in 1924 the various "interests" in Palo Alto agreed upon a scheme of organization, which Wilbur approved and presented to the board of trustees. The plan provided for a ten-member board of directors, to be appointed annually by the president and including (among others) himself, Clark, and representatives of various departments. The directors were required to submit an annual budget (similar to a departmental budget) to Wilbur for his approval; other than this, they were free to determine their functions as they chose. (They were also expected to advise and assist in acquisitions efforts and to "determine upon the lines of development.") In its very first sentence the document stated: "The Hoover War Library is a separate gift and has special endowment funds for the maintenance of certain of its features." In the very next sentence it stated that the Hoover War Library was "under the general administration" of the university librarian.[73]

Not surprisingly, the new organizational framework contained something for everyone. By creating a separate board of directors with responsibility for the budget (and implicitly for acquisitions), it solidified the war library's distinctive status—an outcome all the more apparent when Wilbur appointed Professor Adams the first chairman of the directorate. At the same time, the plan gave Clark authority to appoint all members of the library's staff and established Wilbur's ultimate control over the entire arrangement: he, after all, would appoint the directors and approve or disapprove the budget.[74] Hoover, too, could be pleased; at his request Wilbur appointed him a director—a position Wilbur promptly made ex officio.[75]

In one respect, however, the library's founder was not satisfied, as he speedily informed the president:

> I am not at all certain that this plan maintains the definite separation of the War Library from the general Library of the university because under the plan, the Directors have no power over the staff and no power to budget what they consider necessary or proper in this connection. It would seem to me that they should have some veto power over the librarian's appointments and his budget proposals. As he sits on the Directorate this should not be disagreeable to him.
>
> In other words . . . the action of the committee, not the action of the librarian, should be the controlling action.[76]

Apparently Hoover worried that Clark, in his anxiety to process the mountain of war documents, would hire too many catalogers, thereby soaking up the budget and leaving little money for new accessions. To Hoover it was the directors (including himself), not Clark, who must make the final decisions.

Wilbur immediately yielded. Instead of giving Clark a free hand to appoint the war library's staff, Wilbur proposed that Clark be empowered merely to *nominate* staff "subject to the veto power of the directors."[77] Hoover assented to this amendment since (he said) "it keeps perfectly clear to the donors the independence of the [war] library."[78] Wilbur thereupon made the alteration.[79]

With the arrival of the ARA's endowment gift and the adoption of the reorganization scheme of 1924, a new era for the Hoover War Library commenced. During its first five years of existence its financial sustenance had come almost entirely from its founder.[80] By late 1924, in fact, Hoover had expended more than $85,000 of his personal fortune on what Wilbur called the "upbuilding" of the war collection.[81] By one account the precise sum was $89,311.90—nearly twice what he had promised in 1919.[82]

This figure may have been too low. In mid-1924 Hoover told a friend that he had spent "upwards of one hundred thousand dollars" on his library.[83] In 1937 he recalled that at the 1919 Paris peace conference he had spent at least $100,000 acquiring source material through his aide Robert Taft, using an account evidently separate from the one drawn upon by Adams.[84] Hoover did not specify what purchases he made through this hitherto undisclosed channel, and his operations on this front remain obscure. (Adams seems never to have mentioned it, and Taft apparently kept no records.)[85] When Ralph Lutz learned of Hoover's recollection, he simply added $100,000 to the known and verified $89,311.90—making a grand total of $189,311.90, a figure which was duly entered on statements of account later prepared by the university.[86]

Even this amount, large as it was, may have been an underestimate. In 1946 Hoover declared flatly that it did not represent the entirety of his direct expenditures for the war library in its earliest years. His own accounts, he told the president of the university, revealed that his contribution had actually been $221,000.[87] But whatever the exact figure, there could be no denying that without Hoover's tremendous expenditures in 1919 and the early 1920s, a historic opportunity would have been lost.

The war library's restructuring of 1924 and the creation of a permanent endowment did not portend any loss of interest by its founding father. Determined to foster its growth, he paid $8,000 out of his own pocket that year for a journey by Professor Adams to Europe, with the proviso that three-fourths of this sum be reserved for acquisitions.[88] "The day will go by," he warned Wilbur, "when new material will be available and if the library is to develop, now is the time it must be done."[89]

Then, in mid-1924, came a crisis that nearly set Hoover at odds with his best friend. The CRB and ARA bequests of 1922 and 1923 had explicitly stipulated that income from these trusts must be used to service these record groups and then to acquire more. Ray Lyman Wilbur, however, had a different understanding: he told Adams in late 1923 that income from the combined endowments would go for *all* Hoover War Library expenses, including acquisitions, administrative appointments, and general maintenance.[90] Now, in the summer of 1924, Hoover discovered from his faculty allies that the CRB/ARA income was not being used to administer these two collections at all. Instead, 70 percent of it was being used to catalog, bind, arrange, and supervise *other* materials in the war library: the materials that Hoover himself had paid for and donated since 1919 through Adams, Golder, and Lutz. Only 30 percent of the endowment income was being used for acquisitions.[91]

Hoover was angry. Back in 1919–1920 he had offered his personal war collection to Stanford on the condition that it be maintained as a separate entity, in separate stacks, and in a separate room—an understanding that the trustees had formally confirmed. Did not this agreement mean that the university should incur the costs of maintenance? To Wilbur he communicated his displeasure: "The original conception of my gift of the library was that the *University* was going to pay the administration expenses of all *my* collection. Today the CRB and ARA are doing it. Surely so great a purpose is worthy of much more liberal support from the University itself."[92] Hoover therefore prepared a draft letter to the board of trustees requesting confirmation that in accepting his gifts the university "assumes the obligation" to provide adequate facilities and support services, including salaries for the collection's administrative staff.[93] He thereupon showed his draft to Wilbur.[94]

It is easy to understand the university's perspective on this simmering conflict. In barely 60 months the Hoover War Library had developed on a scale, and at a pace, anticipated at the start by no one—and the end was by no means in sight. In 1923, in fact, Hoover had unilaterally expanded its scope and had remarked that the task of collection must continue for another 25 years.[95] Clearly the efficient management of this resource was going to entail far more expense than the trustees (or anyone else) had probably ever contemplated. Moreover, Stanford in the 1920s had precious little surplus income. How, some of its administrators must have wondered, would it finance this ever-growing giant in its midst?

It is also easy to comprehend Hoover's viewpoint. In five short years, and principally with his own resources, he and his friends had created one of the great archives and libraries of the world—a treasure that had raised his alma mater to global eminence. Certainly the beneficiary of his generosity ought to be able to find a way to care for an incomparable gift, one which could only enhance Stanford's prestige in the future. Furthermore, only by relentlessly acquiring new materials could the library maintain its lead over its competitors. This was the moment for collecting; said Hoover to Wilbur, it was "now or never."[96]

Hoover apparently did not mail his draft letter to his fellow trustees, and it is not clear whether the board acceded to his demand. Instead, President Wilbur moved with alacrity to mollify him. Barely a month after receiving Hoover's message, Wilbur urged the board to appropriate $5,000 from the university's general revenue fund for the purchase of books and documents for the Hoover War Library in the current academic year. There was a "unique opportunity" to make such acquisitions at present, he said, echoing what Hoover and others had been noting for some time.[97] The trustees approved the request, thereby adding to their appropriation of $4,000 earlier in the year for the war library's administration.[98]

Wilbur's maneuver was only a temporary palliative. During 1924 the feud between Clark and his rivals worsened, with the university librarian demanding (among other things) that the costs of shipping and binding new materials be charged to the Hoover acquisitions budget, not his. When Frank Golder suggested that Clark reduce his cataloging staff for the war library to save administrative expense, Clark countered by suggesting that its reading room be closed.[99] Well aware of these festering tensions and of the problems of uncoordinated growth, President Wilbur decided to intervene. The time had arrived, he told the war library's directors in early 1925, to draft a "tangible plan" for the library's future development. At his request the directors created a committee to recommend policy and procedures.[100]

A few months later the three-member committee (which included Lutz and Clark) submitted its report, which was immediately adopted. In careful detail it defined the functions of the directors, the duties of Librarian Clark, the scope of the Hoover collection, and the division of labor between it and the general university library. Many of the recommendations were noncontroversial. Some—such as the call for systematic publication of Hoover War Library monographs—anticipated the library's eventual evolution. One, however, seemed to point in a different direction: no longer would Adams and Lutz have an unfettered right to acquire items they deemed desirable. Henceforth all decisions on purchases of source material were to be made *jointly* by the chairman of the directors (Lutz, as of mid-1925) and the university librarian. If they disagreed, the directors as a group would decide. Despite this restatement of the directorate's ultimate authority, for the first time George T. Clark obtained a formal role in the war library's accessions program. It remained to be seen whether this was a formula for harmony or for paralysis.[101]

The news of this latest modus vivendi was quickly overtaken by developments of a more exhilarating nature. By early 1925 the Hoover War Library had outgrown its allotted quarters. Less than six years after its founding, it occupied one fifth of the available stack space in the entire main library;[102] long before then Adams and Lutz had been forced to squirrel away excess documents in nooks and crannies all over campus.[103] One historian later described the war library's reading room as a "rabbit warren of one-way footpaths" among the heaps of papers—an embarrassment aggravated by its disagreeable proximity to the men's room.[104] Never one to beat around the bush, Adams informed Hoover in mid-1923 that the collection would soon require a separate building. The Chief was astonished, but soon he, too, realized that the international archive carrying his name deserved—nay, demanded—a more dignified and commodious home.[105]

Toward the end of 1924 an enthusiastic Professor Adams took the initiative. First he approached Hoover's personal financial manager, Edgar Rickard, who opined that the requisite building funds could be raised if Hoover would give the signal to his friends.[106] Conferring next with the Chief himself, Adams found him eager to proceed; so, too, was President Wilbur, whose ideas for the new structure mirrored Hoover's own.[107]

Adams's intensive lobbying soon produced results. First, Rickard agreed to take charge of the fund-raising.[108] Then, in the spring of 1925, the Stanford trustees approved the War Library building project, and the university's architects—Bakewell and Brown—were invited to draw up the plans.[109] Finally, in October, Rickard launched the solicitation drive with a circular letter to every man and woman who had worked for the CRB, ARA, and U.S. Food Administration.[110]

During late 1925 and 1926 Rickard's fund slowly accumulated. While the response (as he expected) was broadly based, the total contributions were but a fraction of the $750,000 that Hoover estimated would be necessary.[111] One problem was that Hoover himself refrained from direct involvement; as a public official he was reluctant to endorse anything that might be denounced as a monument to himself.[112] Yet in order to succeed, the campaign would have to attract wealthy contributors,[113] the kind of donors for whom a Hooverian "sales pitch" might be needed. As 1926 passed into 1927, fulfillment of the quest for cash remained elusive.

Meanwhile, back on the campus, Clark was behaving more aggressively than ever. Under the terms of the "constitution" of 1924 and the policy understandings of 1925, the war library was placed under the "general administration" of the university librarian. Furthermore, although the board of directors prepared the budget, it was Clark who now controlled disbursements. And he construed his authority to include the right to *approve*—not merely honor—Chairman Lutz's requisitions.[114] Long frustrated by Adams's and Lutz's independent source of income (Herbert Hoover), Clark proceeded to use his power of the purse (and coordinate authority over purchase of new materials) to obstruct, alter, and veto every plan of Lutz's involving an expenditure of money. As a result, wrote Lutz in 1927, the university librarian had successfully delayed and even blocked the acquisition of new collections, at considerable damage to the Hoover War Library's development.[115] Bent on curtailing its growth if he could, Clark even argued at one point that the postwar reconstruction period should be defined as ending in 1924, thus confining future purchases to documents generated before that date.[116]

In 1927, two events occurred that augured the kind of future for which Adams and Lutz ardently yearned. In March the Laura Spelman Rockefeller Memorial awarded Stanford University a $250,000 grant, in part to establish two new research institutes: one on the Russian Revolution (to be headed by Golder) and one on the postwar German Revolution (to be headed by Lutz). Although not technically a part of the Hoover War Library, both centers depended upon its unique resources and hastened the fulfillment of Hoover's dream of a library that would be more than a simple assortment of books and papers.[117] Three months later, George T. Clark, who had been hospitalized in 1926 for an operation, announced his retirement as university librarian.[118]

Elated by this turn of events, Adams, Lutz, Golder, and Fisher decided to make an outright bid for independence. In a letter on July 25, Lutz asked

President Wilbur to designate the Hoover War Library a "research institution at Stanford" entirely separate from every other library or department. He argued that the institution Herbert Hoover had founded could not realize its "full possibilities" as long as it remained a "subsidiary department" of the general library. "For example," he wrote, "the encouragement and direction of research, which play a part of increasing importance in the Hoover War Library, are not functions of the general library. . . ." The two entities had different purposes and perspectives and should not therefore be yoked.[119]

Professor Adams, ever the master strategist in the art of academic warfare, promptly showed Lutz's letter to Herbert Hoover, who was visiting Palo Alto at the time. Hoover read it in haste and declared that he agreed with its contents.[120] The patron, the Chief, was on the side of the insurgents.

To the chagrin of Lutz and his colleagues, Ray Lyman Wilbur was not. In a conversation on August 8, Adams found the president sharply opposed to "eliminating the librarian from a pretty considerable control of the affairs" of the Hoover War Library. "He acknowledges past difficulties" (Adams wrote to Lutz), "but says those all were based on personality and that with a new librarian we ought to expect to have a man who will see eye to eye with us and who will contribute the essential business knowledge and control which the President evidently thinks necessary." So rapidly and vehemently did he express himself that Adams was unable to present the arguments for separation. It was not an auspicious sign for the history professors. Wilbur, however, did promise to consider the question further and to consult with Hoover about it.[121]

On September 15 Wilbur delivered his verdict: there would be no change in the status quo until he saw how the new university librarian worked out. "I spoke to Mr. Hoover about the situation," said the president pointedly, "and he seemed satisfied."[122] For Adams and his associates it was a disappointing rebuff, one made all the more painful when Clark's successor, Nathan van Patten, turned out to be as antagonistic toward the war library as the man he replaced. But without the support of Hoover, there was little the historians could do.

Hoover, in fact, was preoccupied with another matter that summer. On August 2, 1927 an event occurred that transcended and transformed his relationship to Stanford University: Calvin Coolidge, vacationing in the Black Hills of South Dakota, announced that he did not "choose to run" for President in 1928. Hoover was at the Bohemian Grove when the electrifying news arrived. Within an hour friends gathered among the redwoods to urge him to seek his party's nomination.[123]

Hoover had been out of college nearly a third of a century. Throughout these years he had done much for his alma mater. Now it would have an opportunity to reciprocate for its "favorite son."

III

Early in 1928 Hoover formally announced his candidacy. Quickly Stanford-for-Hoover Clubs sprang up across the country as alumni everywhere rallied to his cause.[124] Will Irwin ('99) wrote a campaign biography.[125] President Wilbur addressed a mass meeting in San Francisco and became an alternate delegate from California to the Republican national convention.[126] On March 20 the Stanford Alumni Association, through its executive committee, took the unprecedented step of publicly endorsing Hoover for President. It urged alumni to support him without regard for party affiliation.[127] In less than a week approximately 1,700 responses poured in; only three were negative.[128]

The enthusiasm permeated the campus. Departing from its tradition of avoiding politics, the *Stanford Illustrated Review* devoted its April issue to Hoover's campaign. The Class of 1928 dedicated its yearbook to him.[129] And when in mid-June he won the Republican nomination, the faculty itself wired him a telegram of congratulations. "We rejoice over the great honor that is rightfully yours," they said, "and appreciate that it reflects on Stanford through you."[130]

In mid-summer Hoover returned to California. For a few days the mood of celebration was interrupted by the sudden death of Mrs. Hoover's father, who was buried following a funeral in Stanford's Memorial Church. Out of respect for the family, students at first refrained from demonstrations; some even kept guard around the Hoovers' home. Finally, unable to restrain themselves any longer, a group of high-spirited matriculants staged a rally at the Hoovers' doorstep. The Republican nominee thanked them with pleasure. "I would rather have a greeting from Stanford men and women," he declared, "than from any other group!"[131]

After a "nonpartisan welcome" in San Francisco, followed by a parade back down the peninsula, through the streets of Palo Alto, and on up to his house on San Juan Hill, Hoover was no doubt ready for a quick trip with various old Stanford friends and political allies to the trout streams of far northern California. It would be his last surcease before the rigors of the coming campaign.[132]

In the 1920s, presidential nominees did not address the conventions that nominated them. Instead, following a custom dating back to the nineteenth century, the nominee waited for formal notification from his party weeks later, often in a small ceremony on his front porch. In 1928 President Wilbur and various party leaders hit upon an innovation appropriate to a new era: why not hold the ceremony in Stanford's football stadium and invite the public to attend? This, Wilbur telegraphed Hoover, would allow "popular participation in greatest event in California" and "start campaign on new basis." It would offer a "vent for California enthusiasm" and be a symbolic break with "old style politics."[133]

And so, on August 11, 1928, one day after his 54th birthday, Herbert Hoover delivered his acceptance speech before 70,000 admirers in the Stanford stadium—and an audience of uncounted millions by national radio hookup. David Starr Jordan was there, as were some of the university's first professors and many members of the Pioneer Class of '95.[134] Shortly afterward the nominee journeyed east on his arduous path to the White House.

On November 5, the day before the election, a confident Herbert Hoover returned home. The portents were promising as his campaign train steamed down the peninsula. A few days before, a straw poll of Stanford students revealed that 75.9 percent favored the university's most successful graduate, while only 20.5 percent supported his Democratic opponent, Alfred E. Smith. A similar poll of the faculty disclosed 192 for Hoover, 35 for Smith.[135] Here, more than almost anywhere, the candidate was among friends.

Ten thousand people, including virtually the entire Stanford student body, cheered the Chief at the Palo Alto railroad station that day. Overhead an airplane pilot dropped "bombs" that broke into parachutes flying the flags of the world's nations. Up Palm Drive Hoover and his family rode as students and adults lined their path. That night the nominee addressed the nation by radio from his campus home.[136]

The next day, Tuesday, November 6, the Hoovers, their two sons, and their daughter-in-law cast their ballots in mid-morning at their campus precinct. How fitting it must have seemed that their polling station was the Women's Clubhouse of the Stanford Union. Here, too, they were among friends; the precinct voted 410–50 for its leading resident. Then, its civic duty done, the family retired to its home, where special Associated Press and Western Union wires were in place to convey the returns.

Early that evening old friends from Stanford, Palo Alto, and the Bay Area gathered at the house of the nominee. As it happened, many months before—before, in fact, it was known that Hoover would be a presidential aspirant—the university had booked an election night concert by John Phillip Sousa and his 70-piece band. The venerable "March King" (who turned 74 that very day) agreed that if the returns showed Hoover victorious by the close of the performance, he would lead a parade to the candidate's home.

And thus, in late evening, an exultant crowd of 2,000 Stanford students ascended San Juan Hill, a tired and puffing Sousa at their head. Cameras whirred, reporters scrambled, a special radio hookup broadcast the scene. Out onto the roof and terraces came Hoover's family and friends. The candidate himself and his wife thanked Sousa at the front door and then mounted to the second floor to survey the scene.

Across the breadth of America—even as far away as Tahiti—owners of radio sets heard the jubilant sounds. Sousa struck up the band; it was the "El Capitan" march. Then came "Stars and Stripes Forever." Then two thunderous yells for the President-elect.

Next the throng sang the "Star Spangled Banner"—not yet the national anthem (it would become so designated during Hoover's administration). As the crowd lifted its collective voice, a pilot from the Palo Alto School of Aviation fired a 21-gun salute of fireworks from an airplane circling overhead. And then the Stanford hymn:

> Where the rolling foothills rise,
> Up t'wards mountains higher,
> Where at eve the Coast Range lies,
> In the sunset fire,
> Flushing deep and paling;
> Here we raise our voices hailing
> Thee, our Alma Mater.
>
> From the foothills to the bay,
> It shall ring,
> As we sing,
> It shall ring and float away;
> Hail, Stanford hail!
> Hail, Stanford hail!

As he heard the words of the anthem, Hoover was transfixed. He did not sing. He seemed "wrapt in thought." Tears filled his eyes. Never was his identification with Stanford as complete as it was at this, the most triumphant moment of his life. [137]

And never was Stanford's identification with Hoover more joyful and unrestrained than it was that starlit November evening. His glory was also its own. A few days later an old British friend expressed the sentiment well: "I do hope and believe that a hundred years hence Stanford men will point back to Hoover with the same sort of pride that the University of Virginia now points back to Jefferson." [138]

Herbert Hoover as a Stanford University sophomore. Courtesy NLH.

Herbert Hoover (standing, second from left), his fellow geology students, and their professors, ca. 1893 (Dr. John C. Branner, seated, middle). Courtesy NLH.

Herbert Hoover addresses Stanford University's
50th anniversary exercises, October 1, 1941
(Ray Lyman Wilbur seated, left). Courtesy NLH.

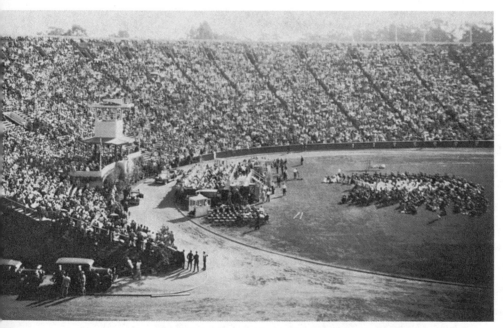

Hoover accepts the Republican presidential nomination,
August 11, 1928, in the Stanford stadium. Courtesy HIA.

President and Mrs. Herbert Hoover, 1931. Courtesy NLH.

Lou Henry Hoover House, Stanford University, 1934. Courtesy NLH.

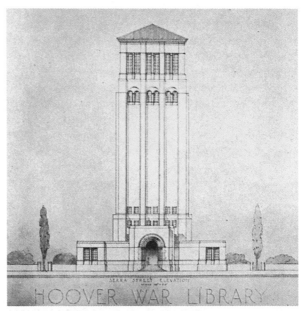

An artist's rendition of the proposed Hoover
Library building, ca. 1938. Courtesy NLH.

Herbert Hoover and his sons Herbert, Jr. and Allan during the 1928 election campaign. Left to right: Herbert, Jr., Herbert, Allan. Courtesy NLH.

The Hoover Library tower
completed, 1941. Courtesy NLH.

Herbert Hoover dedicates the Hoover Library
building, June 20, 1941. Courtesy NLH.

Herbert Hoover in his office in the
Hoover Tower, ca. 1960. Courtesy HIA.

Herbert Hoover, J. E. Wallace Sterling, and
W. Glenn Campbell, 1962. Courtesy NLH.

· 6 ·

The Lengthening Shadow

I

As Hoover took his oath of office on March 4, 1929, he could look back on a career whose trajectory had curved ever upward. The orphaned son of an Iowa blacksmith, he was now the 31st President of the United States. His relationship with his alma mater had followed a parallel path: from the obscurity of a seventeen-year-old freshman to unrivaled influence as an alumnus and trustee. In the eyes of his countrymen and his university, Hoover was at the zenith of his prestige.

As he prepared to occupy his high office, Hoover tendered his resignation as a trustee of Stanford University; his fellow board members refused to accept it.[1] And so, for the next four years, he remained on the board, although he attended none of its meetings. The chief executive's distance from the West Coast, however, was purely geographical. At the outset of his administration, his bonds to his alma mater grew even more intimate when he asked Ray Lyman Wilbur to come to Washington with him and serve as secretary of the interior. At first Wilbur demurred, citing his duty as Stanford's president to complete its postwar program of renewal. But Hoover was not a man to take no for an answer. He quickly persuaded his fellow trustees to grant Wilbur an overdue sabbatical (later changed to a leave of absence with full pay) in order to accept the proffered cabinet post. Professor Robert E. Swain, another close friend of Hoover, became acting president in Wilbur's place.[2]

The appointment of Wilbur to the cabinet brought new honor to Stanford and no doubt enhanced its growing reputation as one of the principal academic institutions in America. Residence in the nation's capital also gave Wilbur an exceptional opportunity to "widen the circle of friendship and support" for his university.[3] Such were the advantages of having Stanford's president and pre-eminent alumnus at the summit of governmental power. But as the months passed, the administration, faculty, and students in Palo Alto discovered that the singularly close Hoover-Stanford connection had an unexpected and dis-comfiting consequence. Not only was the President of the United States in the unremitting glare of publicity; the university, as his home and booster, was as well.

The spotlight of journalistic sensationalism first fell on the President's brother. On May 15, 1930 the editor of the student newspaper, the *Stanford Daily*, reprinted an excerpt from Professor Theodore Hoover's syllabus for Mining and Metallurgy 101:

PREPAREDNESS

The human race develops by war and succeeds in war in proportion to its use of metals; races perish in peace. Culture is increased by invention of new weapons.

The pacifist errs in assuming that peace is desirable.

Emerson says everything we have must be paid for. We Americans are living in unpaid luxury and must pay in the future by blood and hard work.

Denouncing Hoover's views as a "shocking" manifestation of "militarism" on a campus "where men and women are supposed to think in terms of humanity," the pacifistic editor, Robert Speers, demanded that the school of engineering (of which Theodore Hoover was dean) "wipe out this statement at once."[4]

Speers's editorial triggered an instant uproar. Shortly before printing it, he or one of his student associates alerted the San Francisco area newspapers, which soon dispatched swarms of reporters to cover the story. Confronted by the impending blast, the outspoken dean defended his syllabus statements as a "somewhat depressing and saddening" truth, expressed the fear that at-tempts to achieve "perpetual peace" would be "ineffectual," and accused Speers of a "flagrant violation" of "the inviolability of the class room and all that it implies." The next day Speers's editorial and Professor Hoover's protest were reported in newspapers from coast to coast. That night a group of Stanford engineering students unsuccessfully attempted to kidnap the *Daily*'s editor.[5]

The tempest in Palo Alto had immediate repercussions in Washington, where President Hoover was struggling to persuade a balky Senate to ratify a naval disarmament treaty. As Ray Lyman Wilbur confessed to Robert E. Swain, Theodore's remarks had come at an "inopportune time." Very possibly at the request of the White House, Wilbur immediately instructed Swain by telegraph on the way to control the damage:

Freedom of classroom is vital and essential. Since there has been breach of confidence in presenting classroom work publicly, it seems to me desirable that it should be made clear that these statements are propositions put up for thoughtful debate among students and not final declarations of opinion.[6]

Swain followed Wilbur's advice with alacrity. To the acting president of the university the issue was not Theodore Hoover's opinions about war or peace but his mistreatment by the local news media.[7] Within hours of receiving Wilbur's telegram Swain issued a statement deploring the fact that an "able and highly esteemed member of the faculty" had been subjected to "nation-wide publicity without being given the courtesy of an interview before the excerpts [from his syllabus] were released." Swain also denounced the *Stanford Daily's* "violation of the freedom and the spirit of the classroom" by printing the controversial passages. "The greatest teachers," said Swain, "are those who provoke students to the thoughtful consideration of important issues. They present propositions for thoughtful debate and study which are not final declarations of opinion." To focus on "isolated sentences" out of context could be "positively misleading." "The work of the university classroom," he declared, "should be kept free from this type of public criticism."[8]

Chagrined but unrepentant, Speers protested that he had acted in "good faith." The so-called unwritten rule against quoting a professor's classroom statements, he argued, applied to the spoken word only, not to a written syllabus that had been in circulation for several years.[9] To the embattled editor, Theodore Hoover's comments were no hasty effusion but a well-considered statement of conviction. (To Swain's distress Theodore Hoover had admitted as much.) A few days later Swain called in Speers and orally condemned his journalistic ethics but decided not to take "summary action" against him.[10] The immediate campus crisis was over.

Back in Washington, Secretary Wilbur agreed with Swain that the case could now be allowed to drop. "Every so often it is inevitable that we will run into those newspaper people who think they are going to save the country by talking their heads off," Wilbur observed. "It is a little more important than usual to us now because of our peculiar position in the limelight." As for the editor of the *Stanford Daily*, Wilbur said:

> If a student like that could grasp how much trouble he is making that goes far beyond any possible range of understanding that he can comprehend, he might be willing to let the older heads look over what he is trying to do before he goes too far.[11]

The editors of the student newspaper, however, were not about to submit their copy to the university administration for prior approval—as Wilbur, before long, would discover.

The Theodore Hoover/"militarism" incident soon subsided; on Swain's anxious urging, the feisty professor of mining (and patron of Stanford's R.O.T.C. program) refrained from further comment on public issues.[12] But the university's newly perceived vulnerability made a powerful and lasting impression. So identified was the President of the United States with his alma mater that any statement on campus differing with Hoover administration policies was liable to be seized upon by the press to tweak and disturb the White House. In the autumn of 1930 a leading American magazine portrayed Stanford as an unhappy "presidential fief" whose denizens were silent, sullen, and afraid. More and more members of the faculty, it alleged, had retreated into a shell of prudent reticence, lest they embarrass their President/hero or incur Dr. Wilbur's retribution.[13]

The deepening malaise soon found focus in the question of the status of Stanford's absent president. To many trustees and faculty, the arrangement occasioned by Wilbur's entry into the cabinet had not worked satisfactorily at all. Although Professor Swain was nominally the acting president, in practice he referred nearly every issue, great and small, to Wilbur for decision. The result was administrative uncertainty and delay. The mood on campus did not improve with disclosure that since March 1929 Wilbur had been drawing two full-time salaries: one as secretary of the interior and one as Stanford's president on leave.[14]

In the summer of 1930 Wilbur asked the university's trustees to extend his leave of absence for one year.[15] At once a movement arose among certain trustees to compel him to return to his post in Palo Alto within six months.[16] At the White House, trustee Herbert Hoover was alarmed—and determined to thwart the rebellion. On August 29 he telegraphed his fellow board member, Harry Chandler, owner of the *Los Angeles Times*, that Wilbur's forced homecoming would be a "great mistake." The university, said Hoover emphatically, gained more "credit" from Wilbur's success and stature in Washington than it could derive "in many years by the ordinary course of its work." The state of California also benefited from Wilbur's prestige, Hoover stated, while from a "national point of view" Wilbur was the first secretary of the interior ever to take the department "out of politics" and onto "a basis of complete esteem." To Hoover the agitation for Wilbur's return was the work of a "small coterie" that had always opposed Wilbur as university president. He therefore asked Chandler for his assistance.[17]

Unable to muster a quorum, the trustees did not act immediately on Wilbur's request.[18] Instead the issue simmered until mid-autumn, when, once again, the *Stanford Daily* provoked a crisis. On October 13 the *Daily* boldly called upon Ray Lyman Wilbur to choose. Stanford University was without a president, it editorialized, and was suffering accordingly. Wilbur, it said, should either resign as president or resign as secretary of the interior. In a separate statement, the *Daily* reported that the trustees might refuse to renew Wilbur's leave.[19]

For the second time in five months Stanford's student newspaper generated national headlines—and a response from the highest levels of the Hoover administration. The very next day President Hoover informed a news conference that Wilbur most certainly *would* remain in his cabinet. "The University will gladly extend his leave as long as it is necessary," he declared bluntly, "and he is too valuable a man to lose out of the Federal service." Then, with a smile, Hoover added: "Being one of the trustees of that institution myself, I can speak with more authority than the student daily."[20]

Hoover's speedy rejoinder to the student newspaper placed his fellow trustees in a quandary. At this point the board had not met to resolve the issue of Wilbur's leave of absence, nor, so far as is known, had it decided informally what to do. Yet Hoover had just predicted its course of action—and in a forum as public as could be. If the board now convened and demanded Wilbur's return or resignation, it would be openly defying and humiliating the President of the United States.

Faced with Hoover's possibly preemptive maneuver, the trustees on October 23 extended Wilbur's leave of absence for one year but without salary. Privately the board requested Wilbur to indicate before his leave expired when he would be able to return to Stanford.[21]

Despite this decision, dissatisfaction at the Hoover-Wilbur nexus continued to surface. In October the undergraduate humor magazine known as the *Stanford Chaparral* published a satirical article referring to Secretary Wilbur as the university's "President-by-mail." The student publication even printed a cartoon in which the gateway on Palm Drive was portrayed as containing two vertical columns on which, Mount Rushmore-like, the visages of Wilbur and Hoover were carved in stone.[22]

By early 1931 the campus was awash with complaints about the "headless University."[23] Hoover, meanwhile, was feeling out-of-sorts with his alma mater. During the Christmas vacation of 1930 the president of Stanford's student body, Thomas Pike, visited the White House for lunch as a guest of the president's son Allan. During the meal the President, preoccupied with affairs of state, said virtually nothing until Allan launched into a spirited description of the panacea he had just learned at Harvard Business School for the ills of the Great Depression. When Allan finished, his father uttered one word: "Bosh!" Then, turning to Pike, the president asked, "How's that Country Club getting along out there?" Before Pike could respond, the President left the table.[24]

Hoover's annoyance did not preclude his participating in symbolic acts of identification with his university. Thus in November 1931 he posed for photographers on the White House lawn with members of Stanford's 1894 football team, whose finances he had supervised as student body treasurer.[25] Another Stanford tie was religious. At his request a Stanford classics professor, Quaker, and old friend—Augustus T. Murray—served as a resident minister of the Friends meeting that the Hoovers attended in Washington. Murray had come East for this purpose in 1929. For the next four years he spent part of the year in Palo Alto and part in the nation's capital; the university granted him leaves of absence for his pastoral assignment.[26]

The Wilbur controversy, meanwhile, simmered on. If the trustees of the university thought that they could force the secretary of the interior to come home in 1931, they were soon to find themselves mistaken. That spring Hoover asked his fellow board members to extend Wilbur's leave of absence again, this time to the end of Hoover's first term. Whatever their earlier misgivings, most of the trustees were amenable,[27] although they took no action until two of their members, Leland Cutler and Paul Shoup, could journey to Washington. Calling first on Wilbur, Cutler found the secretary of the interior an unhappy man—torn between his (and his ailing wife's) yearning to return to Stanford and his feeling of duty toward his friend, who was contending with the ever-worsening depression. But when Cutler pleaded personally with Hoover to let his cabinet secretary go back to the university that needed him, the President was sternly unyielding. Finally, almost poignantly, the man in the White House explained:

> Le, people forget that Dr. Wilbur and I have been close friends for forty years. In this job I need a friend. [Senator] Borah is unreliable, Hiram Johnson is vindictive. I can talk to Dr. Wilbur without fear of being misunderstood and he can talk to me. He never repeats anything I say. I need him.[28]

To Trustee Shoup the President reiterated Secretary Wilbur's unique value as a confidant. The nation, too, needed Wilbur—more (said Hoover) than Stanford did—as a crucial cabinet officer and voice of good sense during the continuing economic downturn. Furthermore, the university in time would garner a harvest from Wilbur's ever-expanding contacts.[29]

On June 18, 1931 the board of trustees yielded to Hoover's request and extended Wilbur's unpaid leave of absence until the end of 1932. The board did so, it said, in recognition of "the outstanding importance to the nation" of the secretary of the interior's successful completion of his work. Professor Swain continued on as acting president.[30] Later the trustees again prolonged Wilbur's leave until the end of the Hoover administration in March 1933.[31]

Not all such campus issues were as satisfactorily resolved for Hoover as his retention of Wilbur in Washington. By early 1929 the Hoover War Library contained more than 1,400,000 items and needed space more urgently than ever[32]—a condition exacerbated by increasing hostility from the university's imperious librarian, Nathan van Patten (whom Ralph Lutz and his friends privately nicknamed "The Patroon").[33] At the start of Hoover's presidency, success for Edgar Rickard's fundraising efforts seemed imminent, with the still-to-be liquidated ARA, among others, promising substantial sums.[34] But as the months passed and the Great Depression set in, the necessary $500,000 remained elusive, as pledges failed to materialize and securities in the form of stocks and bonds depreciated in market value. Rickard's labors were complicated by President Hoover's aversion to any solicitation that smacked of "strong-arm methods" or exposed him to potential embarrassment.[35] At one point E. D. Adams enthusiastically proposed that the War Library raise $200,000 from twenty wealthy friends of the Chief in the Chicago area on condition that they seek no presidential favors. Hoover at once quashed the idea. He knew very well what would happen, he said: within ten days at least three of the donors would smilingly call at the White House to tell him how happy they had been to make the donation.[36]

Stymied by the continuing dearth of funds, and by the president's refusal to exploit his high office for personal purposes, Rickard and the Hoover War Library's directors were forced to reconsider their plans. Back in late 1924, when Adams had again proposed separate housing for Hoover's war collection, the Chief had suggested combining the facility with the long-proposed Stanford War Memorial, for which more than $100,000, at that point, had been raised. The resulting structure, he said, could be called the Stanford War Memorial Building and could include his War Library (with all its stacks, research rooms, and offices), as well as a lecture hall and central entrance hall for honorific displays.[37] The early architectural designs had reflected Hoover's views: one sketch (prepared by Bakewell and Brown and circulated by Rickard to potential donors in 1926) projected a two-story building with two wings and an approximately four-story memorial tower in the middle.[38]

By the end of 1929 this original, "monumental" conception seemed unattainable. And so arose a plan for a simple, inexpensive "utilitarian building" that would adjoin, and in fact be connected to, the main library. This prospect apparently delighted van Patten, who at one point suggested that the new building contain no book stacks; the War Library, he said, could simply leave its books in *his* library![39] Not surprisingly, the cost cutting substitute thoroughly displeased Professor Lutz; the last thing he wanted to erect was a mere annex to the domain of the Patroon.[40]

Aesthetics soon triumphed over economics. When one of the principal donors back East objected that the proposed "utilitarian building" looked like a Ford factory, the scheme very speedily collapsed.[41] No one around the Chief was going to settle for anything like that. In May, Rickard (in all likelihood with Hoover's approval) announced that he had decided to revive the original

(1925) conception and to try to raise the additional funds required.[42] The "improvised" (utilitarian) plan, he informed Lutz, "was not quite dignified enough for the Hoover War Library."[43]

Nor, it seemed to Lutz and others, was the new location. Soon a committee that he chaired approved a return to the site that Hoover and the trustees had approved several years before.[44] It was on this spot that the War Library eventually would be built.

The discussions and decisions of 1930 had one other crucial consequence: the Hoover War Library undertaking was now definitively severed from the proposed Stanford War Memorial with which, since the mid-1920s, it had been entwined. Hoover and his associates agreed that his library (in Rickard's words) should "stand on its own."[45] In 1937 the Stanford War Memorial project reached fruition separately in the building known today as Memorial Hall.[46] This structure, however, contained no commemorative tower; that motif was to appear instead in the Hoover War Library—in honor, not of Stanford's World War I dead, but of Hoover himself.[47]

The renewed fundraising efforts of 1930 soon foundered. Stanford University could not afford to erect the War Library building on its own,[48] and Edgar Rickard was unable to raise enough from the increasingly straitened private sector. While willing to contribute heavily to put the campaign over the top, President Hoover would not permit certain of his friends to be approached.[49] By 1932 it was clear that success would have to await a revival of the nation's faltering economy.[50]

The Hoover War Library's travails emboldened its principal adversary. In 1931 and 1932 Librarian van Patten intensified his guerrilla warfare against the quasi-autonomous institution in his midst. His relationship with Professor Lutz deteriorated into a daily spectacle of confrontation and harassment, including the withdrawal of needed staff assistance.[51] Aware that the War Library's cherished freedom depended upon outside financial support, Lutz turned desperately to Hoover's right-hand man, Edgar Rickard.[52]

On March 3, 1932, Rickard—probably with Hoover's approval—intervened in a subtle but effective manner. Informing Acting President Swain that the American Relief Administration had $200,000 in readiness for the War Library's building fund, Rickard proposed to convert this sum into a temporary endowment, the interest from which could support the Hoover library's operations until the construction project was resuscitated. Such an infusion of cash, of course, would liberate Lutz from the constraints imposed by van Patten. Rickard also proposed that the new sum be combined with the earlier CRB and ARA bequests into a single trust fund for the War Library's maintenance. But, he added, if all these and other arrangements were to be effected, there must be a "definite statement" that he be consulted about any plans involving the War Library's "building operations." Rickard intended that he—and the interests he represented—have a share in shaping its future.[53]

It was not until autumn that the Stanford administration finally responded, not with acquiescence but with a request that the War Library's endowment be merged into the university's general funds.[54] Such consolidation was not at all what Rickard wanted. In a letter that bore certain hints of Hoover's draftsmanship, Rickard informed Ray Lyman Wilbur that the War Library had been established by agreement as "a separate entity" and that the university had not fulfilled its legal obligations toward it. Thus "although stipulated in the [CRB and ARA] contracts," Stanford had never completely accounted for its stewardship of these bequests. It was desirable to attain "a clear understanding of the whole relationship surrounding the Library," said Rickard (in Hooveresque prose). If the university were to receive any more grants from Hoover's family of charitable foundations, its trustees should specify how they proposed to meet their obligations.[55]

Wilbur rushed to placate his correspondent—and, behind him, the Chief. Stanford indeed wished to protect the War Library's funds and collections and to preserve its special "identity," Wilbur wrote by return mail. All "obligations entered upon," he promised, "will be maintained."[56] Once again the Hoover War Library's distinctive status had been reaffirmed.

It was not his war collection, however, that preoccupied the nation's President that autumn; it was his own strenuous battle for re-election. On Tuesday, November 8, 1932, as the electorate went to the polls, Hoover returned home to California for the first time since 1928. For all the stresses of the preceding four years, the students of his alma mater were still with him. A straw poll conducted by the *Stanford Daily* disclosed 63.4 percent for Hoover, 19.4 percent for Franklin Roosevelt, and 16.7 percent for the Socialist, Norman Thomas—not quite as overwhelming a margin for Hoover as in 1928, but a substantial majority nevertheless.[57]

Once more the city of Palo Alto welcomed its distinguished citizen home. At 3:00 P.M. that election day classes at the university were dismissed. Minutes later the presidential motorcade arrived from San Francisco, stopped at Palo Alto's Community House for an official reception, and then approached the Stanford gates under escort. Up Palm Drive, lined with schoolchildren and troops of Boy and Girl Scouts, the President and First Lady rode, in a car festooned with flowers and an American flag. Upon reaching the sunken garden oval, the couple was met by the Stanford University band and led in procession to the Memorial Arch. Here, near the Quad in which Hoover had walked 40 years before, 2,000 waiting students stood and cheered. Weary and hoarse from the punishing campaign, the President thanked the throng.

After voting at the Women's Clubhouse in the Stanford Union, the Hoovers drove on up to their home, where Ray Lyman Wilbur, three university trustees, and various associates and relatives joined them for supper. Following the meal the Hoovers invited their neighbors in for a reception. All was in readiness for election evening: the special telegraph wires, the blackboard for recording the state-by-state returns, the friends, the candlelight, the fire.

Hoover's university-dominated precinct cast 176 ballots for its favorite son, 45 for Roosevelt, and 17 for Thomas. Across the country, however, it was a different story: in every state but six, Roosevelt and the Democrats were victorious. At 9:35 P.M. Pacific time, from his study in his home on San Juan Hill, the President telegraphed his congratulations to FDR.

In the driveway outside the Hoover home, a crowd of Stanford students had gathered. The President and his wife now appeared on the second-floor balcony to acknowledge them. Immediately the assembly below burst into four minutes of continuous cheering, while some among their number lit powder candles that illumined the nocturnal scene. When the noise and smoke subsided, a cheerleader led a yell for the chief executive and his lady. Then there was silence, and Hoover struggled to speak: "I thank you for your fine loyalty," he said, "and I deeply appreciate this very hearty greeting. Thank you." And that was all. Fighting to control his emotions, the President as he finished turned away.

By a little past ten o'clock all the guests had departed. By eleven the mansion on the hill was dark. Only the evening's memories remained, including a telegram from Hoover's secretary of agriculture. It said simply: "Your shadow will lengthen in history."[58]

II

In 1933 Ray Lyman Wilbur resumed his full-time presidency of Stanford, and Herbert Hoover, now an ex-President, returned to his alma mater to live. For the next several years the former chief executive was a familiar, though unostentatious, campus figure. Inveterate entertainers still, he and his wife frequently invited faculty friends and neighbors to dinner. From time to time also Hoover had groups of Stanford undergraduates in for evening visits at which he answered questions submitted by the students in advance. Sometimes he attended the climax of Stanford's football season, the annual "Big Game" against Berkeley.

As the titular leader of his party and a trenchant critic of the New Deal, Hoover could not escape controversy that occasionally produced local echoes. So often did Republican leaders visit him at Stanford in 1935 that a San Francisco newspaper printed a cartoon depicting his San Juan Hill home as an armed fortress surrounded by a moat and inhabited by the GOP's Old Guard.[59] On June 16, 1935, Hoover was the principal speaker at the university's first-ever outdoor commencement, held in the football stadium where he had launched his presidential campaign seven years earlier. His address—an analysis of the true path to social security—evoked some complaint that it was a "political speech" inappropriate to the occasion.[60] But such discordant notes were rare in the 1930s. For most members of the university community he remained a respected public figure.

Back on their beloved home terrain, the Hoovers renewed their unobtrusive benevolence. They contributed books to the university library and money to the scholarship fund for student aid.[61] In 1937 Mrs. Hoover took a leading part in founding the Friends of Music at Stanford, which underwrote a series of chamber music concerts and substantially enriched the university's music program. When the group was formally organized in 1940, Lou became its first chairman and tirelessly helped to foster its good works.[62]

In other ways also Hoover cemented his diverse ties with his alma mater. He hired Stanford graduates as secretaries and assistants.[63] In 1937 he donated a collection of volumes on business and economics to the library of the Graduate School of Business.[64] One listener never forgot the night in the early summer of 1940 when Hoover advised an assembly of graduating Stanford MBAs: "Buy all the real estate you can, and buy it on the San Francisco Peninsula." The area around the university, he predicted, would someday become a magnet for businesses and industrial research.[65]

Meanwhile Hoover and his fellow trustees endeavored to cope with the Great Depression's impact on Stanford's finances. In March 1933 the university was obliged to impose a 10 percent pay cut on every faculty member earning more than $1,000 per academic year.[66] Two and a half years later Hoover warned an audience of alumni that the Roosevelt administration's massive borrowing policies, its bank credit inflation, and its devaluation of the dollar were threatening to depreciate the endowment of the nation's independent colleges and universities.[67] For Stanford the danger was especially acute, for from the very beginning the trustees had invested almost exclusively in bonds and first mortgages, including millions of dollars in railroad bonds that were now increasingly going under. By early 1936 approximately 15 percent of the book value of Stanford's endowment consisted of securities in default.[68]

To avert further contraction Hoover believed that the trustees must diversify their portfolio by investing in common stocks and other equities as a hedge against inflation—a risky course but one that seemed essential under the circumstances. On the board he became the "prime mover" in seeking such a radical change of investment policy. But did Stanford's founding grant permit it? On February 10, 1936, the trustees—unsure of their legal authority under their charter—petitioned the superior court in San Jose for a judicial determination that they could indeed so deviate from their practice of half a century.

Hoover himself appeared in the courtroom to testify. The problem, he said, was "grave." Arguing that the federal government's inflationary bank credit policies had caused a steep decline in interest rates, he stated that if these low rates persisted Stanford would lose about 25 percent of its endowment income. Currency inflation, too, was a "menace." The university's trustees, he declared, "should have the freedom to protect the endowment as best they can." [69]

Two weeks later Judge William F. James of the superior court confirmed the petitioners' power to invest their trust funds in common stocks and certain other equities. [70] Later that year the finance committee of the board initiated a partial shift away from bonds. [71] As a result the university's tottering endowment fund ceased to diminish and soon generated an additional annual income of $100,000. [72] Without this Hoover-induced change of direction, wrote one trustee years later, Stanford's endowment would have suffered "permanent shrinkage." [73] Once more—and in a manner few have realized to this day—the board's dominant trustee had pulled his alma mater back from an abyss.

Of all Hoover's university-related interests in the 1930s, the one that remained paramount was the welfare of the institution that carried his name. Not long after his return to campus the Hoover War Library set out in new directions. In October 1933, at his initiative, its range of collecting was broadened to encompass no fewer than 21 post-Armistice categories, including Hitlerism, taxation and national debts, and the New Deal. [74] This enlargement of focus reflected Hoover's contention that the roots of the Great Depression lay in World War I. It also implied an increasingly open-ended acquisitions policy and a relative diminution of the war itself as a field of concentration. [75] Such breadth and dynamism appealed to the library's founder. Eventually, in 1938, he proposed that the entity be named the Hoover Library on War, Revolution and Peace. "This will transform it from a dead collection to a live one," he said.

> It has been suggested that we use the title—"War, Peace, and Revolution." This is a little less optimistic. Perhaps we had better have the title wind up with Peace. [76]

The university's trustees agreed, and the change of name was made. [77]

As the library's scope expanded, so also did its functions. In 1930, with Hoover's and Wilbur's approval, it offered its first course of instruction; eventually it presented several more. [78] In 1932 the Hoover War Library Publications series was launched with two scholarly tomes, augmented by seven additional volumes in 1934–1935. [79] Meanwhile plans were set in motion to publish 24 volumes of documents on Hoover's European relief work between

1918 and 1922.[80] Slowly—but now at an accelerating pace—the archive-cum-library of the Chief was becoming the research center he desired.

All this, of course, required money—more money than either a beleaguered Stanford or the CRB/ARA endowment funds could supply. Although the university in the 1930s contributed an average of about $6,500 per academic year (exclusive of utilities and janitorial service) to the War Library's maintenance, this sum was always less than 25 percent of the library's total income.[81] To supplement these revenue sources Hoover tapped the still-liquidating American Relief Administration. Thus in 1933 the ARA gave Stanford $15,000 for purchase and installation of steel library stacks to house a new infusion of Hoover-related records, provided that the university promise to furnish an identical sum for the War Library building (if and when erected). The university accepted these terms.[82] The ARA simultaneously appropriated $9,000 for the acquisition of further materials for the War Library. With this sum, and by prior agreement, Stanford established a Hoover War Library collecting office in Washington, D.C., under the direction of the Chief's long-time confidential secretary, Lawrence Richey.[83] Approximately two years later the ARA donated $10,000 to the War Library in support of certain publishing ventures.[84]

Hoover himself drew on his personal savings for his library's benefit—more so, he later acknowledged, than he had "the right to do in view of the natural obligations of one's family."[85] Although Lawrence Richey, for instance, was nominally a "special agent" of Stanford University in the 1930s, the ARA and Hoover actually paid his salary and expenses; Hoover's personal share was at least $4,000 a year for eight years.[86] When Richey was forced to retire from the Washington office in 1941 because of ill health, Hoover arranged to pay him $400 a month for up to three years after office funds were exhausted.[87] As always he rewarded personal loyalty.

Still, the most ambitious project of all—the long-deferred building plan—remained moribund. For a time, in a mood of discouragement, Hoover even contemplated deeding his home on San Juan Hill to the university so that it could install his Hoover War Library there.[88] Certainly *something* needed to be done. By the late 1930s its incomparable holdings comprised 5,000,000 items, many of which (thanks in part to van Patten) were scattered in basements across campus.[89]

In 1937 and 1938 the financial logjam at last broke; once more Hoover's foundations were responsible. In 1937 the American Relief Administration finally liquidated, leaving more than $140,000 to Stanford for erection of a War Library building.[90] In late 1938 the CRB Educational Foundation—recently renamed the Belgian American Educational Foundation—came forward in even more generous measure. After amending its certificate of incorporation to permit such a gift, the foundation (of which Edgar Rickard was president) offered Stanford $300,000 toward construction of the proposed building, provided that the university pledge the $100,000 still needed and assume the eventual costs of maintenance. The university's trustees agreed.[91]

Meanwhile Hoover himself had been soliciting funds on his own, stressing the uniqueness and value of his library. It now possessed "the largest collection of war materials and of materials bearing upon the economic and social consequences of the war that there is in the world," he told one potential donor. The archive included vast numbers of items that "would not have been preserved except for the unique circumstances of the collection."[92] Its documentation on Bolshevism was without peer.

> I am convinced that we are establishing here a real, important cultural center in the United States; that it will furnish a continuous source of research not alone in history but in social and economic forces, and as such is a distinct addition to the whole educational fabric of the country.[93]

Hoover was a supremely accomplished fundraiser; his exertions soon paid off in the form of a $50,000 contribution from John D. Rockefeller, Jr.[94]

With success in sight on the financial front, preparations now accelerated for what Lutz, Rickard, and other Hoover intimates envisaged as a "permanent memorial" to the Chief.[95] The sketches and blueprints were entrusted to Arthur Brown, Jr. of the old firm of Bakewell and Brown. Using the tower motif that had been abandoned for Memorial Hall (and which Hoover indicated that he favored), Brown designed a monumental structure that, in Hoover's words, "would add to the ornamentation of an open space campus."[96] At last, on December 8, 1938, President Wilbur publicly unveiled the $600,000 building plan.[97]

At this point Brown's design included an entrance hall and two stories of offices, out of which would arise a high tower topped by a sloping red-tiled roof.[98] As revised into final form a few months later, the blueprint called for a higher tower still, capped by a domelike, red-tiled belvedere that resembled the twin towers of the Stanford Union.[99] Both the library tower and its crown were patterned after the cathedral of Salamanca in Spain.[100] According to Hoover some years later, this cathedral was "a most perfect development" of the "Romanesque Renaissance" style that unified the Stanford campus.[101]

The proposed new building won some admirers. According to the university's alumni magazine, Stanford's "physical structure," held "close to the ground since the disaster of 1906," would "once again . . . soar into the heavens, a fitting flight, both as an architectural development, and as a symbol of Stanford's intellectual achievements."[102] Ray Lyman Wilbur later characterized the tower as "a great shaft of light up into the blue for the long look of history." [103] At least a few seemed to find in it a worthy rejoinder to the campanile at the Berkeley campus across the Bay. [104]

Such signs of approval, however, were outnumbered by cries of protest. To many on campus, the edifice was a glaring anomaly—in the *Daily*'s words, a "peristylic giant" that violated Stanford's aesthetic integrity in "an apparently purposeless departure from traditional Quad architecture." [105] Some called it a "tower of Babel"; one labeled it "a monument to wounded vanity." [106] A student theatrical production lampooned it as the "Boulder War Library." [107] Even some trustees had misgivings. At one point Wilbur instructed one of the project's engineers to confer with him and Hoover alone (and not the trustees) about certain details; two of the board's members, Wilbur reported, "take a crack at it when they can." [108]

If Hoover was affronted by such criticism, the available record does not show it. It is possible, though, that the decision in early 1939 to alter the tower design (to make it resemble the one in Salamanca) was a response to the initial outpouring of complaints. On the other hand, it is also possible that the architect's revision was done simply to permit installation of a carillon. (In this respect, too, Stanford would have a rival to Berkeley's campanile.) [109] Whatever the case, neither Hoover nor his entourage appeared unduly nettled. Wrote Wilbur with satisfaction to the Chief in November 1939: "The building is going to be the Stanford Trademark within a dozen years." [110]

Only two weeks after the library's groundbreaking in mid-August 1939, World War II broke out in Europe. Even before then, Hoover had taken cognizance of the gathering storm. On March 9, 1939 another of his foundations, the American Children's Fund, appropriated $50,000 to Stanford University for his library. With this sum, and at Hoover's instruction, Professor Lutz embarked on an ambitious collecting journey to Nazi Germany, Fascist Italy, and other countries. Before he left in June, he learned from Hoover that a second $50,000 would be forthcoming; in due course the American Children's Fund provided it. [111]

Lutz was in Europe when the war came. For three more months he traveled across the continent in an unflagging quest for documentation on the cataclysm. In nearly every country he visited, the professor, at Hoover's urging, established networks of collecting agents—booksellers, librarians, government officials—who agreed to amass propaganda and other items of value for Hoover's library. Lutz promised to compensate them for their acquisitions when peace returned. It was a brilliant innovation. No other library had ever employed such a strategy; no other even had representatives in Europe at the time. Once again, thanks to the founder's farsightedness and timely financial support, and to Lutz's own astuteness and zeal, the Hoover Library would reap a historical bonanza and remain unchallenged in its field. [112]

By early 1941 the great structure that would house this institution was nearing completion. Its impressive tower rose 285 feet from the basement floor, rendering the building the dominant feature of the Stanford landscape. The construction costs exceeded $600,000, more than five-sixths of which emanated from nonuniversity funds: a tribute to the prestige and resourcefulness of the Chief. [113]

The year 1941 also marked his alma mater's 50th anniversary. As the Stanford community prepared to celebrate this milestone in its history, Hoover requested that the formal dedication of his library building be included in the ceremonies. [114] The university accepted and went further: it made its most honored alumnus a focus of the observances.

From June 16 to 21, 1941 Stanford presented itself to the nation in an elaborate Academic Week of Commemoration. The events opened with a four-day symposium on "The University and the Future of America," at which fifteen distinguished scholars and men of affairs from across the land delivered lectures to a total of approximately 9,000 people. [115] To Hoover was given the privilege of offering the concluding and synthesizing address. It was a plea for American universities to raise "the lamp of freedom" in a world ravaged by tyranny and war. In the current time of unprecedented peril, he argued, universities had responsibilities that exceeded "their major purpose of the training of our youth." They must "fight every impairment of intellectual and political liberty." They must be "the insistent guardians of truth and intellectual honesty." They must expand "the boundaries of knowledge" and "stand for orderly progress, for evolution, not for the revolution of violence." They must affirm "certain standards of ethics and the great domain of human values." They could and should "give guidance to constructive forces in time of crisis." No doubt thinking of the conflict in Europe, and of those who would have America plunge into it, he declared:

> The Universities should sit in judgment upon those who claim the need of war . . . . They can apply the weights of objectivity and experience to the arguments of the fanatic and the foolish. They can and must oppose that submergence of freedom of speech and press which has already come upon this country with the madness of war psychosis. [116]

The next day, June 20, Stanfordians, visitors, and guests gathered for what Ray Lyman Wilbur considered the climax of the entire symposium: the dedication of the new Hoover Library building. Speaker after speaker acclaimed what one journal called "the world's hugest collection of social and political documents" [117] and the man who, most of all, had made this resource possible. Professor Sidney Fay of Harvard, perhaps the leading living historian of the causes of World War I, pointed out that in its scope, its manuscript archives, its publications, its accessibility, and its fruitful proximity to a

university, the Hoover Library had outstripped its only two significant European counterparts. [118] President Charles Seymour of Yale observed:

> The significance of the collections here housed cannot be overstated, for
> they will serve not merely historians but mankind . . . . [F]or his early
> conception of the importance of such a collection to human welfare, and for
> his unlimited activity in building it up, we are every one of us under
> inestimable debt to Mr. Hoover. [119]

Before the final dedication exercises, a concert of carillon music rang forth
from atop the stately tower. The magnificent, nine-ton carillon had been built
in Belgium and exhibited at that nation's pavilion at the New York World's
Fair. The Belgian American Educational Foundation had then purchased the
instrument from its owners and presented it to the Hoover Library—a musical
memorial to the humanitarian achievement that had created a hero a quarter
of a century before. [120]

Rising at last before the outdoor assembly seated in front of the tower,
Hoover noted the treasures to be stored inside. His mind that afternoon,
however, was on the present and the future:

> I suppose some one will wonder why all this trouble and expense to
> preserve these records. . . . If we assume that humanity is going to abandon
> the lessons of its own experience, the whole of this collection is useless,
> except to the casual visitor. But sometimes the voice of experience does
> call out to stop, look, and listen. And sometimes peoples respond to that
> call . . . .
>
> The purpose of this institution is to promote peace. Its records stand as a
> challenge to those who promote war. They should attract those who search
> for peace.
>
> I therefore dedicate this building to these purposes. [121]

A little over three months later the men and women of Stanford convened
to celebrate the university's official opening on October 1, 1891. Once more
Herbert Hoover, Pioneer, was a featured participant. This time his mood was
mellow and full of reminiscence:

> I might mention to you, without undue pride, that I have the dubious
> title of being the first resident student on this campus. That timely arrival
> was not pure idealism—it was a practical job in the effort of cramming to be
> admitted at all . . . .
>
> I was one of those, 50 years ago, who stood over there about 200 feet
> away and watched the ceremony of the opening of this University.
>
> I had at that time never listened to great speeches on public questions

before, and it was all very wonderful. It was one occasion when I was warranted in believing everything that was said . . . .

After it was all over I went across the Quad and resumed my job in the Registrar's office—where with three days' experience, I gave advice to the registering freshmen.

But Hoover had a serious message also. A university, he told his audience, "is more than just to help you. It is a great living thing radiating truth, justice, service and freedom. And if you work for it and care for it and serve it in these next fifty years, it will give even greater service to mankind." [122]

III

Even as he spoke, however, Herbert Hoover's world was quaking, and with it his relationship to his alma mater. On June 22, 1941 Nazi Germany had attacked Soviet Russia. That summer and autumn the United States drifted ever closer to belligerency.

On campus, too, the currents of change were accelerating. In 1940 Ray Lyman Wilbur had reached the age of retirement. The university's trustees had extended his tenure so that he could preside over the institution's 50th anniversary observances. But the days of his presidency were now waning. [123] Since 1939, in fact, Hoover had been chairman of the trustees' committee in search of a successor.

Hoover could not yet know it, but June 20, 1941 in some ways was the zenith of his long association with Stanford University. It was indeed fitting that he should play so visible a role in the events of its semicentennial. In Stanford's first 50 years of existence, no other unaffiliated alumnus had contributed as substantially and as continuously to its welfare. Only Leland and Jane Stanford, David Starr Jordan, and Ray Lyman Wilbur had done as much or more.

But now Wilbur, his best friend, was leaving, and the future was gray with uncertainty. Abroad and at home the winds of war and ideology were rising to the force of a gale. Not even the sturdy sandstone campus bathed in California sunshine would be untouched. Hoover's benefactions for Stanford had not ceased. But never again would his influence over its destiny be as strong or as substantially uncontested as it had been before 1941.

· 7 ·

The University and
Its Benefactor Diverge

I

The first portents of an altered relationship between Hoover and his alma mater appeared on the horizon on the eve of the semicentennial. In the preceding decades, campus criticism of Stanford's greatest living benefactor had been rare. And when it had surfaced, it had been largely unrelated to his public philosophy. The outcry against Ray Lyman Wilbur's retention of his cabinet post in 1930–1931, and against the design of the Hoover Library tower in 1939, had been essentially university issues, not ideological ones. As far as any observer could discern, Stanford and its noted alumnus were still politically compatible.

This perception was soon to be shattered. In 1939–1941 Hoover emerged as one of the most powerful opponents of American entry into World War II. The contumely heaped upon him by political enemies during the years of the Great Depression now acquired new intensity and venom. And between him and his university there developed an ideological breech that became an ever-widening chasm.

In 1940 and 1941 Hoover directed a national campaign to bring humanitarian food relief to the civil population of several European democracies overrun by the armies of Nazi Germany. Arguing that the innocent citizens of these captive nations were suffering from famine and starvation, he obtained German permission to organize a CRB-style relief mission for the occupied lands. The British government under Winston Churchill, supported by the Roosevelt administration, refused to sanction his scheme. In the British view such an effort would inevitably benefit the Germans.[1]

To Hoover's embarrassment some of the most determined opposition to his plan emanated from the Food Research Institute at Stanford University. According to one of the institute's economists, an anti-Nazi German refugee named Karl Brandt, there was *no* famine occurring or impending in the German-occupied countries, and, if one developed, it would be the fault of Adolph Hitler.[2]

Hoover reacted angrily to this unexpected criticism. "I don't see any reason why Brandt should be constantly throwing stuff into the press that makes our problem more difficult," he told Ray Lyman Wilbur in October 1940.[3] Two months later he complained to Wilbur again:

> Professor Brandt is still going on making statements that are wholly without any basis of fact . . . . He is contributing directly to the starvation of millions of people by stating things of which he has no knowledge and situations with which he has no touch. What his political motivation can be I do not know, but it is not a worthy function of any professor of Stanford University.
>
> In view of his German exile background it is not well for him to be taking part in American public questions in this fashion.[4]

Nevertheless Brandt continued to speak out, asserting in the summer of 1941 that the occupied European democracies faced no food emergency and that their food reserves would probably increase in the coming months.[5] Hoover, in a rejoinder, stated that Brandt was not only factually wrong, he was an irresponsible "propaganda operator" whose behavior was inconsistent with the "scientific and objective attitudes" and "humanitarian professions" of Stanford University, under whose "label and title" he spoke.[6]

All this was extremely irritating to Hoover, especially since he had established the Food Research Institute, had secured its first ten years of funding, and, in early 1940, had helped Brandt and his colleagues obtain major funding for their work from nonuniversity sources. Without his endorsement their drive would probably have failed.[7] It therefore galled him when, in mid-1941, Joseph Davis, a director of the Food Research Institute since its inception, asserted that Hoover had never contributed to the support or development of the FRI. It was a "regrettable misapprehension," said Davis, to believe that the institute had ever operated under Hoover's "special influence."[8]

The contretemps with Brandt was the first overt manifestation of Hoover's growing estrangement from the enterprise in which he had once placed great hopes. In one respect Davis was right: determined to stay aloof from political controversy, the institute's directors had never listened much to Hoover's advice. And that, for its founder, had been part of the problem. In 1942 he wrote that the Food Research Institute had been "a great disappointment." Ignoring his demands that it "investigate and state boldly the fallacies or wisdom" of various political "panaceas" for the farm problem, it had instead "degenerated into a mostly statistical body, reassembling known figures in new forms." Then, in 1940–1941, it had suddenly reversed its stance and entered the political fray—against *him*. The reason, he claimed in 1942, was simple. The institute's staff was controlled by two "elements": a faction headed by the zealous Professor Brandt and a "Left Wing near-Communist group, who took the 'party line.'" The institute's figures about European food conditions had been "faked," said Hoover, "but the real proof lay in the millions who died." [9]

Bitterly disillusioned, Hoover vowed never again to create a public policy institute:

> This experience in the way such endowed research agencies in economics and social sciences can go wrong was such that I have opposed the permanent establishment of them ever since. Such research is vital, but it should be done by men chosen for special tasks, and released when that task is over. [10]

Some years later he declared that such institutions "need a strong directing hand of public men," lest they slip into professorial control and the wastes of "squirrel-cage scholasticism." [11]

As far as is known, Hoover never again assisted the Food Research Institute. He did not forget how (as he put it) "under the cloak of academic freedom" it had expressed opinions in 1940–1941 on subjects for which it was "entirely unfit." [12] Nor did he forget or forgive Karl Brandt. In late 1945, after the close of World War II, the refugee scholar asked Hoover for help in ameloriating the suffering of the women and children of Germany, now under Allied occupation. Hoover was willing, but not before delivering a scathing rebuke:

> I well recall the visit you mention and the press statements which you subsequently issued undermining my efforts to secure food for the women, children and unemployed men in the German-occupied democracies.
>
> Not only were these statements untrue, but they were at once seized upon and used effectively against us by opponents to the humane proposals we made. Events have proven that our statements were accurate. Aside from a mass of evidence of our own, Archbishop Spellman, on the authority of an investigation by Church authorities, issued a statement that at least a million children in the Western Democracies have died as a result of insufficient food throughout the period of occupation. Your actions contributed to that result.
>
> I am aware of the need of German women and children. But it seems to me that a request from you to me and from you to the public comes from unclean hands. Your first approach to me should be an abject apology for the

infinite harm you have done and for the way you prostituted the Food
Research Institute which I created as a contribution to feeding the hungry.[13]

The wrangle with the Food Research Institute was the first skirmish in an
ideological war that pitted Hoover against his university in the months just
prior to Pearl Harbor. On August 5, 1941 Hoover, Ray Lyman Wilbur, and
several other Republican leaders publicly urged Congress to "put a stop to
step-by-step projection of the United States into undeclared war." Accusing
the Roosevelt administration of unsanctioned "warlike steps" that undermined
the "constitutional powers" of Congress and "the fundamental principles of
democratic government," Hoover and his associates insisted that America
remain apart from the Eurasian conflict. America should concentrate on protecting its own liberties, they declared. Its freedom did not "depend on the
outcome of struggles for material power between other nations." [14]
A few weeks before this declaration, Nazi Germany had invaded the Soviet
Union. To Hoover this startling development rendered the case for American
intervention less tenable than ever. No longer, said he and his colleagues on
August 5, was the contest "purely a world conflict between tyranny and
freedom." [15] No longer was Great Britain in danger of military defeat. To
Hoover and many others, the two great totalitarian powers, Germany and
Russia, were equally abhorrent and would now proceed to destroy each other
if left alone. America need not take sides.
The Hoover/Republican manifesto had immediate reverberations on the
Stanford campus. The fact that the university's president and most prominent
trustee had just ringingly condemned Roosevelt's foreign policy disturbed
many anti-isolationist faculty members who wanted the United States to do
whatever it could to aid the Allies.[16] On August 21 a group of these professors,
citing "patently increasing confusion of thought" about the nature of the
current world war, circulated a rejoinder in the form of a faculty petition. The
document urged all Americans, "regardless of party affiliations," to give "unified support" to President Roosevelt as commander-in-chief during the present
"national emergency." Rejecting the "utter futility" of "economic and political
isolationism" and the "fallacy" of "passive defense," the statement called instead for "a more dynamic policy of action as the most effective means of
security against the totalitarian menace." [17] A total of 176 Stanford professors
signed the petition.[18]
Hoover, predictably, was appalled. To Ralph Lutz he wrote:

> The confusion of mind in American intellectuals over the United States
> supporting Communism is almost beyond belief. And that is what these
> Stanford professors are doing. I wonder if it ever occurred to them what

would happen to the world if we entered the war and brought victory to Russia.[19]

When the faculty petition was released in mid-September,[20] Hoover responded with a questionnaire that he mailed not just to the 176 signatories and others of professorial rank but to what he called the "whole faculty" (including instructors, visiting and part-time faculty members, secretaries, and librarians). What did the term "dynamic policy of action" really mean? This was what he proposed to ascertain. Did the Stanford faculty, he asked, want to send munitions to England in ships flying the American flag? Did it want to convoy these ships all the way? Did it approve "complete naval action against Hitler in all waters"? Did it wish to send an American expeditionary force to fight Hitler on the European continent? Would it give Japan an ultimatum to withdraw from China and declare war on her if she did not?[21]

Approximately ten days later Hoover announced the results of his personal poll: 60 percent of the Stanford faculty, he asserted, "taken as a whole," did not concur with the August statement of the 176 petitioners. Hoover did not disclose how many of the 800 people he canvassed had actually replied—only that the response had been "extraordinarily generous." On every point, he said, a majority of the respondents had rejected the interventionist policy options that he had presented for their consideration. Elated by his findings, he told the press that "the winds of freedom" still blew at his university.[22]

If Hoover was delighted by his "market research," many in Palo Alto were not. The unprecedented poll, in fact, deeply offended a number of residents of the Stanford community. Some were outraged that a university trustee (and especially Hoover) should canvas faculty members for their opinions on public questions.[23] Beyond this, many faculty interventionists were convinced that for all its specificity the questionnaire did not truly clarify the issues at stake and in fact was potentially misleading. In other words, the poll was flawed.[24] Hence Hoover's poll data, said Professor Lewis Terman bluntly, were "not to be taken as seriously representing the real opinions of the faculty on isolationism."[25] Privately some professors suspected that Hoover's figures had been deliberately falsified.[26]

Under Terman's leadership a committee of faculty interventionists now countered with a poll of its own, designed, in its words, to be "brief, direct, and unambiguous." Sidestepping the constitutional question entirely, the pollsters asked three questions. Did the respondents support the measures already taken by the Roosevelt administration against the Axis powers? Did they favor further measures, specifically revision of the neutrality acts and additional lend-lease legislation? Would they support unspecified "stronger measures" if these were needed "to defeat the Axis powers"? The new survey was mailed to past and present members of the university academic council and to all others of professorial rank: a total of 483 persons. Those holding temporary positions or not belonging to the "regular teaching staff" were excluded.[27]

And so, politely yet unequivocally, the interventionists prepared to test Hoover's claims. Who spoke for Stanford University? As the day of the poll count approached, Hoover's indignation seemed to rise. On October 21 he told a friend that "our Stanford colleagues have stepped off the deep end into emotional psychosis where all sense of proportion is lost."[28] The very next day the Terman group released its results. Of the 341 respondents, nearly 84 percent endorsed without reservation the Roosevelt administration's anti-Nazi foreign policies. More than 80 percent favored additional pro-Allied legislation. And more than 75 percent unqualifiedly approved even "stronger measures," if necessary, to defeat the Axis evil.[29]

In the battle of the polls the interventionists had triumphed. Or had they? In the ensuing analysis of the data, it apparently occurred to no one that there might be a divergence in political sentiment between the full-time professors reached by Terman's group and the secretaries, librarians, and draft-age instructors who had been included in Hoover's sample. Nevertheless, one fact was now indisputable, and it was one that could give Hoover no comfort: a substantial majority of Stanford's principal faculty was in the Rooseveltian, interventionist camp.[30]

For the second time in three months Hoover stood publicly repudiated on the campus he called his home, and he did not take kindly to the experience. To Professor Terman he wrote on October 30:

> I could comment upon the poll of your Committee. The policies you perhaps innocently are supporting will lead this country into sending millions of American boys to die on battlefields in Europe. You did not put that question to the Stanford faculty. I have concluded that it is no use engaging in such discussion with friends who are uninformed of what they are doing. I shall, however, file away the whole of these papers to be produced ten years hence and examined for (a) the wisdom of your Committee's proposals, (b) the intellectual honesty or dishonesty of these policies you are promoting, (c) the fidelity or repudiation of the spirit of democratic process, Constitutional and statutory law that lies in your proposals.
>
> In the meantime, forces greater than any of us will save or destroy the foundations of freedom in America, so that we do not need to spend ten years quarrelling among friends.[31]

As it happened, the traumatic issue that divided the two men very shortly became moot: only a few weeks later the Japanese attacked Pearl Harbor. But the isolation/intervention controversy that autumn had exposed a deepening fissure between Hoover and most of the Stanford faculty. It remained to be seen whether time and new political configurations would heal or exacerbate the rift.

II

With the entry of the United States into the Second World War, political contention at Stanford disappeared, and Hoover resumed his traditional role of trustee/benefactor. Early in 1942 he approached his fellow alumni with an innovative fund-raising scheme called Stanford Futures. Pointing out that the average student at the university in the past had received an indirect subsidy of $1,500 from endowment and other sources, he asked the alumni to pledge to return this sum to the university during their lifetime. The money would be earmarked for scholarships for needy undergraduates.[32] It was a quintessentially Hooverian undertaking—an attempt to provide educational opportunity to those, like himself half a century before, who had to scrape and struggle to "make it." And the response revealed that his name was still "magic" among the alumni. Within a few months, and despite the onerous new burdens of wartime, the Stanford Futures campaign garnered more than $350,000.[33]

Quietly, in ways none but intimates were aware of, Hoover endeavored to sustain his alma mater's momentum. Thus in 1942, for instance, he pursued funding for a badly needed new chemistry building.[34] Even the board of trustees did not escape his eye; working with the newest trustee, Donald B. Tresidder (class of '19), he strove to alter its membership and energize its all too perfunctory procedures.[35] It was not easy. "I have tried, time and time again, to get something done," he told Tresidder, "but it seems as if one runs against an implacable wall of opposition. It is not particularly personal, but just completely reactionary."[36] Still, in 1942, Tresidder, with Hoover's backing, accomplished some internal reforms and became the board's own president.[37]

The most important responsibility confronting the trustees, however, was the selection of a successor to Ray Lyman Wilbur. On December 5, 1941 the board formally offered the Stanford presidency to the head of the Carnegie Institution of Washington, Vannevar Bush.[38] Two days later the events at Pearl Harbor thwarted its desire; absorbed in wartime service for the government, Bush, a noted scientist, had to decline. At the beginning of 1942 Wilbur became chancellor as scheduled but agreed to act also as president until his replacement could be found.[39] In the circumstances of war, qualified and available candidates were hard to find; that spring Hoover's search committee disbanded without success.[40]

A new trustees' committee chaired by Tresidder resumed the quest. Before long, and (so far as is known) without his encouragement, Tresidder himself emerged as the preference of many faculty and alumni. The personable physician-turned-businessman also impressed Herbert Hoover, who on the night of August 2 "made a suggestion" to two trustees. A few months later, with Hoover's wholehearted approval, the board invited Tresidder to become the university's fourth president.[41] When the 48-year-old alumnus accepted, Hoover the veteran president-maker was pleased. "Your letter," he wrote, "lifted a large load from my mind."[42]

The university's change of leadership in 1943, however, did not occur without a measure of strain. Repelled by the enormous and austere president's house in which Wilbur and his large family had lived, Tresidder and his wife, a childless couple, asked permission to make the Hoovers' home their official campus residence. (The dwelling was usually vacant; for some time the Hoovers had been spending most of their year at the Waldorf Astoria Towers in New York.) The incoming president's request apparently annoyed the Hoover family, but Tresidder pleaded and soon received his wish.[43] At first Hoover intended to sell the home outright but eventually decided to lease it instead.[44] He arranged for Tresidder's payments as tenant to go to the Stanford Futures, so that (he told Wilbur) "I shall not be in position of taking anything directly or indirectly out of the University."[45]

Then, on January 7, 1944, Hoover's wife of nearly 45 years died suddenly, two months short of her 70th birthday. A few days later her California friends and neighbors assembled for a memorial service on the Stanford campus. In a simple but moving address Ray Lyman Wilbur eulogized the unaffected woman who herself had brought luster to her alma mater. "There is no finer example of how to live," he said, "than was given to us by Lou Henry Hoover."[46]

Later that year Hoover offered his campus home to the university for its official president's residence, provided that it be named the Lou Henry Hoover House and provided that Stanford contribute $6,250 per year for ten years to document-collecting efforts of the Hoover Library in her memory.[47] A grateful board accepted his bequest.[48]

It was, in fact, his incomparable library that absorbed most of Hoover's Stanford-oriented energies as the war progressed. Within days of Pearl Harbor he initiated a new campaign to acquire "fugitive material" on the current conflict.[49] The files of the America First Committee, which he personally solicited, were among his earliest prizes.[50] His principal financial ally in the document hunt was an old friend, businessman, and philanthropist, Jeremiah Milbank, whose contribution of $2,500 in late 1941 helped make it possible for Hoover to reopen his library's Washington office.[51]

Meanwhile the institution itself was evolving in ways that its founder approved. In 1940 its teaching and research functions had been combined into a "Research Institute," renamed the "Hoover Research Institute on War, Revolution and Peace, Hoover Library" in 1941.[52] Later in the war, at the request of the U.S. government, the library's staff conducted intensive training schools for armed services personnel about to be assigned to occupied countries in Europe and Asia.[53] Hoover was gratified; at last his library's resources were being put to productive use.

By the end of 1944 Hoover had secured about $235,000 in gifts and pledges (including $50,000 from Milbank) for acquisitions related to World War II.[54] With this reserve he was able to finance a monumental collecting drive in the critical years just ahead. As the world recovered from its torment, dedicated agents of the Hoover Library (many of them Stanford professors and alumni) scoured Western Europe, Japan, and even China in a successful search for historical treasure. By 1950 the library's ever-burgeoning holdings were more than double what they had been before the war.[55]

The Chief himself participated actively in the campaign, at times using his political influence to achieve results. Thus even before the fighting in the Pacific was officially over, he asked General Douglas MacArthur to provide staff assistance to a representative of the library who was traveling in the Far East.[56] When Hoover's collectors in China were unable to transport precious documents out of disrupted areas, he asked the assistant secretary of war to authorize the American military to aid them.[57] Time and again Hoover's prestige, and the international reputation of his archive, enabled him to obtain unique assets that might otherwise have been lost forever. On a relief mission to Europe for President Truman in 1946, he personally acquired the diary of Nazi Germany's propaganda minister, Joseph Goebbels, as well as files of the wartime Polish underground.[58] Said one admirer of him: "Other people collect antiques and china in Europe, but he bought living history."[59]

Even the Soviets, no friends of him or his politics, acknowledged his library's distinction, although this time (unlike the 1920s) they closed their borders to its representatives. In the spring of 1945, during the founding conference of the United Nations in San Francisco, Foreign Minister Molotov and his cohorts came down the peninsula for a look. In the words of Ray Lyman Wilbur, they "just smelled the outside of the Hoover Library building and went away."[60]

In mid-1943 Ralph Lutz was forced by illness to retire as chairman of the Hoover Library's directors; Professor Harold H. Fisher succeeded him.[61] This transfer of authority, and the impending growth of the library's holdings and public policy potential, inspired Hoover in 1944 to seek the library's administrative independence. On September 2 he wrote to President Tresidder:

> I have never been satisfied that the purpose of the War Library was really recognized by placing it under the University Librarian and thus casting it

in the mould of just a library adjunct. That is not its purpose. Its purpose is to build up a great research institution upon the most vital of all human questions—War, Revolution and Peace.

The library, said Hoover, should now have a full-time director who should report directly to the university president and not be "subject either to the History Department or the University Librarian."[62] The "major purpose" of his institution, said Hoover in a later letter, was "research, training of men in foreign affairs, and the development of scholarship and knowledge." It should also become "a center of Pacific relations." "All this," he concluded, required "an institution with its own Director, personnel, and budget"—an entity, he added pointedly, "no longer . . . a mere adjunct to the University Library."[63]

President Tresidder was amenable to this proposal.[64] But Hoover shortly discovered that the university's chief executive, though outwardly sympathetic, was not as complaisant as his predecessor. It soon developed that Hoover wished to reorganize the library's board of directors, which had not met as a body for several years. As of 1945 the board consisted of himself, Edgar Rickard, and eleven Stanford professors and administrators.[65] Hoover now proposed to replace them with a body comprised principally of himself, his son Allan, and a few close faculty and nonfaculty friends.[66] It was clear from this action that he planned to maintain or even increase his influence over the library he had founded.

To Professor Fisher, however, and apparently to Tresidder also, Hoover's plan implied a power shift that was unacceptable. In Fisher's view the moribund board of directors should be abolished and replaced with a merely advisory board and a largely honorific council of academics.[67] Writing privately to Tresidder, Fisher argued that the library's director should function like the head of a university department.[68] In such a scheme of things there would be little role for outsiders.

There now ensued a behind-the-scenes tug-of-war. Twice, apparently, Hoover pushed for the creation of an administrative committee, and twice President Tresidder apparently buried the idea.[69] Finally, on March 15, 1946, Hoover unleashed his heaviest weapon via a letter to Tresidder from Edgar Rickard. After expressing his unhappiness at being a member of a board of directors that had not convened since he had joined it five years before, Rickard announced that he was prepared to give Stanford University $30,000 for the Hoover Library, *if* the university accepted two conditions: all of the money must be spent on further acquisitions, and the trustees must appoint "an administrative board which shall have an active part in determining the policy of the Library." Rickard suggested that this board consist of Tresidder, Ray Lyman Wilbur, Robert E. Swain, Jeremiah Milbank, Herbert Hoover, and

Allan Hoover. Rickard's message was polite but unambiguous: unless the university granted the library's founder the role that he wished to have, there would be no $30,000.[70]

Unknown, probably, to Hoover and Rickard, President Tresidder immediately sought the reaction of Director Fisher. In a reply marked "personal," Fisher made it plain that the proposed "administrative committee" was a distasteful proposition. If it must be accepted (as he clearly feared would be the case), the committee, he hoped, would be confined to fund-raising and solicitation efforts only. Presumably, he noted, it would have no jurisdiction over research, publication, and teaching.[71] In a word, Hoover wanted his institution to be independent of the university library; Fisher wanted it also to be independent of its founder and his friends.

It now fell on Stanford's president to attempt to square the circle. After conversations with Hoover in the summer of 1946, Tresidder proposed a reorganization plan superseding the library's mode of governance since the middle of the 1920s. Hoover pronounced the scheme "entirely satisfactory," and the university's trustees duly ratified it in September. The board's resolution (approved beforehand by Hoover) changed the name of the institution to the "Hoover Institute and Library on War, Revolution and Peace" and declared it to be "a separate division of Stanford University." The resolution also created an advisory board consisting of Herbert Hoover (for life), the university's president ex officio, and others appointed annually by him. This body was to advise "the University administration" on such matters as "general policies," acquisitions, and the library's "lines of development." A separate council of distinguished scholars and public leaders, also appointed by the president, would be formed for consultation, when asked, on subjects of special interest to its members. Finally, the resolution stipulated that Stanford's president would appoint the library's chairman, who would be responsible to him and would "function in a manner similar to department heads throughout the University."[72]

For the Chief and such long-suffering allies as Ralph Lutz, the trustees' action was a signal victory. Physically separate since 1941, the Hoover Library was now administratively free as well—free from van Patten and the university library bureaucracy. The trustees' resolution also contained a broad and satisfying mandate. The library/institute's functions, it said, included collection of materials on war, revolution, and peace; "promotion and organization of research"; "publication of the fruits of research"; and the offering of instruction, "chiefly at the graduate level."[73] Pleased by the outcome, Hoover asked Tresidder to notify Edgar Rickard.[74] Tresidder did, and the $30,000 was apparently released.[75]

On closer inspection, however, Tresidder's plan contained a number of curious features, and one is forced to wonder whether Hoover fully grasped its implications. After all the discussions of the preceding months, including Rickard's well-aimed salvo in March, the final resolution explicitly created an *advisory* board (not an "administrative" one) whose functions, for the most part, were nebulous. Furthermore, the resolution unequivocally vested in the president the right to appoint the chairman of Hoover's library; nothing was said on paper about any role in this process for its founder. Why, when all was said and done, had Hoover settled for such an apparent circumscription of his influence? Did he consider the distinction between an "advisory" board and an "administrative" one merely semantic? Did he expect to exercise as much power over his library as he ever had, regardless of the resolution's phraseology? Had he and Tresidder worked out a supplementary gentleman's agreement on their own? Or had Tresidder in his genial way outwitted him?

For Hoover the precise wording of the resolution may have seemed less consequential than the relationship that he thought he had with the university's president. On one issue, at least, the two men had reached an understanding that was not incorporated in the formal trustees' minutes: the first advisory board of the Hoover Institute and Library was to include Hoover, his son Allan, Rickard, Wilbur, Swain, Milbank, and Perrin Galpin (of the Belgian American Educational Foundation).[76] But on another issue—selection of the first group of councillors—Tresidder showed signs that he might not always be so amenable to Hoover's wishes. At Fisher's private urgings, and evidently to avoid difficulties with the Chief, Tresidder drew his first appointments entirely from those on campus who had already been serving on the library's directorate. Hoover apparently had no objection. But precisely by being so cautious, and by listening to Fisher's advice that he be cautious, Tresidder revealed that he perceived Hoover as a problem, and not simply as a great man and a friend.[77]

Hoover could not yet know it, but the reorganization scheme of 1946 was a symbolic watershed in his relationship with his alma mater. Until now, in the recurrent territorial battles between his institution and the university library, he had enjoyed the unwavering support of some distinguished faculty associates, particularly in the department of history. But now, 27 years after his library's founding, the campus environment was changing. Adams was gone, Lutz was semiretired, Wilbur was only the chancellor. What if it should transpire that the faculty was no longer with him? While the current president seemed friendly, what would come to pass if Stanford selected a leader who was not as accommodating as Wilbur? Hoover's library was at last a "separate division," a consummation for which he had yearned. But what if he should someday discover that an adversary lurked within?

III

Hoover's activities in behalf of his alma mater during the Tresidder years took place against the background of a Stanford faculty gliding slowly toward the left. So, at least, it appeared to the university's foremost alumnus. As early as 1943 he complained to Tresidder about a member of the staff who had just received newspaper publicity for leftist activities:

> I suppose that academic freedom requires that we keep a few Communists on the faculty, but nevertheless, when [a certain professor] admits that he joined the Communists in signing a protest without ever reading a document, it indicates a very considerable lack of both character and academic standards.[78]

In 1946 he attempted unsuccessfully to postpone Tresidder's appointment of the new dean of the law school until Hoover could forward information about the man's past. Hoover's telegram came too late. Ingenuously or otherwise, Tresidder replied that the dean (who had been on the job for six weeks) had shown no signs of being an extremist.[79]

In 1947 Hoover again was disturbed, this time by a Stanford economist's textbook that had come under public attack by certain conservative authors. Tresidder responded that while the author was clearly a Keynesian, his book was not subversive. The university's president professed to discern an increasing national reaction against Keynesian philosophy.[80]

It is not clear whether Hoover accepted Tresidder's explanations, considered him naive, or suspected that Tresidder was fending him off with sophistries. The question, in any case, soon and sadly became moot: in early 1948 Tresidder died suddenly at the age of 53. The board of trustees soon appointed a committee to recommend a successor; not surprisingly, Hoover was member of the panel.[81]

For several months in 1948, despite advancing age and a staggering burden of governmental duties, Hoover joined actively in the search for a new Stanford president.[82] At one point a Stanford alumnus protested against the possible appointment of the university's acting president, Alvin C. Eurich, whom he termed an ardent New Dealer.[83] Hoover promptly assured him that Eurich was not being considered for the position.[84]

The trustees' opposition to Eurich may or may not have been ideological; in the eyes of certain faculty members, the acting president was not a sufficiently qualified candidate. But to at least a few of the trustees, including Hoover, political considerations were undeniably critical. One of the individuals they were considering was the new director of the Huntington Library, J. E. Wallace Sterling, a Canadian-born historian who had received his Ph.D.

from Stanford in the 1930s. On August 25, 1948 Hoover's friend and fellow trustee, Seelye G. Mudd, called on Sterling to ascertain his political convictions. Sterling declared that he had never voted for Franklin Roosevelt, considered him egotistic and intellectually dishonest, and favored Thomas Dewey for president. As for the New Deal, Sterling stated that while he admired some of its social objectives, he considered that the programs themselves had usually been badly implemented. What Washington, D.C., needed now, he said, was a thorough housecleaning. On the strength of these and other remarks, Mudd concluded that Sterling's academic and political ideology were to the right of center.[85]

For Hoover this was conclusive. "I believe this is our man if we can get him," he told the chairman of the search committee. As a trustee of the Huntington Library Hoover promised to put pressure on his colleagues to let the new director go.[86]

Some years later Hoover declared that it was he who provided the critical vote that put Sterling's nomination through; without Hoover's switch the board would not have made the selection.[87] If so, he could now claim a crucial, perhaps decisive, role in the selection of four consecutive presidents of his alma mater. On April 1, 1949 Sterling duly took the helm of Stanford University; within weeks he was invited to join Hoover's Caveman Camp at the Bohemian Grove.[88]

Not all the news from campus, however, was so encouraging. On June 26, 1949 Ray Lyman Wilbur died at 74. To the very end he and Hoover had remained close, with offices on the same floor of the Hoover Tower. With his passing Hoover lost not only an intimate friend of nearly 57 years but an irreplaceable personal link to the university.

Despite this blow, the summer of 1949 was for the Chief and his Stanford admirers a time for festive celebration. On August 10 more than 12,000 people assembled in the Laurence Frost Memorial Amphitheater on campus to salute him on his 75th birthday. During the ceremony a local friend named Fred A. Wickett presented a birthday gift of more than $155,000 collected from more than 1,200 people—all for the use of the Hoover Institute and Library. Even Hoover's nationally broadcast address to the gathering—a somber warning that pressure groups and profligate government spending were driving America down the "back road" to collectivism—did not dissipate the relaxed atmosphere or dilute his joy at being home. Prior to speaking he lunched at the Stanford Union and reflected on what his country had given him. "There is no place on the whole earth except here in America where all the sons of man could have this chance in life," he said.[89]

But again, as in 1941, the mood of celebration did not last. In the autumn of 1949 the mainland of China fell to the communist armies of Mao Tse-tung. A few months later, after a trial that stunned the nation, a man named Alger

Hiss was sent to prison—convicted of perjury and in effect of espionage for the Soviet Union while serving high in the Department of State in the 1930s. Just weeks later a senator from Wisconsin named Joseph McCarthy accused the State Department of harboring dozens of Communists.

Abroad and at home the winds of ideological warfare were blowing at hurricane force. From the effects of this deepening rancor neither Hoover nor his university would be spared.

· 8 ·

The Tower Tilts to the Left

I

By 1949 Herbert Hoover was an old man. But even as he approached and then entered his 80s, Stanford's most honored alumnus did not fade silently away. Though he now made only occasional visits to the campus and attended trustees' meetings but rarely, his interest in his alma mater's welfare remained deep.

And yet, despite appearances, all was no longer the same. In the final years of his life, Hoover's relationship to his university grew increasingly tense and discordant. Outwardly Stanford acclaimed its venerable alumnus and invoked his immense prestige in its quest for gifts from persons who admired him. Privately, however, a growing number of faculty bemoaned the campus influence of a man they scorned as a meddlesome reactionary. As for Hoover himself, his continuing impulse toward philanthropy clashed with a disheartening awareness that the university he loved had profoundly changed. Public honor, private acrimony: this was to be the pattern of his active twilight years—until suddenly the bitterness erupted and obscured a lifetime of benefaction.

No casual observer of Stanford's public relations mechanism, of course, would have noticed this deepening dissonance. Public relations does not emphasize the negative, and during the late 1940s and 1950s the university labored hard to maintain the image of an institution in harmony with the Chief. In 1949 Hoover was made a lifetime honorary member of the Stanford student body.[1] In 1951 he was invited to write the foreword to a university publication; his contribution promptly appeared in the alumni magazine.[2] In 1956 and 1957 he addressed the graduating classes at commencement.[3]

Stanford also did not hesitate to make use of his financial connections. In 1956 it asked him to serve as honorary chairman of a committee to raise more than $42,000,000 for a medical center to be located on campus. The aging alumnus agreed, and the campaign was successfully launched.[4] Despite his "honorary" status, Hoover actively solicited contributions.[5]

Even as Stanford benefited, however, from the aura of Hoover's reputation, tension at times surfaced behind the scenes. In September 1956 he formally protested to his fellow trustees against the proposed architecture of the planned medical school. It was "a complete departure from the Romanesque which has been the architectural motif of the University since the beginning," he wrote.[6] Once upon a time his objections would have carried the day. But Hoover was no longer as dominant as he once had been, and the board decided not to change course.[7]

The Chief did not give up easily. A year later he strenuously reiterated his disapproval of the university's growing break with its architectural past. The medical school and post office were a "sorry departure from the Romanesque," he charged; so, too, was the proposed new addition to the physics complex, which would be "an eyesore" until the university tore it down.[8] He urged the trustees to revise their plans for the physics buildings now, when only a few thousand dollars had been expended.[9] Stanford, he declared, was "one of only two or three American universities having a distinctive and consistent architecture. Its architectural motif is singularly appropriate for California as it memorializes the spirit of learning and religious faith which the Spanish Fathers brought to this State." It was also "an essential part" of the Stanford family's gift to the university.[10]

This time Hoover's protest, in which at least one other trustee joined,[11] had a noticeable impact on his brethren. Although the board did not modify its current projects, in November 1957 it did decide that all future structures erected adjacent to or facing the original Quad should "conform, as nearly as possible" to the modified Romanesque form of architecture of "the original Inner and Outer Quadrangles, due allowance being made for modern costs and materials."[12] Thanks in considerable measure to Hoover, the erosion of Stanford's architectural integrity—at least on the inner campus—was stopped.

On a related issue, however, he did not make headway. In 1957 Hoover suggested that Stanford someday erect a second Hoover Library–type tower at the opposite end of the Quad. Such a building, he believed, would provide not only useful storage space for the university but, more important, a balanced, aesthetically appealing facade from the perspective of Palm Drive. "Towers are a usual part of Romanesque," he observed, and many Spanish missions had pairs of them. If a second such tower were built, he argued, Stanford "would certainly be unique among all universities as to its architecture." Hoover was enthusiastic about his proposal. But as it happened, the placement of the medical school and other buildings on that side of the campus rendered his idea somewhat impractical. [13] No duplicate of the Hoover Tower seems ever to have been seriously considered.

To a fellow trustee Hoover called his suggestion an "amiable thought," [14] and perhaps there was a trace of whimsy in it. Alas, in his final years there would be fewer and fewer occasions for him to contemplate his library so benignly.

II

When Harold H. Fisher became chairman of the Hoover Library's board of directors in 1943 he had known the founder for nearly a quarter of a century. It was in fact Hoover who had arranged for him to come to Stanford in 1924 to complete a history of the American Relief Administration. Since then he had become a popular professor at the university and a published scholar on Soviet Russia. Throughout the years he had remained friendly with his early patron—friendly enough to address him as the Chief. [15]

The new chairman, however, was a different man from his predecessor. A self-styled "Vermont Republican" and member of the GOP since 1912, Fisher was also an outspoken liberal. In the 1920s he had worked for a time on the staff of the *New Republic*. [16] In the early 1940s he had signed a petition urging the House of Representatives to abolish the Dies Committee investigating un-American activities. [17]

But far more revelatory of his overall viewpoint was a book that he published in 1946 under the title *America and Russia in the World Community*. In it Fisher argued that "American and Russian aims are not irreconcilable with each other" and that Stalinist Russia was evolving in ways that increasingly facilitated Russo-American "collaboration" in the "world community." For one thing (he claimed), the USSR had officially abandoned its "program of world revolution" as well as the doctrine of two irreconcilable worlds—one communist, the other capitalist. For another, the celebrated Soviet constitution of 1936, while failing to guarantee "what we regard as essential freedoms for true democracy," nevertheless represented an "advance" toward American ideals of "democracy and legal and economic equality." In fact, it even mentioned certain rights—such as the right to medical care—that were "just becoming issues" in American political life. To be sure, Fisher continued, the "Soviet interpretation of the freedom of the press does not correspond with our interpretation." And the communist monopoly of political power, as well as the "important role" of the "political police," meant that "Soviet democracy will be far removed from American democracy." Still, he said, the Soviet constitution had "great educational value" and was evidence of Russia's "recognition" of liberties that the West regarded as essential. Furthermore, observed Fisher, the atheistic communist regime had relaxed its once-hostile policies toward religion—a change that "surely makes her membership in the world community easier."

Not surprisingly, Fisher vigorously criticized those "opinionated" individuals—both communist and noncommunist—who continued to believe in the existence of "two worlds" in inevitable conflict until one or the other had changed. Asserting that there were no "inseparable barriers" to Russo-American cooperation in "the realization of a true world community," he argued that the choice was stark; it was "one world or none."[18]

In quieter times Fisher's political vision and optimistic assessment of Soviet behavior might have gone unnoticed. But the period of Cold War into which America was entering was not such an era of tranquillity. An international ideological and even military struggle was underway, in which scholarship itself was a weapon. In addition, Fisher was no longer simply a professor at a peaceful campus in California; he was the caretaker of the free world's greatest repository of data on the Bolshevik revolution. He had taken his post, moreover, at the very moment in which Hoover was seeking to transform this library into an instrument of public service and enlightenment. But what constituted "enlightenment," particularly on the subject of communism? On this the Chief and his onetime protégé came markedly to disagree.

It was not long before Fisher's stewardship of the Hoover Library fell under the scrutiny of hard-line anticommunists with whom Hoover was increasingly associated—and whom Fisher in his book labeled a threat to world peace.[19] In 1945 the executive editor of the anti-Stalinist *New Leader* informed Hoover (through a friend) that "a well-known fellow traveler" was about to take charge of a Russian studies publications program at his library.[20] After showing that this report was inaccurate, Fisher in reply denounced the *New Leader* "crowd" as an intolerant remnant of Trotskyites and other fanatics who "probably should be examined by a psychiatrist."[21]

A year later, in a statement reported on the front page of the *New York Times*, Fisher (conspicuously identified as chairman of the Hoover Library) joined several other public figures in criticizing American military support for the Nationalist government of Chiang Kai-shek in the Chinese civil war. "We cannot promote American ideas of democracy by giving exclusive support" to the Nationalists or their communist enemies, the signers claimed. Instead the United States should convene an international conference to terminate the hostilities.[22] This manifesto led to an acrimonious exchange between Fisher and Alfred Kohlberg, publisher of the anticommunist monthly *Plain Talk* and later the catalyst of the so-called "China Lobby." Fisher accused Kohlberg (who had complained about him to Hoover)[23] of dishonesty and fanaticism.

Kohlberg in turn accused Fisher of behaving as an apologist for "Russian aggression and terror." For Kohlberg, being a "noncommunist" (as Fisher labeled himself) was not enough. It was "a position either of uncertainty or ignorance as to which side to take in the present struggle between the totalitarian and the free world."[24]

Meanwhile Fisher was beginning to leave his imprint on the Hoover Institute and Library. In April 1947 he brought in as vice-chairman a former graduate student named C. Easton Rothwell, then on the senior staff of the liberal Brookings Institution. Between 1941 and 1946 Rothwell had worked in the State Department, where he had become a friend and close associate of Alger Hiss.[25] A few months after moving to Stanford, Rothwell received a project proposal from Hiss, who had recently become president of the Carnegie Endowment for International Peace. Shortly thereafter, the Hoover Library initiated a Carnegie Endowment-funded survey of the use of motion pictures to educate the American people about international affairs. This study, Hiss explained to Rothwell, should attempt to foster the production of movies in America that enhanced international understanding. It should also try to persuade moviemakers to pledge to refrain from including in their films anything that might engender hatred or misunderstanding.[26] The guidelines for such self-censorship, of course, would presumably reflect the political stance of the survey's sponsors.

On another front, in 1948 the Carnegie Corporation (a separate entity from Hiss's) awarded the Hoover Institute $180,000 to conduct a three-year multidisciplinary study of the impact of revolution on international relations since 1890.[27] In planning the RADIR project (as it came to be called)[28] Fisher and Rothwell consulted a variety of established scholars—all of them, however, on the center-to-left on the political spectrum. One, in fact, later became a self-styled "Marxian economist," another a contributor to the fellow-traveling periodical *PM*. Still another, an eminent authority in his field, was soon to be publicly accused of belonging to the Communist Party.[29]

Until now the Hoover Library had usually published books of an essentially documentary character—books drawn directly from manuscripts in the library itself. With the advent of the RADIR project, Chairman Fisher abandoned this policy and set the library on the path of publishing interpretive studies by social scientists. He did not yet know it, but this was a formula for trouble.

In the meantime the institute/library continued its unprecedented expansion. With the aid of a $200,000 grant from the Rockefeller Foundation in 1947, Fisher awarded fellowships to numerous scholars in Slavic studies.[30] One of these was an unabashed Soviet sympathizer.[31] Fisher also increased the library's curatorial staff to six,[32] including Mary Wright, then a Harvard doctoral candidate who had acquired invaluable materials in China for the

Hoover Library at the end of World War II. Competent in her professional duties, Wright was also outspokenly sympathetic to the Chinese Communists led by Mao Tse-tung.[33]

Not every Hoover Library staff member stood politically to the left of center. In February 1947 a Polish émigré diplomat, Witold Sworakowski, came to the library as a Slavic studies fellow and remained to become one of its most successful collectors.[34] But Sworakowski's presence initially seemed somewhat anomalous, as he himself probably felt after a conversation with Rothwell in 1947. It turned out that another scholar had recently informed the visiting Polish ambassador that there were Communists among the Slavic studies fellows. The charge had gotten back to Fisher, who had Rothwell call in Sworakowski to determine if he was the source of the accusation.

In their ensuing interview it developed that both men had attended the founding conference of the United Nations in San Francisco in 1945— ·Sworakowski as an observer for the Polish government-in-exile based in London, and Rothwell as the conference's executive secretary under the secretary-general, Alger Hiss. Somewhat naively, Sworakowski revealed to Rothwell that he had been told by a colonel in Polish intelligence to beware of Hiss at the conference since Hiss was known to be a Soviet agent. At this Rothwell exploded, telling Sworakowski not to repeat such "hearsay." Thus was opened a permanent rift between the East European exile and his American superior, who disbelieved the growing suspicions about Hiss.[35]

By early 1948 the Hoover Tower under Fisher and Rothwell was a hive abuzz with busy scholars, virtually none of whom shared the political philosophy of the founder. At his residence in suite 31A in the Waldorf Astoria Towers, Hoover heard a rising crescendo of complaint from various informants that his library in Palo Alto was falling under procommunist influence. Irritated and depressed by the accusations, Fisher took his case to Ray Lyman Wilbur. It was true, he conceded, that among the fellows was a Soviet sympathizer who had embarrassed the library by his partisan public statements. But the man, said Fisher, had assured him that he was not a party member and had behaved satisfactorily since. The embattled chairman also pointed out that over the years the library had published anticommunist works and that he himself had condemned the Soviets many times in his writings. He also supported the Truman Doctrine and the Marshall Plan, he said, and remained a member of the Republican party. He stressed also that in the current political atmosphere researchers on communism were in danger of being smeared, as (he said) he himself had been. He pleaded for recognition of the principle of free investigation, and he noted what he considered the reckless overextension of the theory of guilt by association.[36] In a separate memorandum Vice-chairman Rothwell defended his own record of loyalty by citing his years of service in the State Department.[37]

Ray Lyman Wilbur interceded with Hoover,[38] who replied a few days later with a letter to Fisher based on a draft that Wilbur had prepared. Not for one moment, wrote Hoover, "do I consider you or Dr. Rothwell to be communists or fellow-travelers, or 'left wingers' or anything of the sort, but honest Americans trying to do a first-class and difficult job." In explaining the source of the difficulty Hoover observed that American revulsion against the Soviet Union since "the Roosevelt era" had "risen to a high emotion." "The world," he said (perhaps alluding to Fisher's recent book) "is now certainly two worlds with an implacable division." He emphasized also that communist and fellow-traveling professors deliberately sought not to advance the cause of true scholarship but "to infiltrate, undermine and pollute objective truth and real freedom in American institutions." This "is a new phenomenon in history," he warned, and it lent "a certain validity" to the imperfect efforts of people "on the lookout for these activities."[39]

For Fisher and Rothwell, Hoover's words of assurance were a welcome reprieve.[40] But the tension unleashed by America's growing "inner civil war" did not cease. In the summer of 1948 the long-simmering Alger Hiss case broke wide open. In testimony before the House Un-American Activities Committee a former Communist named Whittaker Chambers publicly declared that he had known Hiss as a Communist in the 1930s. The former State Department official vehemently denied the accusation. Within months he was on trial—nominally for perjury but in reality for having stolen classified State Department documents for transmittal, through Chambers, to the Soviet Union.[41]

At one point in the congressional hearings it appeared that the Hoover Institute and Library would become entangled in the unfolding drama. As a former assistant to Hiss, Vice-chairman Rothwell fully expected to be subpoenaed. According to Sworakowski, Rothwell thereupon went to New York and asked the Chief to intervene so that the Hoover Library's name could be kept out of the proceedings. Anxious to avoid such sensational publicity, Hoover promptly contacted someone close to the congressional committee. As a result Rothwell was not called upon to testify.[42]

Some months later J. E. Wallace Sterling arrived in Palo Alto. Initially well regarded by Hoover, the new Stanford president was also a former student of Fisher as well as a friend, since graduate school days, of Easton Rothwell.[43] At the time of his selection Sterling remarked that a candidate for a college presidency must fall within a "narrow margin" of intelligence: he must be "bright enough to be considered and stupid enough to accept."[44] In the years ahead he walked an increasingly frayed tightrope between Hoover and the Stanford University faculty.

Professor Fisher did not make Sterling's status as buffer any easier. On issue after issue in the late 1940s and early 1950s the Hoover Library's chairman took public positions at variance with the library's founder and patron. In 1950 Fisher and Rothwell signed a letter to the *New York Times* implicitly denouncing Senator McCarthy and asserting that "the right of dissent" and "the right to a fair trial" were more imperiled in America than at any time in the last 150 years. The current drive for national security, they claimed, was jeopardizing constitutional rights.[45] In 1951 Fisher joined hundreds of other social scientists in a public defense of Secretary of State Dean Acheson against his critics from the Right.[46]

The issue that most rankled Hoover, however, concerned China—specifically, Fisher's association with the Institute of Pacific Relations (IPR) and his persistent defense of his friend Owen Lattimore, director of the Walter Hines Page School of International Studies at Johns Hopkins University. The IPR was a private international association that had been founded in 1925 to facilitate scholarly study of the Far East. In the late 1940s and early 1950s it was exposed in congressional hearings as having been for years a communist-controlled organization—indeed, an "instrument of Communist policy, propaganda and military intelligence"—that had significantly abetted the cause of the Chinese Communists in American policymaking circles as well as the "interests of the Soviet Union in the United States."[47] Lattimore, an active associate of senior American policymakers in the 1940s and at one point Franklin Roosevelt's personal emissary to Chiang Kai-shek, was accused of being a procommunist (if not worse) who had worked assiduously to subvert the Chinese Nationalists and to turn American policy against them. In 1950 Joseph McCarthy accused Lattimore of being "the top Russian spy" in the United States. Two years later, after hearing voluminous testimony, a subcommittee of the Senate Judiciary Committee unanimously concluded that Lattimore had been, since the 1930s, "a conscious articulate instrument of the Soviet conspiracy."[48]

All these charges were heatedly contested, and Lattimore later portrayed himself as a victim of "McCarthyism." But in the words of one historian, "The evidence was overwhelming that the Institute and its journal [edited for seven years by Lattimore] were tightly linked to Communist, and specifically to Soviet, circles and that its line was Stalinoid." Lattimore himself, as his own writings demonstrated, was "an apologist for the Soviet regime" of Joseph Stalin.[49]

It was little wonder, then, that among Hoover and his friends Harold H. Fisher's conduct evoked distaste and even suspicion. From the perspective of civil liberties, of course, Fisher had every right to express his views, and Hoover never challenged that right. But the political debates of the early 1950s were ones of exceptional intensity and fraught with more than academic significance. Were the Chinese Communists simply "agrarian reformers" (as some in the Hoover Tower maintained),[50] or were they bloody and hostile revolutionaries? Had Lattimore and the leftist-dominated IPR spread disinformation about them and otherwise adversely influenced American policy, to the eventual detriment, indeed enslavement, of a nation? Had the State Department in the 1940s harbored a clique of dupes, anti-anticommunists, and fellow travelers, whose combined influence had benefited Soviet imperialism? The peace of the world, the survival of American liberty, might hinge on the answers to these questions.

But the issue for Hoover was more personal than that. As a frequent public speaker and weekly news commentator on radio station KNBC, Professor Fisher was very much a public figure, regularly identified as chairman of the Hoover Institute and Library. To Hoover this raised the embarrassing prospect that the public might infer that Fisher was speaking as a representative of the Institute and thus of Hoover himself. Worse still, as the institute's administrator, with power over staff appointments and consultancies, Fisher was in a position to shape the contours of the publications that emanated from the library and that bore its prestigious imprimatur.

Increasingly the question of the relationship between Hoover Library personnel and the institution that provided them a living nagged at and worried the Chief. It was one thing, he believed, for scholars to engage in public controversy as individuals, however "fuzzy-minded" their views. It was quite another thing for them to flaunt their institutional affiliation and thus exploit (in his view) its prestige.[51]

Hoover was not alone in his apprehensions. In 1951 a new member of his library's advisory board, Fred A. Wickett, protested to President Sterling along similar lines. Sterling acknowledged that Hoover Institute staff had taken public positions contrary to those of the founder. But the president insisted that they had done so as individuals and that a cherished principle of American life and higher education was "the right for an individual to express honest conviction after honest investigation."[52] It might be honest, Wickett commented, but was it sound?[53] In Wickett's opinion the founders of Stanford University had made it clear that the university should uphold certain standards and convictions to which its faculty and all other employees should subscribe.[54]

It is uncertain to what degree Hoover shared this "confessional" conception of Stanford's institutional purpose. But Hoover had long been a critic of the actual workings of the campus orthodoxy of academic freedom. Too often he had seen the *doctrine* of academic freedom invoked, in his view, as a cover for intellectual dishonesty and even subversion. When a former fellow at the Hoover Institute refused to tell a congressional committee in 1952 whether he had been a member of the Communist Party, Hoover's private reaction, expressed to Wickett, was swift: "My conviction as to academic freedom is that when people claim immunity on the grounds of self-incrimination, they are as guilty as Benedict Arnold or Alger Hiss."[55]

The vexing question of individual/institutional boundaries surfaced publicly in 1951–1952 when the first books in the RADIR project were published. Hoover was appalled by what he considered their strongly left-of-center bias and, even more, by the thought that his institute had sponsored them. Each book, in fact, carried a notice that it was a part of the "Hoover Institute Studies" and that the studies had been "conducted by" the Hoover Institute and Library. The books also stated that while the Carnegie Corporation had funded the project, the corporation must not be construed as approving the books' contents. The publications contained no such disclaimer in the same prominent place by the Hoover Institute. To an anguished and angry Chief the omission seemed to signify that his library—perhaps he himself—was endorsing the viewpoints expressed.[56]

By 1951 Harold H. Fisher was persona non grata at suite 31A.[57] Theoretically this estrangement was irrelevant; the charter of 1946 gave Hoover no role in the selection of library staff. In reality, however, Hoover retained considerable influence if he wished to use it. The institute might reside on a university campus, but he and his friends remained responsible for much of its annual revenue. Whatever the 1946 trustees' resolution said on paper, the facility in the tower was more than a "division of the university." It was his creation, his institution, his legacy.

Upset by the drift of things in Palo Alto, a number of Hoover's friends—in all likelihood at his instigation—now reduced or withheld their contributions to his library. Why, they evidently reasoned, should they finance "fuzzyminded intellectuals" (Hoover's term) and other leftists who were embarrassing the Chief with their activism? In some cases, stalwart contributors such as Jeremiah Milbank continued to donate but restricted their gifts to acquisitions (not administration) or to Hoover's personal archive.[58] In response, the university, which hitherto had supplied only a fraction of the library's operating budget, was forced to increase its subsidy at a time of overall stringency—to the annoyance of many professors. Among certain faculty the institute now became known as "Hoover's Folly." In the tower itself an anti-Hoover curator was heard to remark, "It is only a question of a great funeral, and our trouble will be over."[59]

Lamenting his financial dependence on people he perceived as right-wing extremists, Fisher decided to resign.[60] For a time Sterling apparently dissuaded him; the president told both Fisher and Hoover that he could not "yield to external pressure in the matter of defending a man's right to express his views as a loyal American."[61] At a tense meeting of the advisory board in July 1951 Sterling declared that he could accede to Fisher's request "only on the full understanding that the principle of academic freedom was in no way whatever involved."[62] For Hoover, however, the issue was not Fisher's opinions per se but the *promulgation* of those opinions under the aegis of the library. In the words of the minutes of the advisory board meeting:

> Mr. Hoover said that he fully supported the rights of expression and the principle of academic freedom but the Library had a peculiarly personal relationship to him and that in view of this relationship he felt that the members of the staff should be sufficiently loyal to him not to express their opinions publicly in a way that causes distress and embarrassment to him and his friends. He said that statements by the staff had deprived the Library of financial support it might otherwise have had.[63]

Attempting to placate his critics, Fisher assured the board that every member of the library staff was "entirely loyal to Mr. Hoover and to the institution and all it stands for." Most of the staff were "specialists," he said, many of them of "exceptional competence and great promise," who had been called upon to speak publicly on current issues. They had done so "honestly," he asserted, but their views had been "sensationally or inaccurately reported in the press."[64]

Fisher's protestations were ineffectual. Well before the meeting, Hoover had indicated that he regarded Fisher's departure as a foregone conclusion,[65] and nothing occurred afterward to suggest any change of attitude. Finally, in March 1952, under pressure from Hoover and the advisory board, Fisher at last surrendered his administrative responsibilities.[66]

Still the controversy did not end. For some reason Fisher retained his title of chairman of the Hoover Institute and Library, a designation he evidently continued to use in public forums. In one such instance, during the 1952 election campaign, he delivered on his radio program what Hoover regarded as a false and slanderous attack on the Republican vice presidential candidate, Richard Nixon. On another occasion Fisher again defended the Institute of Pacific Relations. To Hoover these broadcasts, made by Fisher "under title of Chairman of the [Hoover] Library," had brought "great embarrassments to all friends of the Library and the University." "This Library," he wrote Sterling, "is not supposed to be in politics nor engaged in slander."[67] As late as 1955 Hoover complained to Sterling about Fisher's "speaking under my name" and warned that "I may have to publicly declare that I do not agree with anything he says."[68] Only in that year was the issue finally resolved with Fisher's retirement both as a professor of history and as chairman of the Hoover Library.[69]

III

Meanwhile a change of administration had occurred in the tower. In 1952, at the departing Fisher's suggestion, President Sterling immediately appointed Rothwell to be the library's director, without first consulting Herbert Hoover. This decision was promptly ratified by the university trustees.[70] Although less publicly visible and more discreet than his predecessor, Rothwell, too, stood politically far to the left of the Chief. Under the 1946 trustees' resolution, Sterling had no formal obligation to solicit Hoover's opinion in advance. Nor, so far as is known, did Hoover verbally protest this fait accompli, although he was evidently angered by what he considered a betrayal.[71] Instead he made known his displeasure in another way: the "sit down strike" of the library's financial backers continued.[72]

Underlying the ideological conflict was a "constitutional" one that had been present since 1919. To whom did the Hoover Library belong—to its founder and tireless benefactor or to the university that provided it a home? Officially it was a branch of the university, but upon terms that conferred a special status. By custom and precedent, moreover, Hoover had repeatedly exerted influence over its development and was responsible for most of its funding. Under the relentless pressures of the Cold War this symbiosis now threatened to dissolve. To a growing number of faculty, and evidently to Sterling as well, the library was essentially a university property that must be protected from Hoover's interference. To Hoover it was an autonomous institution that must not become a haven for a gaggle of academic leftists using his name to propagate their cause.

The day before he accepted Fisher's resignation, Sterling, again without consulting Hoover, appointed a faculty committee to investigate conditions in the tower.[73] Two months later the committee reported that relations between the Hoover Institute/Library and the rest of the university were in a "deplorable" state, aggravated by the Hoover facility's growing reliance on general university funds. The fundamental cause of the problem, the faculty investigators asserted, was the Hoover Institute and Library's "extreme autonomy" and "separatist tendencies." The committee therefore proposed a broad set of measures designed to merge the institution into the university system and to put it under faculty control. Among other things, the committee suggested a feasibility study of "administrative unification" of the Hoover Library and the general university library—in other words, a repudiation of the resolution of 1946.[74]

The new Hoover Library director seemed inclined to move in this direction. Unable to raise money from Hoover or his allies, Rothwell curtailed the library's hours of operations in 1953 and even signed an agreement with the university librarian to transfer English-language books from the Hoover to the main library. The two institutions, he told his curators, were only one hundred feet apart and should be treated as a single entity. Only after this agreement became final did Hoover himself learn about it. Not surprisingly, the Chief was dismayed. Rothwell's transfer "experiment" was eventually terminated, but his failure to consult Hoover strained relations between the two men.[75]

Sterling's formal interjection of the Stanford faculty into Hoover Library affairs annoyed Professor Emeritus Lutz. For eighteen years as library chairman, he told Hoover in 1952, he had been "hampered" by Stanford professors "who had no adequate conception of the possibilities of [its] future greatness." In fact, he added, "nothing would have been accomplished without your constant support."[76] If Lutz was displeased by these developments, one can imagine the distress of the founder.

In 1953 occurred another episode in the worsening hostilities. That year the Hoover Institute published a study entitled *Moscow and Chinese Communists* by a staff member named Robert C. North, a protégé of Fisher and Rothwell.[77] North's book was "interpretive" in character and did not refrain from controversial judgments. Criticizing a recently released congressional report on the Institute for Pacific Relations, North blamed the loss of China not on communist subversion of American policymaking but on honest American errors of judgment and the failures of the Chinese Nationalists themselves.[78] Near the end of his book North urged the United States to reaffirm its "democratic *revolutionary* heritage" in the face of Third World decolonialization. Alluding plainly to Senator McCarthy (whose re-election Herbert Hoover had recently applauded),[79] North declared: "This is no time for Americans to proscribe books, to inhibit unorthodox thought, or, in hunting Communists, to risk injury to innocent people. On the contrary, the moment has come for us all to reread the Declaration of Independence, nail the Bill of Rights over our doors, and demonstrate to the world that we are a bold, imaginative and constructively revolutionary people."[80] It sounded like Harold H. Fisher.

For the Chief and some of his associates, North's book was further evidence of the left-wing anti-anticommunism that had come to pervade the Hoover Library—and that was useless in educating the American people about the communist enemy.[81] To further complicate matters, North's book contained a disclaimer-of-endorsement by the liberal Ford Foundation (which had financed his project) but none by the Hoover Institute itself.[82] Thus once again, at least by implication, Hoover's library appeared to be endorsing a political viewpoint antithetical to that of the founder.

The revolt of the donors therefore continued. At some point in 1953 a frustrated Rothwell offered his resignation; President Sterling evidently refused to accept it.[83] Meanwhile the university, which had contributed less than $33,000 to the Hoover Library's support in 1948–1949, supplied nearly $150,000 in 1952–1953.[84]

The tension spread to other fronts. In the early 1950s Hoover introduced President Sterling to a wealthy businessman and philanthropist named William Robertson Coe. Eventually Coe decided to will 8 percent of his fortune to Stanford "to establish and maintain a Program of American Studies designed as a positive and affirmative method of meeting the threat of Communism, Socialism, Collectivism, Totalitarianism and other Ideologies opposed to the preservation of our system of Free Enterprise. . . ."[85] When the conservative benefactor prepared his bequest, he evidently intended to designate the Hoover Institute as the beneficiary. Instead, Sterling assured him that such specificity was unnecessary and that he (Sterling) would take care of the matter. In the end Coe merely willed his gift to "Stanford University"; when the money finally came after his death, the Hoover Institute received nothing. Sterling's action infuriated Hoover; the wedge between the two men drove deeper.[86]

In 1955, however, a thaw occurred in Hoover's frigid relationship with his library. Despite their divergent politics, Rothwell was able to convince Hoover that he could provide the leadership necessary to make the Hoover Library a source of "true scholarship" (in Hoover's words) on matters "affecting our national policies in this Cold War."[87] This dramatic change seemed to coincide with the advisory board's August 1955 meeting, at which Hoover successfully proposed that the institute/library resume its pre-Fisher policy of documentary publication.[88] At about this time the Stanford University administration (under faculty pressure) announced that it was sharply reducing its subsidy for the Hoover facility to $100,000.[89] Whether because of Rothwell's acceptance of a shift to documentary volumes, the university's sudden financial pressure, or perhaps a combination of the two, Hoover telegraphed Sterling on September 13, 1955, that he could "now see my way clear to raising from $40,000 to $45,000 [in] gifts to the War Library for the next University fiscal year—if the Trustees are willing to restore their former budget."[90] Within 72 hours the board agreed and set its annual appropriation at $125,000.[91]

Hoover was too intelligent, however, to reopen the financial sluice gates unconditionally. He reminded President Sterling that the library's friends had withdrawn their support in past years for a reason:

> They were disturbed by two things: First, the slant of mind of the then Director [Fisher]; second, they point out that in the Library and my personal archives there is the largest collection in the world as to the most dangerous political and revolutionary activity of our times—the Communist con-

spiracy against free peoples. But these materials have never been really used for guidance of the American people, our national policies or the free world in general.

According to Hoover, his friends were "reluctant to aid" unless there were "certain understandings as to the use of these materials"—notably that the resultant publications be "complete, accurate and objective."

Hoover therefore proposed a vigorous new program of documentary compilations on such currently relevant subjects as "the Communist Peace Front," Soviet relations with Poland, and the Russian occupation of Austria between 1945 and 1955. "Our friends wish these materials put into action," he told Sterling. To support this effort, Hoover now pledged to find $100,000 from private sources in the next three years—provided that "our friends" received "certain assurances." Among these: the "proposed publications should be edited by someone to assure that they comply with American ideals." For this role he suggested (with Rothwell's approval) a trusted—and conservative—former research assistant, Professor Arthur Kemp of the Claremont Colleges.[92]

One potential source of revenue, however, the Chief unequivocally rejected. In 1955 the United States Congress enacted legislation permitting the creation of federally funded presidential libraries. For some years Hoover had maintained his personal archives (including the papers of his presidency) in the Hoover Tower at his own expense, with the intention of someday giving these papers to Stanford University.[93] Director Rothwell now proposed that the Hoover Archives be segregated on certain floors of the tower and designated the Hoover Presidential Library, which could then receive perhaps $100,000 a year in federal money. Such a step would relieve the Hoover Institute's financial woes; it would also lessen the Chief's financial leverage, as both he and Rothwell may have realized. In any case, Hoover said no: federal financing would subject his library to possible political influence, the vagaries of congressional appropriations, a loss of independence, a "drying up" of politically sensitive acquisitions, and a shriveling of private financial support.[94]

President Sterling appeared to go along with Hoover's conditions,[95] and in late 1955 and 1956 the founder, now in his early 80s, launched a national fund-raising campaign with his old-time zest.[96] Within weeks he had lined up gifts and pledges amounting to more than $77,000, including $11,200 from himself, $17,500 from his son, Herbert, Jr., and $25,000 from Jeremiah Milbank.[97] Hoover also personally pledged $11,000 more for each of the next two years.[98] Even as the momentum of the new drive increased, however, there were occasional signs that Sterling and Hoover were working at crosspurposes. One case in point concerned a $100,000 contribution from the

Pennsylvania industrialist Joseph Pew, Jr. Sterling wanted Pew to give his money in unrestricted support for the library; Hoover wanted Pew to allocate it specifically for the communist documents publication project. Hoover told Sterling that this was Pew's wish; Pew told Sterling that he was restricting the gift according to Hoover's wish. In this instance Hoover won the duel.[99]

At the library also, the pace of scholarly activity quickened; the "dark years," as Sworakowski called them, seemed to be over.[100] In a significant public relations coup, the library retained the noted Russian exile Alexander Kerensky to prepare a collection of documents on his 1917 provisional government that Lenin and the Bolsheviks had overthrown.[101] A massive study of the Soviet Union's record as a treaty partner was also duly initiated.[102] But Hoover was vigilant. Wary of the left-of-center sentiments prevailing among the library's senior staff, he arranged for the conservative Sworakowski to become the assistant director in charge of research and publications—in other words, to be Rothwell's deputy.[103] At Hoover's insistence also, the advisory board explicitly mandated in 1956 that henceforth the library's own staff studies and publications should be essentially documentary in character, based on the library's own files, and neither "analytical" nor "interpretive."[104]

Even as Hoover strove to energize and redirect his institution, he found still another cause for dissatisfaction with his alma mater. In September 1955 Stanford University accepted a grant from the liberal Fund for the Republic for an "impartial study" by Stanford Law School of the testimony by witnesses in public proceedings concerning communism. In announcing the grant, President Sterling asserted that his law school faculty would adhere to "rigorous standards" of scholarly integrity.[105] Hoover and many conservatives were not so sure. The president of the sponsoring fund, after all, was Robert M. Hutchins, an outspoken critic of congressional committees investigating communism. To the chairman of the Stanford trustees Hoover presented data documenting the left-of-center views and associations of Hutchins and of Stanford's law school dean, Carl Spaeth. If the trustees were going to have "any more dealings" with the fund, Hoover stated, they ought to have "authentic information" about it.[106] The board apparently ignored his protest.[107]

The Fund for the Republic grant, and Sterling's public endorsement of it, may well have reinforced Hoover's determination to see to it that donations to *his* institution went to specific projects that he approved. So it seemed to be with the Pew grant: the Chief was not about to let Sterling funnel it into an unrestricted account that he or Director Rothwell could draw upon without Hoover's consent. The founder was sick of value-free "squirrel cage scholasticism" and of social science "interpretive" studies that somehow always managed to display a left-wing bias.

Hoover's burst of energy in behalf of his library was now accompanied by an increasing emphasis on defining its corporate purpose. In 1957, at his request, the trustees changed its name to the one it still has today: the Hoover Institution on War, Revolution and Peace.[108] Now it would be similar in title to the Brookings Institution and Carnegie Institution, as Hoover himself observed.[109] Again and again he stressed that his was "not an ordinary library nor a 'packrat operation' but a dynamic institution"[110] which sought to offer (in the words of a press release) "effective guidance for the future of our people and of mankind everywhere."[111] It was an institution "unique in the world," he declared—"not a dead storage for documents."[112] To one potential donor he stated that its purpose was threefold. As to war: ". . . to aid the defense of the U.S." As to revolution: "The purpose is, by research and publications, to protect the American way of life from evil ideologies and to reaffirm the validity of the American system." As to peace: "By research and publications to present the world's experience." He added that by publishing its documents "without comment or attempt at interpretation" the institution could provide the "raw materials upon which official action can be guided and historical studies can be founded."[113]

Alas, the thaw of 1955–1956 did not endure. Less than three months after the advisory board promulgated its documentary-only publications policy, Rothwell asked Hoover to broaden it and permit "interpretive" historical monographs once again.[114] Hoover could hardly have been reassured by this untimely request, nor by Rothwell's apparent failure, in the months ahead, to grant any significant role to Hoover's chosen consultant, Professor Kemp.[115] Another issue also began to disturb the Chief: the publication elsewhere by Hoover Institution personnel of interpretive books that did not bear the institution's imprint yet identified the individual author as an institution employee.[116] The problem of differentiation of viewpoints did not seem to die.

The unfolding documentary series aroused other concerns. Hoover initially had high expectations for this undertaking. By publishing the "documentary facts concerning communism," he told the advisory board in 1956, the library was "exposing the evil of ideas that have spread throughout much of the present world" and thus "protecting the American way of life, which is a primary target of communism."[117] Hoover was particularly anxious to publish evidence establishing the record of "Soviet disregard of treaty obligations"—the disjunction between words and deeds. Such a publication, appearing during the current Soviet "peace" offensive, could, he thought, alert the American people that communism was "not dead but is alive and using many tricks, subterfuges, and tactics to advance its aims."[118] Unfortunately for Hoover's hopes, the vast project fell increasingly behind schedule and evolved into an interpretive "content analysis" at odds with his policy-oriented purpose. Sworakowski vehemently protested the shift; Rothwell, siding with the project directors, overruled him.[119]

Meanwhile, in early 1956 Hoover had launched a $2,500,000 endow-
ment campaign (later raised to $4,000,000) for his library under the chair-
manship of Alonzo Peake, a retired president of Standard Oil of Indiana. [120]
By early 1958 the elaborate effort had ground to a disappointing halt, with
receipts but a fraction of expectations. [121] To a friend Hoover attributed the
failure to the recession of 1957–1958 and the reluctance of many foundations
to contribute money for endowment. [122] But behind the scenes the drive was
plagued by dissension between Hoover's conservative fund-raisers (on one side)
and Sterling and Rothwell on the other. The details of the clash remain
obscure, but the result was quietly devastating: angry at Stanford's treatment
of his friends, Hoover abruptly withdrew his support for the project, which
thereupon speedily collapsed. Rothwell was stunned. Donations plummeted.
As a result, in 1958 the Hoover Institution plunged into a financial crisis of
severe and threatening proportions. [123]

At the root of the conflict, of course, was the rift between Right and Left.
In later years the institution acquired a reputation for being monolithically
conservative. In the late 1940s and 1950s, however, nearly the opposite was
the case: with the exception of Witold Sworakowski and Hoover's personal
archivist, Thomas Thalken, every member of the administrative staff of the
Hoover Institution was politically to the left of center. [124] In his unsent letter
of resignation in 1953 Rothwell conceded that the political viewpoint of the
majority of the advisory board was inadequately represented on the library
staff. But he insisted that this was not intentional and that all appointments
had been made solely on the grounds of competence. [125] To Hoover it was more
than a coincidence that virtually all these appointees somehow flocked to one
part of the ideological spectrum.

By 1958, and probably even earlier, Hoover had begun to state openly to
friends that "the leftwingers" had "taken over" his library. [126] How, he must
have wondered, could he convert his institution into a vehicle for anticommunist scholarship when the staff was riddled with "fuzzy-minded" liberals
and even admirers of Mao Tse-tung? One sign of his displeasure was subtle.
Increasingly during the mid- and late 1950s he solicited the personal papers
of prominent persons, not for the Hoover Institution itself but for his personal
archives *within* the Hoover Institution—archives under the supervision of
Thalken. [127] In June 1957, for instance, he tried unsuccessfully to acquire the
papers of the just-deceased Joseph McCarthy. The late senator's collection,
Hoover told an associate, "can be put in my personal archives, which are
separate and locked away from the General Library. There are no left-wingers
on that staff and I have set up conditions where they will not be for at least
twenty years." [128] Lest there be any doubt on these points, Hoover forcefully
reminded the university trustees later that year that his own archives were his
personal property, that title "does not rest with the university," that he had

always paid for their custody, that he had always insisted on approving their caretaker, and that no one could use them without his personal permission. Hoover expressed the "hope" that he would leave most of this material to Stanford University, but he pointedly added that "this is no commitment." [129]

The Chief's frustration with conditions at his alma mater was manifested in other ways. Late in 1957 his secretary, Bernice Miller, released a booklet entitled *What Herbert Hoover Has Done for Stanford University*. For many of his loyal friends it was a long overdue reminder of a legacy that too many in the university either knew not or preferred to forget. [130]

At about this same time the Hoover Institution made public one of its most valuable and sensational acquisitions: a file of long-concealed records of the Paris office (1883–1917) of the tsarist secret police. Ralph Lutz had obtained the huge archive under conditions of strict secrecy in 1926 from the last tsarist ambassador to Paris, Basil Maklakoff. [131] But in a letter to Hoover in 1957 Lutz recalled that it was Hoover who had laid the groundwork for this collecting coup in conversations with Maklakoff in 1919. [132] Hoover's response to Lutz was succinct: "I am glad to have that confirmation. That place doesn't seem to know that I slept there." [133]

The developing "Tower crisis" (as it came to be called in some quarters) now took another twist. For some time Rothwell had been attempting, with President Sterling's approval, to obtain joint appointments in the departments of history or political science for Hoover Institution curators. [134] The six curators currently held professorial rank and privileges within the university but possessed no formal links to specific departments—a situation that Rothwell's scheme would rectify. But his plan would also have the effect of providing university tenure for Herbert Hoover's critics among the curators—something Sworakowski suspected was precisely Rothwell's design. When Sworakowski (who also was approached with such an offer) turned to Hoover for advice, the Chief told him not to accept. A joint appointment, he warned, "will produce split loyalties." [135]

The revolving spotlight of controversy now focused on Robert C. North. On August 30, 1957 Hoover asked President Sterling to dissociate North ("a constant splinter in my mind" whose "leftish instincts are of no help to anybody") from the Hoover Institution if some other opening within the university arose. More important, Hoover said, North "should never have any administrative functions or promotion in the Institution. I do not wish to endure another Fisher episode." [136] Sterling promised to "have an eye open for alternatives." [137] But less than three months later, on Rothwell's quiet initiative, North's name came up for a joint associate professorship with the political science department *and* the Hoover Institution. Hoover was shocked. "I have never interfered before in any kind of appointment to the university staff," he telegraphed Sterling, "but if this is true it is a personal affront to me." [138]

There now ensued a six-month debate by correspondence and conversation between Sterling and the Chief. What title, if any, should North hold in the Hoover Institution? Sterling was in a quandary. How, he asked, could he accede to Hoover's wishes without being unfair to North or evoking a rebellion by the faculty? [139] Hoover conceded that it was "not my business" if Sterling wanted to appoint North to a Stanford University department. But "it must be agreed that neither he nor any other person who is offensive to me may have permanent position in the Institution." [140] While eventually willing to retain North in the tower so long as he did not receive tenure there, Hoover insisted that the central point was something else: nobody "in any way connected with the Institution" should "use any title implying connection" with it on any publication anywhere unless that publication were of the documentary nature prescribed for Hoover Institution publications in 1956.

> That does not limit "academic freedom," as such persons can publish anything they like on their own sole responsibility. Also, it implies *academic integrity* by not using my name as a false color. [141]

North was "only a symbol," Hoover continued, a symbol because of "numerous adverse reports" by many people about the library's "non-objective publications." How much North or other staffers were fellow travelers, said Hoover, was of less importance to him than "the character of publications that were being issued in the name of the Hoover Library. . . ." [142]

The Hoover-Sterling exchanges ended inconclusively,[143] except for one result. On March 20, 1958, at Hoover's suggestion and Sterling's formal recommendation, the Stanford University board of trustees appointed a standing committee (chaired by James B. Black) to oversee the Hoover Institution. [144] A new actor thus entered the drama. The battle was beginning to escalate.

Perhaps sensing the impending showdown, Rothwell now began to consider job offers elsewhere and to reorganize the institution in ways that appeared to isolate his assistant director. In particular, Rothwell seemed intent upon removing the pro-Hoover Sworakowski from control of research and publications and replacing him with a colleague whom Sworakowski regarded as a "yes-man." By this tactic, Sworakowski feared, the emboldened Rothwell would recapture publication policy even before the trustees' investigation fairly commenced, and would thus present the trustees with a fait accompli. Sworakowski also suspected that Rothwell was scheming to line up a successor—without the prior approval of the Chief. Thoroughly alarmed, Sworakowski began to send reports on Rothwell's maneuvers to Hoover's son Allan in Connecticut. [145]

Then, in early April 1958, C. Easton Rothwell made his move. The director presented a comprehensive memorandum to the Black committee—a report that he did not pass on to Hoover until late May. [146] In it Rothwell drew a portrait of a Hoover Institution gradually losing its national preeminence and increasingly unable to generate outside funding (because, he argued, its narrow-minded publishing policy inhibited the kind of research that would attract support from "major foundations"). On campus, too, he claimed, a shift was occurring: "the focus of research and teaching interest formerly centered in the Hoover Institution" was "now moving toward the University." Indeed, he said approvingly, the recent decision to grant tenure in university departments to members of the Hoover academic staff was a "healthy" step, pointing "toward the gradual subordination of the Institution's interest to general interests of the University." Rothwell thereupon proposed a number of fundamental changes. Among them: henceforth the Hoover Institution's academic staff should hold tenure appointments "in their respective disciplines" and should be associated with the institution simply on an annual basis. Hoover Institution publications should again include "analytical and interpretive works" approved by "a competent review board"; the publications program itself should be planned and controlled by a committee or board appointed by the director. From now on, Stanford University should assume "full responsibility" for the Hoover Institution's "total budget." In fact, "all present endowments," said Rothwell, should be allocated toward its current operations. [147]

Rothwell's memorandum was a thoroughgoing challenge to Herbert Hoover—and not just in its bold recommendation for a return to "interpretive" publishing under Rothwell's personal control. The subjecting of all Hoover Institution academic appointments to the departmental tenure process would introduce into the tower an unprecedented measure of faculty influence—at the very time that the Stanford faculty was veering ideologically toward the Left. Above all, the use of endowment *principal* (and not just the interest on the principal) would eventually deprive the institution of an indispensable pillar of its autonomy. All such changes, of course, would have the effect of eliminating Hoover's personal leverage. In short, and without the founder's prior knowledge, Rothwell had recommended nothing less than the absorption of the Hoover Institution—both financially and academically—by the faculty and administration of Stanford University. [148]

Rothwell may have calculated that with the new trustees' committee on the scene, he could make his case successfully to it over Hoover's head. Such at least was the interpretation of his acts by Sworakowski, who privately warned the Hoover family of the implications of Rothwell's proposals. [149] Meanwhile, from mid-April to early May, Hoover was hospitalized in New York for gallbladder surgery. [150] It was an anxious time for his allies.

Sworakowski was not the only Hoover loyalist to express indignation at the director's report. To Fred Wickett it was an act of disloyalty and ingratitude toward the man who had founded, developed, and paid for the Hoover Institution. Wickett also suspected that Rothwell's document had the covert approval of his friend and patron, President Sterling.[151] To Wickett the Chief replied:

> You have a good understanding of these tricks.
> I wonder why my property plus the property I have helped build is subject to the Stanford "Faculty." Why not the Trustees?[152]

It was to the trustees, in fact—not Sterling—that Hoover now appealed. On August 25, 1958 he wrote to James B. Black:

> A fundamental for decision by the Trustees' Committee as to the future of the Institution is whether its independence shall be maintained. The original status of the Institution, and that for many years following, was that it was an independent Institution described as "associated with Stanford University," all appointments and the approval of its budget being made by the President of the University subject to the approval of the Trustees.[153]

Hoover supported his request with a lengthy memorandum written in rebuttal to Rothwell's. He declared that teaching (which Rothwell and some of his curators wished to emphasize) was not a "primary function" of the institution and that its "teaching staff" should be "transferred to the University." He stressed that although the 1946 trustees' resolution made the institution a division of the university, it never before had been subjected to the faculty council. For the founder the issues were clear. Should the Hoover Institution retain its "independent identity within the frame of Stanford University," as he had intended, or should it now be "absorbed by the faculty"? Should it maintain its stated documentary publications policy or revert to "'interpretive' opinion type studies" that "involve responsibility as to their validity and character upon the Institution and the University for their points of view"? Should the "independent entity" he had created "as a body dedicated to history and the historical record be maintained and not confused with teaching functions and the invasion of the University faculty"?[154]

By now Rothwell was not welcome at the Waldorf Astoria; unable to gain an appointment with the Chief, he was obliged to send Sworakowski east instead.[155] Hoover also sent out signals of growing impatience with Sterling. Back in West Branch, Iowa, which had feted Hoover on his 80th birthday in 1954, a group of admirers known as the Herbert Hoover Birthplace Foundation was developing plans for a memorial park in his honor. In May 1958 Hoover indicated his willingness to build a small library-museum in West Branch to house his memorabilia and various books. His Iowa supporters were delighted.[156] As it happened, Hoover's office in the tower was lined with honorary degrees and awards. The redwood-paneled room was also one of President Sterling's favorite showplaces for prospective donors whom he escorted around campus—another way that Stanford profited from its Hoover connection. At first Hoover agreed to send only color photographs of these items to Iowa. Suddenly, in June, he ordered his personal archivist to "forget the copies" and "send the originals to West Branch."[157] In all, memorabilia insured for $500,000 were shipped.[158] But Hoover's gesture was too oblique. Sterling appeared to miss the point entirely.[159]

If Hoover was angry at Rothwell and Sterling, the director was equally incensed at what he regarded as Hoover's irresponsible accusation that "the left-wingers" had captured the Hoover Institution. No one had taken over anything, Rothwell retorted to Sterling. The same people were performing their duties as they had a year before. Such erroneous charges, he declared, were an injustice to himself, to his staff, and to the university's president. The director was also furious at Hoover's abrupt termination of the $4,000,000 fund drive and at what he perceived as the Chief's indifference to the canons of academic freedom. To Sterling, Rothwell confessed that he was becoming tired of having to defend the Hoover Institution against its founder, and the university against one of its trustees.[160] To each side, then, the other appeared the aggressor.

In late October President Sterling journeyed to New York for two lengthy conversations with Hoover. For a time, during the North affair, the two men had had difficulty in subsequently agreeing upon what they thought they had agreed upon earlier. To avoid such a recurrence of misunderstanding, Hoover summarized the results of their conferences in two lengthy memorandum-like letters. According to Hoover, he and Sterling agreed that the Hoover Institution's independence and "setting within the University" would be "restored to its original form"—in other words, free from faculty interference. Furthermore, the institution would retain a rigidly documentary publications policy, institution personnel would not hold fixed tenure, and Stanford faculty would not be members of the institution's staff. The two men also agreed (Hoover recorded) that he would have the explicit right to approve the appointment of the next director of the institution. The founder added that he felt he deserved this privilege during his lifetime.[161]

The two men also concurred about something else: that Rothwell would probably soon be transferred to a planned new Stanford Center for International Studies.[162] As for the rest of the personnel in the tower, Hoover informed Sterling that he "could not leave my personal archives" to Stanford—archives that contained "large amounts of confidential material from other persons"—unless he was "satisfied as to the Institution's principal staff."[163] It was his clearest warning yet that unless Stanford allayed his concerns, it could lose one of the greatest historical collections of the twentieth century.

To buttress his contention that his institution had always been independent of the faculty, Hoover cited an unwritten agreement between himself and Ray Lyman Wilbur at the time of the institution's founding—an understanding that Professor Emeritus Robert Swain confirmed. [164] According to Hoover, from the first he had stipulated that his library should be free from faculty committees or control—not out of disdain for professors but out of a desire for effective, single-headed administration. Reiterating a long-held conviction, Hoover argued that "no productive institution could be conducted by a committee." [165] With Swain backing him up, and with Sterling acquiescent, the Stanford board of trustees, on November 20, 1958, declared its "consensus" that "the relation of the Hoover Institution to the University should revert to the initial relationship that obtained in the early Twenties." The board left it up to its special committee headed by Black to settle the administrative details. [166]

Rothwell's bid to wrest the Hoover Institution from its founder had failed. The Stanford trustees, some of whom (like Black) were staunch admirers of Hoover, were not about to repudiate their colleague. Within days of his triumph the Chief was actively searching for Rothwell's successor. [167] It was obvious to all concerned that the incumbent director's position was untenable. A few weeks later, in fact, Rothwell let it be known that he had accepted an offer to become president of Mills College. [168] Within the next few months, at least four of the Hoover Institution's senior staff (including North and Mary Wright) left the tower for employment elsewhere. [169]

Hoover was magnanimous in victory. He told Sterling:

> I was genuinely happy when I learned that Easton Rothwell received that appointment as President of Mills. He has great qualities for that job and I expect him to rise to head even greater institutions. I have always regretted that I could not agree on some of his points of view and his concept for the policies of the Library, as otherwise he had great qualities. [170]

Hoover, then, had won. Or had he? All now depended on the selection of the next director of the Hoover Institution and on the reorganization plan to be worked out by the trustees. In the battle thus far the Chief had had three primary weapons: his prestige as the university's preeminent alumnus, his influence over the institution's finances, and his ownership of his immense personal archive. In the months to come he would need them more than ever.

· 9 ·

The Final Struggle

I

The year 1959 did not begin auspiciously for Hoover and his alma mater. Back in the preceding October, Sterling had promised Hoover to maintain Stanford University's annual appropriation of $125,000 to the Hoover Institution—a figure amounting to roughly 30 percent of its current budget.[1] But on January 2, 1959, Sterling telephoned Hoover that because of severe financial constraints (including soaring medical school costs) he was recommending a cut in the subsidy.[2]

Hoover was amazed. To "say I am still chocked [sic], indignant and discouraged," he told Sterling by mail a day later, "is a complete understatement"—and not in small measure because of Sterling's previous assurances. How, Hoover asked, could the institution attract an outstanding new director if its "financial base" were reduced? For a university with an annual income of $8,000,000 to do this was to tell the American people that it placed "a trivial evaluation on the importance of the usefulness of this Institution." Hoover warned Sterling that if this budget cut were made, he would inform the institution's loyal donors in order that "they may feel free to reconsider their assurances to me of future support." "I am too far along in life to continue the worries I have endured in respect to the Institution over the past ten years," Hoover wrote.

> For forty-four years I have dreamed of a great service to the American people, to the world, and to Stanford University. For it, my friends and I have worked and made great sacrifices in money, and more importantly, to

the upbuilding of the historical resources of the Institution. And I recognize that any new determination on my part means a confession of failure to the American people.

Hoover now served notice that he was determined to "conclude the situation which is of obvious embarrassment to the Trustees of the University, to you, and to myself."[3]

The president of the university's board of trustees, David Packard, now stepped forward as a conciliator. Late in January he informed Hoover that the trustees had no intention of reducing the university's $125,000 allocation, although budgetary realities made any immediate increase impossible.[4] Sterling, too, hastened to mollify the Chief, and the squall thus rapidly dissipated.[5] But Hoover was clearly becoming provoked at the now seemingly unending difficulties in communication between himself and the man he, as much as anyone, had made president of Stanford University.

Meanwhile, in the tower, C. Easton Rothwell was still presiding—and urging Sterling to appoint a three-member university committee to administer the Hoover Institution after his departure, pending the appointment of his successor. To Witold Sworakowski, Rothwell's plan was not an innocent move but a deliberate attempt to entrench the university in the Hoover Institution's internal affairs—and to lay the groundwork for one of the committee members to become the next director. Deeply dismayed, Sworakowski feared that history was repeating itself—that, as in 1952, another non-Hooverite would slip artfully into the directorship. Abjuring any ambitions for himself, Sworakowski communicated his anxiety to the Chief.[6]

On March 19, 1959 Rothwell formally submitted his resignation to President Sterling; as of April 1 he was gone.[7] That day Sterling—without consulting or informing Hoover in advance appointed Dean Philip Rhinelander of the School of Humanities and Sciences to serve as the institution's acting director until a new director could be named.[8]

Once again Herbert Hoover was shocked. On April 4 he wrote to Sterling from New York:

> Before you left here on March 13, we had agreed . . . that W. Sworakowski, the Assistant Director of the Hoover Institution, who had been Acting Director whenever Rothwell was absent, would be continued in the position of Acting Director.

Furthermore, Sworakowski would have a "temporary Advisory Committee" consisting (among others) of Rhinelander and the Hoover loyalist Fred Wickett. In addition, this "temporary committee" would "in no way . . .

imply faculty control of the Institution now or later." "I need not mention," Hoover concluded, "the half dozen assurances I have had that no one will be appointed Director of the Institution without my approval." [9]

Sterling, however, was unyielding. "I have never agreed," he responded, "and cannot now agree, to asking Sworakowski to assume the responsibilities of Director of the Hoover Institution on either an acting or a permanent basis." For all his "notable and outstanding talents," Sworakowski was not the man for that position. As for the advisory committee, Sterling stated that he had told Hoover that he had rejected a committee directorate in favor of an acting director with the *possibility* of a consultative committee later. As for Rhinelander, Sterling had unequivocally instructed him that he was acting as the president's "designate," responsible through Sterling to the trustees, and without the interposition of faculty committees. "Thus there is in all this," Sterling informed Hoover, "no 'faculty control,' implied or otherwise, of the Hoover Institution." Finally, as to Hoover's precise role in choosing the next director, this, said Sterling somewhat stiffly, should be "clarified," because it was the trustees, not he, "who have the right to grant or withhold such a privilege." [10]

Once again the trustees' resolution of 1946 had come back to haunt Herbert Hoover. In self-defense Sterling told Hoover that he felt he had been "caught in a trap because of the difference between your conception of the Institution-University relationship, of which I had no written record, and the relationships stipulated in the document of September, 1946, which you had approved and which was the only document I had for guidance. I hope that we can soon resolve these differences and put them behind us once and for all." [11] Hoover, of course, thought that he had already resolved these differences in October.

Until now Hoover's multiplying difficulties with his alma mater had been kept "within the family." Even the transfer of his memorabilia to Iowa had gone unreported—so anxious was he (in the later words of his archivist Thalken) to do nothing that would publicly "cast his beloved Stanford in an unfavorable light." [12] But on April 5, 1959—only a day or two after Hoover learned of Rhinelander's interim appointment—this policy appeared to crack. The nation's press carried a story ostensibly from West Branch that Hoover's "personal papers"—indeed, everything except his World War I "war and peace" documents—would be transferred from Stanford University to a museum to be erected near his birthplace. [13] The announcement created confusion in the tower and was denied the next day by Hoover's principal secretary in New York. [14]

The curious dispatch from Iowa may have been a coincidence. It is rather more likely, however, that it was a deliberate, Hoover-engineered "leak."

Certainly Hoover both desired and welcomed the turmoil that the story created in Palo Alto.[15] It was a way of putting Sterling and the trustees on notice that Stanford was no longer the only suitor for the Chief's affections.

That the West Branch announcement was a tactic and not a fixed decision became clearer in the days just ahead. In mid-April a friend expressed sorrow to Hoover that Stanford was "losing your priceless papers."[16] Hoover quickly replied: "If the Trustees of Stanford do right by me and agree to keep the left-wingers out of the Institution, they will be able to keep the papers."[17]

Meanwhile, led by Packard and Black, the trustees were searching for a solution. At Packard's suggestion Hoover, in early April, prepared a set of memoranda specifying the policies and management that he desired for the beleaguered institution.[18] To his distress he soon discovered that Sterling—his apparent promises of the past October to the contrary—was actively resisting Hoover's wishes.[19] Instead of drafting a comprehensive statement that reflected Hoover's conception of the institution's purpose, for instance, Sterling submitted to the trustees a single, anemic paragraph. The purpose of the institution, it said (borrowing some words from Hoover), was "to support the values of freedom of thought and enterprise and the forces which sustain all liberty" and to contribute "to peace and prosperity on earth." More disturbingly still, Sterling's counterproposals to the trustees conspicuously omitted any declaration of the Hoover Institution's independence and allotted to the founder a merely consultative role in the selection of the institution's director. Hoover immediately objected to the board:

> I cannot accept the idea of a mere *consultation* in a matter which reaches to the whole fundamental of my relation to the Institution.
> The Institution is obviously my creation. The major financial support for forty-four years has come from my friends and myself. The largest part of its collections were acquired directly by myself and staffs which I have headed. It is probably my major contribution to American life. . . .[20]

Weeks of anxiety and negotiation passed, in which trustee Packard particularly acted as a mediator. In early May Hoover still did not know (he told a friend) whether "the left-wingers of the University" would "prevail on the trustees" to "seriously amend or delete my proposed resolution."[21]

The trustees did not let him down. On May 21, 1959, with his approval and the formal recommendation of President Sterling, the trustees adopted a comprehensive resolution on the status of the Hoover Institution. On virtually every front the founder was triumphant. The trustees' resolution of 1946 was rescinded; no longer, in other words, would the institution be designated a "separate division" of the university. Instead, the trustees resolved that the Hoover Institution was "an independent Institution within the frame of Stanford University," and with a line of authority directly through the president to the trustees. "There will be no reference," said the resolution, "to any faculty committees between the president and trustees." The faculty, in other words, would have no role in the institution's governance.

The board also affirmed that while the institution itself would publish "objective collections of documents" that will give "guidance to thought on public policies," institution staff must be free to publish interpretive books elsewhere. But if they did and declared their Hoover affiliation therein, then that publication must carry a disclaimer of responsibility by the Hoover Institution. Qualified scholars from outside the Hoover Institution, of course, were free to publish "anything they wish," provided only that they not imply the institution's endorsement of their facts and opinions.

On the crucial issue of the institution's director, Hoover also achieved his aim. The board resolved that henceforth the director of the Hoover Institution would be recommended to it by the university's president "for appointment by the trustees" only after having been "previously approved by Mr. Hoover." The president's recommendation, the board added, "shall not require the approval of the Advisory Board of the Academic Council of Stanford University." The faculty, in other words, was formally excluded from the selection process. Nor, the resolution continued, would the director or his staff have academic tenure; they would have "administrative tenure" comparable to that of the president of the university.

Furthermore, the trustees now pledged that the university, which "receives many benefits in reputation" from the Hoover Institution, would contribute at least $125,000 per year to its support, and that any gift made to Stanford and designated for the Hoover Institution "shall be used for that designated purpose and no other."

At the trustees' request Hoover prepared a lengthy statement of the institution's purposes, which was included in the first paragraph of the resolution. Insisting once again that the facility he founded was not "and must not be" a "mere library," Hoover declared that it must "constantly and dynamically point the road to peace, to personal freedom, and to the safeguards of the American system." And in a paragraph that before long would become famous, he wrote:

> The purpose of this Institution must be, by its research and publications, to demonstrate the evils of the doctrines of Karl Marx—whether Communism, Socialism, economic materialism, or atheism—thus to protect the American way of life from such ideologies, their conspiracies, and to reaffirm the validity of the American system.[22]

For Hoover it was only a concise restatement of what he had been saying for several years.

The trustees' arrangement of 1959—particularly its explicit exclusion of the Stanford faculty from any role in the Hoover Institution's governance—was an unusual one for a university.[23] But then, Hoover's institution had never been a typical university enterprise, nor had Hoover himself been an ordinary benefactor.[24] Still, his victory had not come easily; to win he had had to summon nearly every ounce of his prestige.[25] Reflecting on the struggle several years later, a pro-Hoover trustee observed that "the Chief was trying to deliver awfully tough ultimatums to a new man" (Sterling) who "wasn't accustomed to taking them." Nevertheless, Hoover, "with crystal clarity on his understanding of the issue, knew what had to be done to face up to it, and he just bowed his neck and pushed ahead and with the help of some stout trustees got it done."[26]

But had the board actually acceded all the way? In one of his drafts of the proposed resolution, Hoover had the board declare that it "affirms some statements of the founder . . . as follows."[27] But the final resolution was worded somewhat differently:

> Paragraph 1. The Trustees feel that there should be in their records a statement of the scope, the importance and the purposes of the Hoover Institution. To this end Mr. Hoover has prepared for them the following statement:[28]

Hoover's declaration of purpose then followed. Obviously it was Hoover's statement. But was it also unequivocally the trustees'?

Hoover apparently did not detect the ambiguity. Savoring his accomplishment, he wrote to a friend in June: "All is quiet in Palo Alto. The Trustees took an interest. All left-wingers are out."[29]

Confident that the long controversy was finally over, Hoover took steps to dispose of his accumulated papers. On July 22, 1959 he offered the entire Hoover Archives (except for "personal" papers and certain other materials "not directly relating to my governmental and organizational activities") to the trustees of Stanford University. He pointed out that this collection contained 3,500,000 items and was "the largest individual collection lodged in a public institution. No sum of money could replace it." He proposed to deposit this vast trove in the Hoover Tower and supply it with its own archivist, provided (among other things) that he and certain successors have the right to approve the appointment of any archivist for twenty years. All this, Hoover concluded, he was doing in "full faith" that the trustees' arrangements of May 21 would be carried out.[30] On September 17 the trustees accepted Hoover's gift and stipulations.[31]

But now, all over again, trouble appeared. Upon reflection, Hoover apparently wanted to have his archivist appointed directly by the trustees. Sterling, however, wanted the selection to be made "on the recommendation of the President of the University." Unwilling to risk misunderstandings with Sterling any longer, Hoover insisted upon preparing a definite contract for ratification by the trustees. Sterling insisted that no such contract was necessary.[32]

By now Hoover had lost nearly all confidence in Wallace Sterling.[33] Meanwhile, on campus, a group of professors, no doubt anxious to thwart Hoover's influence, had created an informal search committee to advise Sterling on the choice of the next director of the institution.[34] Ignoring this backdoor involvement of the faculty in institution affairs, Hoover consulted Raymond Moley, a former New Deal "Brain Truster" who was currently a conservative columnist for *Newsweek*. Upon Moley's recommendation, Hoover selected W. Glenn Campbell to be his candidate.[35] A 35-year-old economist with a doctorate from Harvard, Campbell was the director of research at the American Enterprise Association (now the American Enterprise Institute). He was also an unabashed conservative. On October 15 the board of trustees authorized Sterling to extend the invitation to Campbell (whom he had not met) after the economist visited the campus and as soon as Hoover gave formal notice of his approval.[36] Outmaneuvered again by Hoover, the president grudgingly complied.[37]

Campbell assumed his duties in the tower on January 1, 1960. The new director's position, however, was far from secure. For more than a year the impression on campus was strong—an impression which Sterling himself fostered—that the university president was simply biding his time and would dismiss Campbell after Hoover was dead.[38]

II

Meanwhile the Chief had launched a spirited new drive for contributions to his favorite cause. With the status of the institution at last resolved, he succeeded on an unprecedented scale. In late 1959 the foundation of his friend Alfred P. Sloan, Jr. granted $250,000 for the Hoover Institution's general support.[39] A few weeks later his friend Jeremiah Milbank pledged $125,000 more.[40] A few months later the Lilly Foundation donated $100,000—and so it went.[41] Not so many months before, C. Easton Rothwell had argued that the "major" foundations would not contribute to the institution's endowment and operating expenses, nor to narrowly documentary studies. That might be true of *liberal* foundations; it was not true of conservative ones, which rallied to the institution as never before.

To facilitate his campaign, Hoover on his own initiative printed a fund-raising booklet bearing the title of his institution and a picture of the tower. In this brochure he included the trustees' May 21 resolution, which had not been made public heretofore. But Hoover's booklet did not quite replicate the trustees' text. Instead he first printed his statement of purpose separately and then (with one alteration) the resolution itself. In this restructured format the introductory sentences of paragraph one were omitted. As altered, the paragraph read simply: "Mr. Hoover's statement as given in the preceding pages."[42]

Hoover's booklet made it clear that the statement of purpose was his and that the trustees had invited him to prepare it. But some who read the pamphlet soon discerned—or professed to discern—a deception. To them it seemed that Hoover, by not printing the actual first words of paragraph one, had contrived to make it appear that the trustees had endorsed his views.

Early in 1960 copies of Hoover's booklet began to circulate on the Stanford campus—to the mounting concern of certain members of the faculty. Here, for all to see, were the hitherto unpublicized terms of the May 1959 resolution—including, above all, Hoover's assertion that his institution's purpose was "to demonstrate the evils of the doctrines of Karl Marx." Claiming that this view of research violated the canons of objective scholarship, various professors sought clarification from the trustees. On February 16 the advisory board of the faculty's Academic Council asked the trustees for a "positive statement . . . reaffirming Stanford's dedication to freedom."[43]

A month later the board replied. After drawing attention to the actual wording of paragraph one of the May 1959 resolution, it declared:

> The Trustees believe it is entirely proper and desirable to have in the official record of the University and as a preface to and separate from the resolutions on operating policies a statement concerning the desires and aspirations of the man who founded the great Institution which bears his name and who, by untiring work during his lifetime, has personally been so largely responsible for the great collections which have been made there available for the scholars of the world.
>
> The Trustees did not contemplate that Mr. Hoover's statement would be interpreted as university policy or as an abridgement of free inquiry. They stand for the principle, that academic freedom in the highest university tradition is expected to prevail throughout Stanford.[44]

Stripped of its polite and deferential verbiage, the trustees' message was plain: Hoover's controversial statement was a nonbinding one, a mere "preface" expressing one man's "desires and aspirations." This was not at all what Hoover thought that he had written.[45]

Without explicitly repudiating Hoover, then, the trustees had distanced themselves from his statement and had attempted to soothe the Stanford faculty. Unfortunately for the board, its placatory action had come too late. On March 29 the *Stanford Daily* printed a copy of Hoover's brochure and launched an assault on the institution's founder. "The Hoover Institution," it editorialized, "has no right to predetermine the goals of scholarship. It can have no other 'purpose' or 'goal' than to facilitate the qualified scholar in his search for the documents necessary to formulate his own opinion."[46] Hoover's statement, the *Daily* declaimed the next day, was "a flagrant violation of academic freedom" and "detrimental to Stanford's reputation in the academic world."[47]

The *Daily*'s attacks precipitated an avalanche. Hoisting high the banner of freedom of inquiry, a wave of professors filled the newspaper's columns with denunciations of Hoover's position, and even of Hoover himself. One professor charged that the statement "carries a connotation of thought control." Another, alluding to Stanford's motto, asserted that the "Winds of Freedom don't blow" in the Hoover Institution. Still another opined that "it is time we stopped coddling Mr. Hoover" and suggested that Stanford's "honor" had been compromised.[48] The storm on campus caught the attention of the media.[49] The *New Republic* castigated Hoover for his "indifference to a cardinal purpose of a free university, which is free inquiry rather than right-wing or left-wing missionary endeavor."[50]

In all this outpouring of indignation no one appeared to notice the parts of the 1959 resolution that affirmed the freedom of inquiry of all researchers, both inside and outside the institution, who availed themselves of its scholarly resources. Nor did anyone remark that protests at "predetermined" scholarship had not been heard in the Fisher/Rothwell era, when the ideological tilt in the tower had been compatible with that of the faculty. For their part, Hoover's supporters wondered what could possibly be so objectionable about a scholarly enterprise that documented the manifest evils of Marxism and thus sustained the American way of life.[51] As a later member of the institution's advisory board remarked, "[I]f it weren't for the American way of life, these professors wouldn't have any academic freedom—they wouldn't have any freedom at all. . . ."[52] For the Chief and his friends, the furor on campus about "free inquiry" was a smokescreen for the recapture of the Hoover Institution by the forces of the faculty Left.

Like the embarrassed board of trustees, J. E. Wallace Sterling was now very much on the spot. The president had apparently counted on keeping the terms of the 1959 resolution (and his own acquiescence in it) confidential.[53] Instead, to his chagrin and anger, Hoover had released the resolution on his own—and in a booklet that bore the appearance of a university publication. Sterling now informed the faculty that this brochure had been published without his knowledge and (so far as he could learn) without the knowledge or approval of the trustees.[54] Privately Sterling chastised Hoover for not consulting him about the pamphlet, for creating "an accomplished fact," and—most reprehensibly of all—for "falsifying" the first article of the 1959 resolution.[55]

On the afternoon of April 1, 1960, Sterling convened a rebellious meeting of Stanford's faculty council. Reviewing the history of the tangled affair, the president reiterated his commitment to free scholarship and dissociated himself from Hoover's statement of purpose. It was "not a formal part" of the 1959 resolution, he asserted, and the founder's fund-raising pamphlet has misstated the trustees' intent.[56] To the shock of two Hoover Institution staffers present, Sterling confessed that in his many exhausting discussions with Hoover he had yielded when perhaps he should not have but had thought that he would only have to wait "a few more years."[57] It was not enough. By a vote of 78 to 73, the faculty council asked its advisory board to form a committee to draft a *new* statement on the Hoover Institution's purposes—one that could be submitted to the trustees and presumably supplant Hoover's own.[58]

At the Waldorf Astoria Towers Hoover's initial reaction to the distant turmoil was cheerfully defiant. Some months earlier he had agreed to become a trustee of the strongly conservative Americans for Constitutional Action, headed by his friend Ben Moreell. But Hoover had forbidden any announcement of this, lest various liberal foundations use it as a reason to reject his grant proposals for the Hoover Institution. On April 2, however, the Chief authorized Moreell to proceed:

> 1. Now that all the liberal foundations have turned me down on my raising funds for the Institution at Stanford;
> 2. Now that the faculty of my own university have proclaimed me a "reactionary" for opposing "the infection of Karl Marx";
> 3. Now that I have raised, within the last seven months, about $1,250,000 for my Institution from righteous foundations;
> 4. You can add my name to your collection of reactionaries![59]

As further reports came in from Palo Alto, Hoover's mood quickly turned to anger—and anger particularly at Sterling. In a letter on April 18 Hoover bluntly reminded Sterling that the university president, as well as trustees Packard and Black, had all read and approved "that wicked statement of mine" before its submission to the full board of trustees in 1959:

> Not one of you three suggested any change in the paragraph relating to Karl Marx.
> You presented it to the Trustees in this final form.
> I hope these facts may be made clear to your dissenting faculty members and to the Trustees as a whole.[60]

Hoover was even more furious at Sterling's claims about the fund-raising pamphlet. Privately he told a friend that Sterling *had* seen the brochure in Hoover's own office, had read it, had not objected to its distribution, and knew "that I didn't falsify anything."[61] More publicly, in a letter to the trustees, Hoover took issue with a faculty committee's claim (derived from Sterling) that the brochure "purporting to express" the institution's purpose had been "unofficial":

> This "brochure" was printed on September 7, 1959 . . . .
> On September 9, 1959 I wrote President Sterling that I was undertaking a personal appeal for financial aid for the Hoover Institution. On September 10, I wrote to Chairman Black about my drive, enclosing several copies of the brochure. On September 14, I showed [Trustees'] President Packard a sample of the letter I was writing to foundations, and gave him several copies of the brochure. And, also on September 14, I wrote to President Sterling that I had given my solicitation materials to President Packard and that he would show them to President Sterling.[62]

The implication was plain that the relevant university officials could have stopped him if they had wanted to—and that they had evidently not wanted to until the faculty complained.

Meanwhile the faculty genie was out of the bottle and causing Hoover ever more vexation. On May 6 a university committee chaired by Professor Gordon Wright of the history department submitted to the faculty's advisory board the statement on the "scope, importance, and purposes of the Hoover Institution" that the Academic Council had called for on April 1. Asserting that Hoover's pamphlet had "damaged" the university and the institution, the committee asked the trustees to make *its* statement the "official" one on the subject and to distribute it in a brochure to counteract Hoover's. Not content with these requests, Wright and his colleagues went on to advocate "closer integration" of the institution with the rest of the university, as well as changes in this "structural relationship" at what it called "some appropriate future time."[63] Since Hoover was now nearly 87, one could plausibly infer what the committee meant.

On May 19 Sterling delivered the Wright committee's letter to the university's board of trustees. Instead of acting on the document, the board simply referred the matter back to the president and instructed *him* to draft a statement of the Hoover Institution's purposes for the board's consideration at its next meeting.[64] Now, more than ever, Sterling was in the crossfire.

By now the Wright committee's report had reached New York, where its effect was instant and predictable. On June 2 Hoover issued an eight-page letter to his fellow trustees reviewing the unending strife enveloping the institution. Pointing out that he had made no "public statements" about these incidents (unlike his critics, who had enlisted the *New Republic*), he wrote:

> After forty years' advocacy of academic freedom and freedom of research in public addresses, two of which were made on the Campus, and after having received eighty-five honorary degrees from universities equally zealous of academic freedom as Stanford, I was astonished at statements being made that I was restricting academic freedom, etc.
>
> All of which was based on a tortuous and distorted argument over a short paragraph in my statement on "the purposes of the Institution."

As for the institution's much disputed aims and goals:

> It might easily be assumed that I know the purposes of the Institution, since I founded it. But a group of the faculty has demanded that the Trustees expunge my statement on the purposes of the Institution and substitute a statement on the purposes to be prepared by them.
>
> I do not believe that the Trustees will countenance such an insult.[65]

A few days later the Chief was still incensed. "These repeated statements by the Faculty of the purposes of the Hoover Institute" (he told Ralph Lutz) were "designed to replace my statement to the Trustees." And then he added: "Their real feeling is objection to the American way of life."[66]

On June 16 Sterling submitted to the trustees what the board's minutes carefully identified not as a definition of the Hoover Institution's "aims and purposes" (although Sterling himself so labeled it) but merely as a report on "the principles in accord with which he would administer the Trustee resolutions" of 1959 and early 1960.[67] According to the minutes, Sterling's report was "filed in the President's Office."[68] It was *not* printed, however, in the board's record of its meeting. Treading warily, the board was evidently anxious to avert a confrontation with either the faculty or Hoover.

Sterling informed the faculty that the board had approved his four-paragraph statement. Why, then, had the trustees not repudiated Hoover directly? Because, answered Sterling, they felt that the principle of free inquiry was already secure and because they wished to avoid "personal hurt" to Hoover. The president strongly intimated that *his* formulation (not Hoover's) would be the governing statement on the "purposes of the Institution" during his presidency. As far as he was concerned, Sterling told the Academic Council in early 1961, the matter could now be considered closed.[69]

It was not closed, however, for Hoover. Sterling's draft of the institution's "aims and purposes" (Hoover told trustee Packard) was yet another attempt to "break down" the resolution of 1959, on the basis of which he had given his private archive to Stanford.[70] To the Chief and some of his supporters, Sterling was a "chameleon" (as Sworakowski privately called him) who propitiated Hoover in his presence but appeased and colluded with the left-wing faculty behind Hoover's back.[71]

By the winter of 1960–1961 Hoover was nearly at wit's end about the course of events on campus. The university's provost, Frederick Terman, did not help matters when he asked Hoover in November to delete a paragraph from a fund-raising statement prepared by Glenn Campbell. The offending paragraph—one that Hoover himself had written for a similar appeal in 1957—affirmed that the Hoover Institution's purpose was "by research and publications, to protect the American way of life from evil ideologies and to reaffirm the validity of the American system." As a personal courtesy to Terman, Hoover agreed to circulate no more copies of Campbell's document. But the Chief was "astonished" that Stanford University by this action was being "put in a position of suppression of freedom of speech" and of "an expression of fidelity to our American heritage." He warned that if Terman's request ever became public, it "would not benefit the University" in the ambitious national fund drive that it was about to launch.[72]

The recurrent slings and arrows from his alma mater now reaped an unexpected harvest. Early in 1961 Hoover told a friend:

> The left-wing faculty in Stanford University is constantly conspiring to get control of the Hoover Institution. In their communist-pattern operations, they have submitted me to great indignities and anxieties, and I have little confidence of its independence in the future, insofar as my Archives are concerned.[73]

To David Packard he expressed regret that he had ever donated his personal archives to Stanford, since "their retainment was my sole hold upon the future conduct of the Institution."[74]

Even as he uttered these words of reproach and despair, Hoover was contemplating a solution. At his birthplace in Iowa the library-museum that he had authorized was slowly developing, and the federal government was eager to convert it into a full-fledged presidential archival depository, administered by the National Archives.[75] It was a measure of his unhappiness with the Stanford University faculty (and Sterling's perceived capitulation to it) that on December 15, 1960 Hoover took a critical step. He formally offered to the United States government his presidential, prepresidential, and postpresidential papers, several million items in number—in fact, everything but his "war and peace" documents and records of his various relief organizations, which he said he had already donated to his "War and Peace Library" at Stanford. Hoover promised to transfer his gift "as soon as practicable" after the government took possession of the Iowa property.[76] On December 30 the government enthusiastically accepted Hoover's offer.[77]

Now, however, a peculiar difficulty arose. In 1959 Hoover had *already* given his personal archive to Stanford University.[78] Yet now, in late 1960, he offered a portion of this archive to the United States government—unbeknownst to the Stanford trustees. It might in fact be argued that he had just proposed to transfer property that he no longer actually owned.[79]

Despite his letter to the government, Hoover's final disposition of his papers was far from settled. Trusting Campbell (to whom he had promised a presidential library at the Hoover Institution in 1959)[80] yet pessimistic about the institution's chances for survival against its enemies,[81] Hoover groped for a formula that would protect his still-confidential papers and at the same time fortify the institution's independence. One option was to create a presidential library with two branches—one in Iowa, one in the Hoover Institution—with Campbell as the director of the whole.[82] Another possibility was to create a separate presidential archival depository in the tower, thus keeping at Stanford everything that had not already been shipped to West Branch.[83] Still another idea was to deed his archival material to his Iowa library but actually retain the material in the tower—as leverage over the institution's fate.[84] In this way, if the Stanford faculty or administration misbehaved, Hoover could remove his personal archive from their grasp.

To do any of this, however, it was necessary for him to regain unequivocal title to the Hoover Archives from the trustees of Stanford University. On March 24, 1961 he made this request to Sterling and Packard, explaining to them that under the law he could donate his papers to the library in Iowa yet retain them in the tower at the expense of the National Archives.[85] A few weeks later, and undoubtedly with reluctance, the trustees agreed to return the property—with the understanding (they added) that Hoover intended to donate it to the government on terms that would provide for its physical retention in the Hoover Institution.[86]

For Hoover, negotiating with the General Services Administration in Washington, the trustees' conditional action was not sufficient. He needed, he said, a retrocession without strings.[87] After various negotiations between his attorney and the university's, the trustees on May 18 unconditionally confirmed Hoover's title to his archives—which, they added with perhaps a hint of asperity, "he turned over to the Board of Trustees on July 22, 1959." Distressed at the thought that the university might lose such a magnificent historical treasure, the board expressed its "hope and expectation" that Hoover would find a way to retain his archives at Stanford.[88] President Sterling joined in the board's expression of anxiety.[89]

All this stood in ironic counterpoint to the public image of the Hoover/Stanford relationship that the university was projecting that spring. At its invitation Hoover consented to serve as honorary chairman of the most elaborate fund-raising effort in Stanford's history: a $100,000,000 campaign known as PACE.[90] When the drive was publicly announced on April 18, Hoover issued a telegram endorsing it.[91] A few months later, at the age of nearly 87, he journeyed to San Francisco to cohost a fund-raising dinner at the Mark Hopkins Hotel with David Packard and another trustee, Thomas Pike.[92] "Hoover's Passion To Help Stanford Is Undiminished," a newspaper headline reported the next day.[93] Few were aware of the stresses to which that "passion" had been put.

At this juncture the university was fortunate that Hoover's attachment to his alma mater still survived. A few months earlier, the *Saturday Evening Post* had published a laudatory article about President Sterling, an article implying that Sterling's recent statement of the Hoover Institution's purposes now superseded that of the founder. A member of the institution's advisory board, John K. Stewart, had promptly mailed a vigorous rebuttal to the magazine. But at the urging of David Packard, Hoover prevailed on a reluctant Stewart to withdraw his letter, lest the ensuing publicity harm the impending PACE campaign.[94]

At the time of the Mark Hopkins Hotel banquet a similar episode occurred. A friend urged Hoover to ask publicly why Stanford had not taken "dynamic intellectual leadership" in the struggle between freedom and communist slavery. Where, he wondered, did Stanford stand? Hoover replied: "While I sympathize with your question, a proper answer representing my kindred feeling would rile up the Stanford community."[95] Instead, he delivered a speech reminding his listeners (among other things): "It is free social enterprise that has built our privately supported institutions, and it is free economic enterprise which makes possible their support."[96]

Thus twice within six months Hoover had suppressed his inner feelings in the interest of his university's betterment. For all his disaffection from its increasingly left-of-center faculty, the "Stanford tie" (as a friend called it) prevented a total rupture with his alma mater.[97] The lingering Stanford tie . . . . If someone said to him (Stewart later recalled) that a certain action "might hurt Stanford," he would reply, "Well, then, we shouldn't do it."[98] The university was a kind of "foster father and mother" for him, another friend observed.[99] Even in disillusionment he could not break that bond of filial devotion.

Hoover's willingness to raise money for the university did not mean, however, that he would cede to it his personal archive. In the end, despite the aversion to federal financing and control that he had expressed just a few years before, he opted to divide his papers along the lines of his letter to the government of December 15, 1960. His presidential, prepresidential, and postpresidential materials went to Iowa. The rest—including the collections of various friends as well as the records of his numerous relief efforts—remained in Palo Alto. The division was completed in 1962.[100] Later that year, on his 88th birthday, he formally dedicated his presidential library in West Branch. Had it not been for the searing events of 1958–1960, this denouement would not have occurred.

The drama was not quite done. Hoover was now willing to revest in Stanford University the title to the remainder of his personal archives, currently in the custody of the Hoover Institution, but only if certain stipulations were met. Anxious to preserve the institution's hard-won independence from the unrelenting assaults of its foes, Hoover now used his control of his papers to secure its safety in perpetuity. On May 1, 1962 the ever-vigilant Chief offered his remaining archives to the Stanford trustees—*if* they amended their 1959 resolution to provide that after the founder's death any director of the Hoover Institution recommended by the university president must first receive the approval of the Hoover Foundation, a New York corporation comprising various Hoover family members and friends.[101] Well aware of his mortality, Hoover was not about to let the university authorities stage a coup in the tower after his demise. On May 17, 1962 the trustees accepted his offer and his terms.[102]

For Hoover the "Tower crisis" was finally over. To the frustration of his vociferous critics on campus, he had lived long enough to prevail.

III

In the final two years or so of his life, according to one who knew him well, Hoover's attitude toward his alma mater mellowed.[103] Whenever he could, he performed good deeds in its service—taping a message, for instance, for a PACE dinner in California in 1962.[104] As so often in the past, his behind-the-scenes exertions in behalf of the university bore fruit for which he never received publicity. In the early 1960s he persuaded Alfred P. Sloan, Jr. to donate $1,000,000 toward a new building for the Business School.[105] In 1964 a man named William M. Keck gave $5,600,000 in Superior Oil Company stock to Stanford—at the time the largest unrestricted bequest that it had ever received. Few knew that Keck did so in response to Hoover's urging.[106]

The university reciprocated with gestures of affection for its most illustrious son. In early 1961 he had resigned from the board of trustees after more than 48 years of continuous service. The board had thereupon elected him trustee emeritus.[107] In 1962, on the occasion of his 50th year of affiliation with the board, his colleagues resolved to strike a gold medal in his honor.[108] In 1963 the Stanford Alumni Association awarded it—the first Herbert

Hoover Medal for Distinguished Service—to (it could be none other) the Chief.[109]

Several times in his sunset years Hoover told David Packard that the founding of the Hoover Institution was probably the most important thing that he had done in his life.[110] As his health began to fail, the founder took particular comfort from the revival of the institution under Director Campbell.[111] In 1959–1960 it had had a budget of less than $400,000 with a projected deficit of 20 percent.[112] By 1964 its annual expenditure had doubled; nearly all of this increase had come from nonuniversity sources.[113]

For Hoover these last months brought news of promise that helped to mitigate past hurts. On April 28, 1964 David Packard notified him that the trustees were prepared to allot $500,000 to the institution from the nonrestricted PACE funds.[114] Three days later the university announced that the Scaife family of Pittsburgh had made a $750,000 matching grant to the Hoover Institution in honor of Hoover's 90th birthday and 50 years of public service. The grant was designated for an additional institution building; when completed in 1967, it was named in honor of his wife Lou Henry.[115]

On October 20, 1964, Hoover died in New York, more than 73 years after he had entered Stanford University. In all that period hardly a week had passed in which it had been absent from his thoughts.

· 10 ·

"And Their Deeds Are Remembered After Them"

A few months before Hoover's death the Stanford University News Service issued a press release in which it recounted some of his principal benefactions for his alma mater. "No other American President," it noted, "has been more deeply involved or contributed more to the development of a single academic institution for so long a time as Hoover has done for Stanford."[1] Indeed, no other person except the Stanfords themselves had done so much for the university as he.[2]

In retrospect it is not difficult to adduce reasons why his impact was so pervasive and enduring. Hoover and his university grew up together. His was a young institution, with few traditions, little bureaucracy, and, for many years, no large, organized body of alumni. As the first graduate to achieve distinction in the outside world—distinction culminating in his occupancy of the White House—Hoover repeatedly brought prestige to his alma mater and validated its aspiring self-image until (as one observer shrewdly remarked) he became a Stanford tradition himself.[3] The fact that his most intimate friend was the university's president for a quarter of a century enormously enhanced Hoover's influence, as did his unexcelled generosity and access to institutional donors upon which Stanford (like other educational institutions) increasingly depended. Contrary to its reputation, Stanford was not a wealthy university during most of Herbert Hoover's lifetime. All these circumstances combined to make possible a remarkable chapter in the modern history of American higher education.

Yet circumstances alone do not explain everything. The most honored alumnus ever to graduate from Stanford University did not, after all, have to do what he did. All his contributions to its welfare—his nearly half-century of service as a trustee, his gifts great and small, his role in selecting four university presidents, his reform campaign of 1912–1914, his fight to save the medical school, the untold millions of dollars in endowment that Stanford derived from his efforts and his name, the Stanford Union, the Lou Henry Hoover House, the Food Research Institute, the Graduate School of Business, above all the Hoover Institution that he came to regard as the greatest achievement of his life—all this would never have occurred had it not been for a will to achieve and an ethic of practical idealism that had driven him since the days of his youth. Here, indelibly, his alma mater left its mark. "Get into the game." "Remember that life is, above all, practical." "Get into the game." Men and women "are judged by achievements, not by dreams." "In helpfulness alone can wealth or power find consecration." "Stanford is the best place in the world."

It was perhaps inevitable that as Stanford University grew—in the size of its faculty, the number of its students and alumni, the diversity of its scholarly disciplines, and the magnitude of its endowment—Hoover's role in its development subtly evolved. No longer could any one individual dominate the multiplying paths of institutional maturation. Increasingly, in these later years, he concentrated his formidable energies on the great library and research center that carried his name. This trend was exacerbated by the ideological battles that beset the Hoover Institution during the final decade-and-a-half of his life, when, like two tectonic plates, he and the university drifted apart until they met at the other end of the earth, as it were, generating friction, fault lines, and tremors of ascending magnitude. Yet even then his influence and symbolic significance were not negligible, particularly among those who gave—and sought—contributions for the university in his honor.

In an autobiographical fragment written sometime after World War I, Hoover declared: "There is little importance to men's lives except the accomplishments they leave to posterity." It is "in the origination or administration of tangible institutions or constructive works," he wrote, that men's contributions can best be measured. "When all is said and done," he asserted, "accomplishment is all that counts."[4]

Almost since boyhood this philosophy had guided him; a pioneering educational institution on a California senator's ranch had implanted it still deeper in his soul. Stanford University gave much to Herbert Hoover. For the rest of his life he reciprocated. He was the Stanford spirit personified, the epitome of Leland Stanford's ideal of "direct usefulness in life." The result was one of the most extraordinary careers in the history of the American republic.

Bibliographical Note

For the preparation of this volume I have drawn principally upon the rich resources of three repositories. At the Hoover Institution on War, Revolution and Peace, the Herbert Hoover Collection and the Hoover Institution Records, including the personal papers of Hoover relating to the Hoover Institution, proved invaluable. At the Herbert Hoover Presidential Library in West Branch, Iowa, the Herbert Hoover Papers for each phase of his long career (pre-1921, 1921–1928, 1929–1933, and 1933–1964) were equally rewarding. At the Stanford University Archives I examined with profit the voluminous files (and in some cases the personal papers) of the first five university presidents, all of whom Hoover knew well: David Starr Jordan, John C. Branner, Ray Lyman Wilbur, Donald B. Tresidder, and J. E. Wallace Sterling. I also made substantial use of the Stanford University Board of Trustees Minutes for 1912 to 1964, the Board of Trustees Supporting Documents for the same period, and the collections of certain key faculty and alumni, notably E. D. Adams, Birge M. Clark, Paul C. Edwards, and Frederick E. Terman. Also very helpful were various Stanford University alumni publications since the 1890s, the compendious annual reports of the presidents of Stanford University (1914–1948), and the undergraduate *Stanford Daily* since its inception in 1892.

For other items of value, please see the notes that follow.

Notes

CHAPTER 1

1. For a detailed account of Hoover's life before he entered Stanford University, see George H. Nash, *The Life of Herbert Hoover: The Engineer, 1874–1914* (New York, 1983), chaps. 1 and 2.

CHAPTER 2

1. On Leland Stanford and the origins of his university, see Orrin Leslie Elliott, *Stanford University: The First Twenty-five Years* (Stanford, Calif., 1937), pp. 3–99, and David Starr Jordan, *The Days of a Man*, vol. 1 (Yonkers-on-Hudson, N.Y., 1922), pp. 365–93, 480–93.

2. Eleanor Pearson Bartlett, "Beginnings in Palo Alto," in *The First Year at Stanford* (Stanford University English Club, Stanford, Calif., 1905), pp. 17–28; Elliott, *Stanford University*, pp. 81–83, 179; Lucy Fletcher Brown, "Annex Pioneers," *Radcliffe Quarterly* (November 1940): 14–16.

3. Bartlett, *The First Year at Stanford*, p. 19.

4. Ibid.; Herbert Hoover, *The Memoirs of Herbert Hoover*, vol. 1: *Years of Adventure* (New York, 1951), p. 16; Rose Wilder Lane, *The Making of Herbert Hoover* (New York, 1920), p. 104; David Starr Jordan, "Random Recollections of Herbert Hoover," *Stanford Illustrated Review* 29 (April 1928): 336.

5. Jordan, "Random Recollections," p. 336; interview with Lucy Fletcher Brown in *San Francisco Chronicle*, December 3, 1928; Brown, "Annex Pioneers," pp.

15–16. According to Brown, David Starr Jordan recommended Hoover for the job of caring for their horses.

6. Herbert Hoover's academic transcript, copy in Herbert Hoover Collection, Box 5, Hoover Institution (hereinafter HI); Hoover, *Years of Adventure*, p. 16.

7. Ibid.; Lane, *Making of Herbert Hoover*, p. 105.

8. Hoover, *Years of Adventure*, p. 16; Jordan, *Days of a Man*, 1:409. Here Jordan states that he assigned Hoover to Room 38 in Encina Hall. But in the "Random Recollections," Jordan says that Hoover's first room was 18. It is possible that the latter was a misprint.

9. Jordan recalled that Hoover was the first Stanford student to whom he assigned a room in Encina. Jordan, "Random Recollections," p. 336; Jordan to E. J. Wickson, January 17, 1920, David Starr Jordan Papers, Series I-A, Box 98, Stanford University Archives.

10. Jordan, *Days of a Man*, 1:402; Ellen Elliott in *The First Year at Stanford*, p. 43.

11. Jordan, *Days of a Man*, 1:485.

12. Quoted in Elliott, *Stanford University*, pp. 88–89.

13. Ibid., p. 88.

14. The text of Jordan's speech is in his *Days of a Man*, 1:688–90.

15. Hoover, *Years of Adventure*, p. 16.

16. Elliott, *Stanford University*, pp. 93–94.

17. Ibid., pp. 175–77; Charles K. Field in *The First Year at Stanford*, pp. 72–73.

18. Elliott, *Stanford University*, p. 179, and, in general, pp. 174–248.

19. Hoover academic transcript.

20. Ibid.; Hoover, *Years of Adventure*, p. 17. Branner was delayed by commitments as state geologist of Arkansas.

21. *The First Year at Stanford*, p. 72; Ray Lyman Wilbur, *The Memoirs of Ray Lyman Wilbur* (Stanford, Calif., 1960), p. 40.

22. Hoover, *Years of Adventure*, p. 17; Lane, *Making of Herbert Hoover*, p. 107. At the beginning of his freshman year Hoover also evidently served on a crew of twelve student janitors for buildings in the Quad. This was the recollection in 1928 of his classmate Archie Rice. See Rice's compilation, "Fifty-six Anecdotes and Reminiscences of Herbert Hoover" (typescript, 1928), pp. 6–7, in file 8450/895H, Stanford University Archives. See also Carol Green Wilson, *Herbert Hoover: A Challenge for Today* (New York, 1968), pp. 13–14. According to Wilson, Hoover soon gave up his Quad assignment to become a student janitor in Encina. Hoover could not have worked there for long, however, because in December 1891 the university replaced the student help with Japanese, a move that aroused protest in Encina (*The First Year at Stanford*, p. 85).

23. Brown interview, *San Francisco Chronicle*, December 3, 1928; Brown, "Annex Pioneers," pp. 15–16. According to Brown, Hoover resigned this job later in

the year because he had found sufficient employment on campus and wished to save time. He lined up a substitute worker.

24. Hoover, *Years of Adventure*, p. 17; Lane, *Making of Herbert Hoover*, pp. 121–22; John F. Newsom, unpublished article on Hoover (1928), John F. Newsom Papers, Herbert Hoover Presidential Library (hereinafter HHPL). Newsom, who was a graduate student and assistant to Dr. Branner at Stanford at the time, vividly recalled Hoover laboring over the bicycle until it was as good as new. In 1955 Hoover told a newspaperman: "My career as a newspaper carrier was as a student at Stanford University. I performed on a sale contract from another student and we shared the benefits which were not great, but very useful at that time." Hoover to M. E. Fisher, May 5, 1955, "Newspapers and Press Services," Post-Presidential Subject File, Herbert Hoover Papers, HHPL.

25. Hoover, *Years of Adventure*, p. 17; John C. Branner, comments at a banquet in honor of Herbert Hoover on December 28, 1919. Branner's speech is printed in the *Stanford Illustrated Review* 21 (January 1920): 188–89.

26. Vernon Kellogg, *Herbert Hoover: The Man and His Work* (New York, 1920), p. 50; Lane, *Making of Herbert Hoover*, p. 121. John F. Newsom, in his sketch noted in note 24, remembered that eye trouble compelled Hoover to wear glasses. A number of photographs of Hoover as a college student show him with glasses.

27. Jordan, "Random Recollections," p. 336.

28. Interview of Mrs. John C. Branner in the *New York Times*, July 22, 1928, sec. 7, p. 11.

29. Quoted in Will Irwin, *Herbert Hoover: A Reminiscent Biography* (New York, 1928), pp. 48–49.

30. *Sequoia* 1 (May 25, 1892): 354. This was an undergraduate publication at Stanford University.

31. Irwin, *Herbert Hoover*, p. 47; Hoover, *Years of Adventure*, p. 21. The two earliest popular biographies of Hoover (those by Kellogg and Lane) do not mention that he played on any team.

32. For a superb contemporary account of the first Stanford-Berkeley "Big Game," see *San Francisco Chronicle*, March 20, 1892, p. 24.

33. One of the most persistent stories about Herbert Hoover's Stanford days is that he had charge of the arrangements for the first "Big Game" and that he was therefore responsible for failing to bring the football. There is no known contemporary document, however, indicating that Hoover had any special role in the first "Big Game." Extensive research in the Stanford University Archives has failed to turn up such a document, nor have the university archives and contemporary student publications at Berkeley yielded any confirmatory evidence. In *The First Year at Stanford*, Frank Angell contributed a chapter on "The Early History of Athletics at Stanford." In this essay, published only thirteen years after the event, Angell does not mention Herbert Hoover in connection with the March 1892 Stanford-California contest. Nor do such standard histories as J. F. Sheehan and Louis Honig, *The Games of California and Stanford* (San Francisco, 1900) and S. Dan Brodie, *66 Years on the California Gridiron* (Oakland, 1949).

Among the important early biographies of Hoover, Vernon Kellogg's does not refer to the game at all, while Rose Wilder Lane and Will Irwin merely state that Hoover attended; they do not attribute to him any particular responsibility. Lane adds that after the game Hoover attended an entertainment at the Bush Street Theater. All this is noteworthy, since Lane's book was done in close collaboration with Hoover's friend and classmate, Charles K. Field, and Lane herself interviewed several of Hoover's friends and relatives. Moreover, there is some evidence that Hoover himself reviewed and approved Lane's book and at least part of Irwin's book before they were published.

Another potentially valuable source is also silent. In 1928 (as mentioned in note 22) Hoover's classmate Archie Rice collected a large number of Hoover anecdotes from Stanford alumni who knew Hoover as an undergraduate. Interestingly, none of these anecdotes links Hoover with the first "Big Game" and the famous forgotten football.

It was not until the 1940s—more than 50 years after the event—that Hoover was publicly associated with the March 1892 "Big Game." In 1947 President Ray Lyman Wilbur of Stanford University reported that Herbert Hoover had been involved in that first legendary contest. In an interview with Wilbur, Hoover recalled in detail how he and some associates rented the football grounds, printed 5,000 tickets, and then took emergency measures to collect cash admission when unexpected crowds appeared and the tickets ran out. After the game Hoover and his colleagues counted the receipts in the California Hotel. Wilbur's memorandum of this conversation with Hoover is in the Ray Lyman Wilbur Papers, Box 120, HI. It was published in the *Stanford Alumni Review* 48 (April 1947): 17.

Five years later, in the first volume of his *Memoirs* (*Years of Adventure*, pp. 21–22), Hoover described a "Big Game" that he arranged. The details are essentially the same as those given to Wilbur, except that Hoover did not explicitly state that he was describing the first "Big Game." Indeed, he dated it as occurring on "the University's second Thanksgiving Day," which would have been November 1892 (the second "Big Game"), not March 19 (the first). But then he recounted the story about the forgotten football ("We had overlooked that detail")—seemingly a clear reference to the first "Big Game."

In November 1894 Hoover, by then the student body treasurer, certainly did arrange the *fourth* "Big Game" (see below). In fact, some of the details he gave to Wilbur in 1947 and included in his *Memoirs* seem to fit the 1894 contest, not the one in early 1892. Hoover told Wilbur, for instance, that he made arrangements for the game with a University of California student named Bert Lang. The records show that Lang was the California team's manager for the 1894 "Big Game" but had no known role in the 1892 event.

One wonders, therefore, whether we are not witness here to some confusion of memory. In early 1947 Hoover was nearly 73 years old. It seems very unlikely that as a shy young freshman in the spring of 1892 Hoover somehow became partly responsible for the first intercollegiate football contest on the Pacific coast—and left no record of it on paper or in anyone's memory. It seems far more likely that in his *Memoirs* and interview with Wilbur he actually was describing his experiences in handling the *fourth* "Big Game." In the absence of conclusive contemporary evidence, one must doubt that Hoover had any connection with the *first* "Big Game," held on March 19, 1892.

34. Hoover, *Years of Adventure*, pp. 17−18; Hoover, public statement, May 17, 1921, Public Statements File, HHPL; John F. Newsom article (1928), cited in note 24. In the 1921 statement Hoover stated that his monthly salary was $40; in his *Memoirs* he recalled that it was $60. A voucher for Hoover as Branner's assistant in Arkansas Geological Survey work in February 1893 (several months later) shows that Hoover's monthly salary at that time was $40. This voucher is in "U.S. Geological Survey, 1893−1916," Pre-Commerce Papers, HHPL.

35. Hoover, *Years of Adventure*, p. 17; Hoover, May 17, 1921 statement; Newsom article (1928).

36. Newsom article (1928); Newsom to Branner, July 27, 1892, John C. Branner Papers, Box 30, Stanford University Archives.

37. Hoover academic transcript. The change was authorized on September 13, 1892.

38. Ibid. Late in November 1892 Hoover, another student, and Professor J. P. Smith took a trip to the coastal area around Coloma, California, in a search for fossils (*Daily Palo Alto*, December 5, 1892). Hoover's academic transcript for the fall semester of his sophomore year appears to indicate that he was temporarily "conditioned" in inorganic chemistry.

39. *Daily Palo Alto*, October 10, 1892, p. 3; Lane, *Making of Herbert Hoover*, p. 130; Frank B. Wooten ('95) anecdote, in Rice, "Fifty-six Anecdotes," pp. 24−25; Ernest Delos Magee ('95) anecdote, ibid., supplement, p. 15. Romero Hall was on Waverly Street in Palo Alto.

40. Lawrie Tatum, Annual Progressive Report, August 24, 1892, Hoover Legal Records, HHPL.

41. Herbert Hoover to Nell May Hill, August 30, 1892, Hill Family Papers, University of Oregon. This letter, and four others by Hoover to Hill between 1892 and 1895, have been published in *The Call Number* 27 (Spring 1966): 2−12, a publication of the University of Oregon Library. Other Hoover-to-Hill letters cited below are from this source. Miss Hill, a resident of Independence, Oregon, attended Stanford University for a time in the early 1890s. Hoover appears to have been acquainted with her before she entered Stanford.

42. See the voucher for February 1893, cited in note 34.

43. Wilbur, *Memoirs*, p. 40.

44. Ray Lyman Wilbur, "Herbert Hoover: A Personal Sketch" (unpublished paper, 1920), p. 6, Reprint File, HHPL. In his *Memoirs*, p. 40, Wilbur quoted Hoover's advice a bit differently: "Do your work so that the professors will notice it."

45. Hoover academic transcript; Lane, *Making of Herbert Hoover*, p. 139. Branner's 1892−1893 letter book in his papers is full of references to this project. The relief map weighed half a ton. Hoover's *Memoirs* state that he worked this summer for Waldemar Lindgren, but this is incorrect. He first worked for Lindgren in the summer of 1894.

46. Theodore Hoover, *Memoranda: Being a Statement by an Engineer* (typescript: Stanford University, 1939), p. 91, copy at HHPL. In November 1893, back at Stanford, Herbert Hoover spoke to the Geological Club on "the general geological structure, the kind of rocks and the mountains of western Oregon" he had evidently explored during the summer. Geological Club of Stanford University minute book, p. 7, in Miscellaneous University Papers II, Stanford University Archives.

47. Burt Brown Barker, *Autobiography of Burt Brown Barker* (typescript, n.d.), p. 37, copy at HHPL. Barker states that Hoover worked that summer for his Uncle John Minthorn's Oregon Land Company, but no corroboration of this statement has been found.

48. Hoover academic transcript. For an interesting account of a campus survey-ing expedition in which Hoover participated during the fall, see R. E. McDonnell, "A 'Hunch' of '93," *Stanford Illustrated Review* 30 (March 1929): 295–96.

49. Encina Hall Register, September 1, 1893–May 31, 1894, Stanford Uni-versity Archives; advertisement in the Stanford undergraduate journal *Sequoia* 3 (Sep-tember 13, 1893). Hoover's room was 175.

During his junior year Hoover also waited on tables in the Encina dining room—or so some of his classmates later recalled. See Rice, "Fifty-six Anecdotes," pp. 4–5, and supplement, p. 16. Rice cited as his authority a San Francisco restauranteur who evidently had the Encina dining contract in 1893–1894. The restauranteur asserted that Hoover himself recalled his waiting on tables when he happened to meet the restauranteur many years later. By 1928 the waiter story was a common one. A survey that year turned up twelve Stanford alumni who asserted that young Hoover had spilled soup down their necks. This statistic led a newspaper reporter to remark that, if so, Hoover "must have been the most careless student waiter ever to work his way through Stanford" (*Washington Evening Star*, November 25, 1928). Interestingly enough, the two earliest biographies of Hoover (Kellogg's and Lane's) explicitly deny that he waited on tables. Hoover's own *Memoirs* are silent on the subject.

Conceivably Hoover was a student waiter in Encina. But the story may also be an example of the power of apocryphal thinking.

50. Lawrie Tatum, Progressive Annual Report for 1893, Hoover Legal Rec-ords, HHPL.

51. Wilbur, *Memoirs*, p. 63. See also Frank Angell's remarks in *The First Year at Stanford*, pp. 52–53.

52. *Daily Palo Alto*, February 8, 1894, p. 1.

53. See, for example, Theodore Hoover, *Memoranda*, pp. 100, 110; Irwin, *Herbert Hoover*, pp. 52–53; Wilbur, *Memoirs*, p. 63. Theodore Hoover called his brother "the father of the Associated Students and their constitution." Irwin claimed that Hoover returned to campus in September with "a mature plan in his mind—his first creation in organization" and that the others then took it up. Wilbur asserted that Hoover "organized and secured adoption of a new constitution," without mentioning anyone else. Rose Wilder Lane's portrayal of the reform movement as a team effort to which Hoover was recruited by Collins and Hinsdale, and to which he contributed significantly, seems more realistic (Lane, *Making of Herbert Hoover*, pp. 141–42).

Hoover himself cited several others who, with him, "declared war for reform" (*Years of Adventure*, p. 22).

54. *Daily Palo Alto*, February 8, 1894, p. 1, and March 2, 1894, p. 1. In 1910 the *Stanford Alumnus* said of E. R. Zion: "As president of the Associated Students in 1894 he drafted and pressed to adoption the first constitution that provided a complete scheme of student activity and which is still practically in effect." *Stanford Alumnus* 11 (May 1910): 355.

55. *Daily Palo Alto*, January 23, 1894, p. 1.

56. Ibid., February 28, 1894, supplement.

57. Ibid., February 8, 1894, p. 1.

58. Ibid., March 2, 1894, p. 1; March 7, 1894, p. 1; and April 11, 1894, p. 1.

59. Lane, *Making of Herbert Hoover*, pp. 133, 142, states that Hoover had assisted Sam Collins in auditing accounts at Romero Hall in their sophomore year and that Collins, impressed, recommended to Hinsdale that Hoover be nominated for student body treasurer.

60. Ibid., pp. 144–45; Elliott, *Stanford University*, pp. 209–15 (for a history of the "Camp").

61. Lane, *Making of Herbert Hoover*, pp. 145–46; Wilbur, *Memoirs*, p. 63. In *Years of Adventure*, p. 23, Hoover simply recorded that when elected treasurer (or as he put it, "financial manager"), he served without pay.

62. Irwin, *Herbert Hoover*, pp. 54–55.

63. *Daily Palo Alto*, February 23, 1894, supplement.

64. Ibid., April 11, 1894, p. 1. While an undergraduate, Lester Hinsdale spelled his name "Hinsdill." Later he changed it, and I have used the revised version throughout.

65. Lane, *Making of Herbert Hoover*, pp. 146, 147.

66. *Daily Palo Alto*, April 18, 1894, p. 1. At first it was announced that Hinsdale had squeaked through, but a recount nullified the result.

67. Lane, *Making of Herbert Hoover*, pp. 147–48.

68. Irwin, *Herbert Hoover*, p. 55.

69. *Daily Palo Alto*, April 24, 1894, p. 1.

70. Wilbur, "Herbert Hoover: A Personal Sketch," pp. 9–10; unsigned memorandum for Vernon Kellogg, October 28, 1919, in "Stanford 1917–1920," Pre-Commerce Papers, HHPL. The author of this memorandum appears to have been Ray Lyman Wilbur.

71. *Daily Palo Alto*, April 25, 1894, p. 1.

72. Ibid., May 2, 1894, p. 4; May 3, 1894, p. 1; and May 4, 1894, p. 1.

73. Ibid., April 20, 1894, p. 4.

74. Hoover to Nell May Hill, July 19, 1894.

75. Ibid.; Hoover, *Years of Adventure*, p. 19; *Stanford Alumnus* 6 (December 1904): 4; Rice, "Fifty-six Anecdotes," pp. 26, 33–35.

76. Hoover to Hill, July 19, 1894, and November 9, 1894.

77. Hoover to John C. Branner, September 2, 1894, Branner Papers, Box 25; Hoover's 1894 field notebook, HHPL; Waldemar Lindgren to the Director, U.S. Geological Survey, June 30, 1895, copy in "U.S. Geological Survey, 1893–1916," Pre-Commerce Papers, HHPL.

Hoover's 1894 field notebook was published in facsimile in 1979 by the U.S. Senate under the title *Geological Atlas of the United States: Pyramid Peak Folio, California. Compiled by Herbert C. Hoover, 1894* (Senate Document No. 96–24).

78. Hoover to Branner, September 2, 1894.

79. Ibid.

80. Ibid.

81. Waldemar Lindgren, "A President in the Making," *The Tech Engineering News* 10 (March 1929): 53.

82. Hoover to Hill, November 9, 1894; Hoover to Branner, September 2, 1894.

83. Hoover to Branner, September 2, 1894. If this request caused any problems with the university administration, there is no record of it.

84. John C. Branner to Waldemar Lindgren, September 20, 1894, Branner Papers, Box 4.

85. Waldemar Lindgren to Branner, October 11, 1894, Branner Papers, Box 26. In his report of June 30, 1895 to the Director of the U.S. Geological Survey, Lindgren mentioned that Hoover had "efficiently assisted" him in his field work the summer before. In 1896 Lindgren published his Pyramid Peak Folio (Folio 31 of the U.S. Geological Survey's *Geologic Atlas of the United States*). On three folio maps of the Pyramid Peak Sheet, Lindgren placed the words: "Assisted by H. C. Hoover." Hoover felt highly honored. See Hoover to John M. Boutwell, May 31, 1949, Post-Presidential General File, Hoover Papers, HHPL.

86. Lindgren to Branner, October 11, 1894; Encina Hall Register, September 1, 1894–May 31, 1895, Stanford University Archives. The last entry in Hoover's field notebook was October 11 (the first, July 22). Hoover occupied room 179 in Encina on October 14, 1894. Classes had begun on September 7.

87. Hoover to Hill, November 9, 1894.

88. Hoover academic transcript.

89. Elliott, *Stanford University*, p. 117.

90. Lane, *Making of Herbert Hoover*, p. 151; Rice, "Fifty-six Anecdotes," pp. 41–42. Some years later a friend of Hoover's at Stanford recalled that the treasurer "had every detail at his fingers' end" and maintained elaborate card catalogues of student finances. Caspar W. Hodgson, "Campus Days With Herbert Hoover," *Western Alumnus* 1 (July 1928): 3.

91. Lawrie Tatum, Annual Progressive Report, 1894, Hoover Legal Records, HHPL.

92. *Stanford Alumni Review* 48 (April 1947): 17.

93. Lane, *Making of Herbert Hoover*, p. 151, states that Hoover's new voucher system evoked unavailing "howls" from the athletes, particularly the baseball team. See also *Daily Palo Alto*, November 26, 1901, p. 1.

94. *Daily Palo Alto*, November 15, 1894, p. 1.

95. Ibid., October 30, 1894, p. 1.

96. Ibid., November 15, 1894, p. 1.

97. Hoover to Hill, November 9, 1894.

98. Ibid.; Hodgson, "Campus Days With Herbert Hoover," p. 3.

99. See, for example, *Daily Palo Alto* for October 30, November 15, and December 5, 1894, and January 16, 17, 18, 21, and 22, 1895.

100. *Daily Palo Alto*, December 12, 1894, pp. 1, 2.

101. *Sequoia* 4 (January 25, 1895): 211. Ten years later, in *The First Year at Stanford*, Frank Angell described treasurer Hoover as "a reformer to whom the Student Body is exceedingly indebted for starting it on the straight and narrow road of business-like methods in its business affairs" (p. 53). This assessment is especially significant since it was rendered long before Hoover became a public figure, the subject of retrospective myth making by both admirers and detractors.

102. *Stanford Alumnus* 14 (December 1912): 126; Wilbur, *Memoirs*, p. 63.

103. Tatum, Annual Progressive Report, 1894.

104. Irwin, *Herbert Hoover*, pp. 57–58; Hoover, *Years of Adventure*, p. 357; Edith Harcourt to Victor Rhein, February 21, 1938, "Stanford—re HH's Days at Stanford, 1921–1959," Pre-Commerce Papers.

105. Irwin, *Herbert Hoover*, p. 58; Will Irwin, *The Making of a Reporter* (New York, 1942), p. 17.

106. See, for example, the impressions of Hoover recorded by Lane (who, be it remembered, relied heavily on Hoover's classmate Charles K. Field) and Irwin, who knew Hoover as an undergraduate. See also Rice, "Fifty-six Anecdotes," p. 38.

107. Irwin, *Herbert Hoover*, pp. 59–60; Irwin, *Making of a Reporter*, p. 17.

108. Irwin, *Herbert Hoover*, p. 63.

109. Ibid., pp. 63–64.

110. For Lou Henry's background, and Hoover's courtship, see Hoover, *Years of Adventure*, p. 23, and the popular biography by Helen B. Pryor, *Lou Henry Hoover: Gallant First Lady* (New York, 1969). For Hoover's earliest known sign of appreciation for her, see Hoover to Hill, November 9, 1894. The class card file for Lou Henry in the Special Collections department of the San Jose State University Library establishes that she graduated in 1893 and held jobs in Monterey before attending Stanford. In 1920 Hoover's cousin revealed that Hoover wrote letters to her while at Stanford concerning Lou Henry, whom he admired greatly from the start. Hoover was "desperate" about the thought of losing her. Harriette Miles Odell to Theodore Hoover, February 18, 1920, "Odell, Harriette Miles," Genealogy File, HHPL.

111. Hoover to Hill, November 9, 1894.

112. Ibid.; Hoover to Hill, September 7, 1895; interview with Professor C. D. Marx, March 5, 1920, "Hoover Genealogy," Ethel Rensch Papers, HHPL. The interviewer was probably Rose Wilder Lane.

113. *Daily Palo Alto*, January 25, 1895, p. 1.

114. Ibid., January 15, 1895, p. 1.

115. On January 5, 1932, George J. Bancroft wrote to his classmate, President Hoover. Bancroft recalled that he nominated Hoover for membership in the Stanford chapter of the SAE fraternity and personally invited Hoover to join. Hoover accepted. But a week or two later, Bancroft recalled, Hoover notified the fraternity that on further thought he felt he should remain a "barb" through college, since the "barbs" had voted for him in the student elections. Accordingly (Bancroft remembered) Hoover withdrew his acceptance. In this 1932 letter, Bancroft acknowledged that his memory might not be accurate "in all details." In his reply, President Hoover told Bancroft: "I think your memory is at fault in the belief that I ever accepted such a pledge. Otherwise, the story seems to me to be correct."

A few days later, a fraternity official reported to President Hoover that an article in a national fraternity magazine stated that "you were pledged to the Sigma Alpha Epsilon fraternity" but that "several of your close associates asked you to resign from this pledge and that you subsequently did so." To this letter Hoover's secretary replied: "He [Hoover] tells me that to the best of his recollection he was never pledged in the matter [sic; manner?] you mention. He was approached, gave it some consideration, and declined."

See: George J. Bancroft to Herbert Hoover, January 5, 1932; Hoover to Bancroft, January 15, 1932; Carl J. Rice to Hoover, January 21, 1932; Lawrence Richey to Rice, January 26, 1932. All in "President, personal data concerning," President's Personal File, HHPL.

116. Hoover to Hill, November 9, 1894.

117. Hoover academic transcript; Hoover to Hill, July 9, 1895; Hoover, *Years of Adventure*, p. 20.

118. Hoover academic transcript.

119. Ibid.; Hoover to Hill, July 9, 1895. In this letter to Hill, Hoover gave the following graphic summary of his senior year:

Having run Athletics the first semester after I reached college I recied [sic] as a reward two conditions and no other credit for semesters work. Hence 2d semester I must carry 23 hours and remove these two cond. which I did and passed English 1b besides and graduated. I also ran base-ball field athletics and did about as much politics as ever. Went to every ball given, Sophomore, Junior, Charity & Senior in fact quite a social swell. Enjoyed myself better than ever before in my life.

Hoover's academic transcript indicates that in fact he took eighteen credit hours in his second semester, not twenty-three, but in this letter he may have been counting the "conditions" he had to remove.

120. Hoover's academic transcript indicates that he took the examination unsuccessfully more than once.

121. See, for example, his letters to Nell May Hill.

122. This story is told in detail by Vernon Kellogg in *Herbert Hoover*, pp. 52–55. Professor Kellogg explicitly cites Lou Henry Hoover as his source. Other early biographers repeat the story with some variations. David Starr Jordan recalled in 1928 that English composition was Hoover's "great stumbling-block at college" and that it was a committee which "decided to pass him at last in freshman English." It did so "mainly because it was claimed that the University could hardly refuse to graduate one who wrote such excellent theses in his major subject and who was reported to be the best student in the department" (Jordan, "Random Recollections," p. 336). Hoover himself, in his *Memoirs* (*Years of Adventure*, pp. 23–24), stated that without the "active intervention" of Professors Branner and Smith, "who insisted among other things that I could write English," he would not have graduated with his class.

123. *Daily Palo Alto*, April 29, 1895, p. 1.

124. Theodore Hoover, *Memoranda*, pp. 93–94.

125. Hoover to Hill, July 9, 1895.

126. Ibid., September 7, 1895.

127. Ibid., November 9, 1894.

128. *Daily Palo Alto*, April 24, 1895, p. 1; April 25, 1895, p. 1; and May 1, 1895, p. 1. Two sources indicate that Hoover was a key figure in arranging for a salary for his successor: Henry D. Sheldon, "The History of the Student Body," *Sequoia* 7 (April 22, 1898): 142; *Stanford Alumnus* 14 (December 1912): 126.

129. *Stanford Quad '96* [for Class of 1895], p. 240.

130. Interview with Professor C. D. Marx, March 5, 1920.

131. Unpublished autobiography of Guido Marx, pp. 85–86, Guido Marx Papers, Box 2, Stanford University Archives. Marx, an engineering professor at Stanford, was the brother of Professor C. D. Marx. See also the recollection of Dr. Branner's wife, *New York Times*, July 22, 1928, sec. 7, p. 11.

132. Branner speech, December 28, 1919, printed in *Stanford Illustrated Review* 21 (January 1920): 188–89.

133. Kellogg, *Herbert Hoover*, pp. 48–49.

134. David Starr Jordan's commencement address, in *Daily Palo Alto*, May 29, 1895, pp. 4–5.

135. Irwin, *Herbert Hoover*, p. 44.

136. Hoover academic transcript.

137. Hoover, *Years of Adventure*, p. 24.

138. Joseph D. Grant, *Redwoods and Reminiscences* (San Francisco, 1973), p. 194.

CHAPTER 3

1. Herbert Hoover to Burt Brown Barker, October 25, 1897, Burt Brown Barker Collection, Herbert Hoover Presidential Library (hereinafter HHPL).

2. Hoover to Harriette Miles, August 5, 1897, extract in "Mining—Australia, Herbert Hoover's Accounts of Western Australia," Pre-Commerce Papers, Herbert Hoover Papers, HHPL.

3. *San Francisco Chronicle*, October 24, 1901, p. 14.

4. F. H. Bathurst, "Hoover in Australia: A Personal Sketch," *The Argus* (Melbourne), November 3, 1928, p. 6.

5. *Years of Adventure* is the title of the first volume of Hoover's *Memoirs*, published in 1951.

6. Herbert Hoover, "And Their Deeds Are Remembered After Them," *Sequoia* 5 (January 10, 1896): 225–26.

7. *Stanford Alumnus* 1 (June 1900): 164.

8. Jordan visited the Hoovers at length during his trips to Europe before World War I.

9. David Starr Jordan, *The Days of a Man*, vol. 2 (Yonkers-on-Hudson, N.Y., 1922), p. 223.

10. For more on Hoover's pre-1914 mining career see George H. Nash, *The Life of Herbert Hoover: The Engineer, 1874–1914* (New York, 1983).

11. Professor Guido Marx, unpublished autobiography (ca. 1941), Stanford University section, p. 89, Guido Marx Papers, Box 2, Stanford University Archives.

12. E. D. Adams, "Snap Shots of Herbert Hoover" (typescript, 1929), p. 24, E. D. Adams Papers, Stanford University Archives.

13. Anne Martin and Mary Austin interviews, 1931, Walter W. Liggett Papers, New York Public Library.

14. Ralph Lutz to Bernice Miller, March 24, 1958, Hoover Institution Records, Series F-01, Box 6, Hoover Institution on War, Revolution and Peace (hereinafter HI).

15. Ibid.

16. David Starr Jordan to Charles D. Norton, October 7, 1910, quoted in Henry F. Pringle, *The Life and Times of William Howard Taft* (New York, 1939), p. 614.

17. Nash, *Life of Herbert Hoover: The Engineer*, p. 512.

18. Will Irwin, *The Making of a Reporter* (New York, 1942), pp. 182–83.

19. The capacity to do this was Hoover's definition of "executive ability." Hoover, lecture to Stanford University engineering students, quoted in *Daily Palo Alto* [Stanford University student newspaper], February 5, 1909, p. 4. In *Principles of Mining* Hoover used slightly different wording to define executive ability: "that capacity to coordinate and command the best results from other men" (p. 186).

20. David Starr Jordan, commencement address to the Stanford class of 1905; printed in *Stanford Alumnus* 6 (June 1905): 16–18.

21. Nash, *Life of Herbert Hoover: The Engineer*, pp. 69–70.

22. Hoover to Lester Hinsdale, July 9, 1897, Hinsdale Collection, HHPL.

23. Hoover to Hinsdale, April 14, 1897, ibid.

24. Ray Lyman Wilbur, *The Memoirs of Ray Lyman Wilbur* (Stanford, Calif., 1960), p. 74.

25. Newton B. Knox reminiscences in *Sunday Oregonian* (Portland), February 17, 1929, sec. 2, p. 14.

26. Jordan to Hoover, May 12, 1905, "Stanford—David Starr Jordan," Pre-Commerce Papers.

27. Hoover to John C. Branner, n.d., John C. Branner Papers, Box 38, Stanford University Archives.

28. Hoover telegram to Branner, May 5, 1910, Branner Papers, Box 42. See also Hoover to R. A. F. Penrose, Jr., April 29, 1910, printed in Helen R. Fairbanks and Charles P. Berkey, *Life and Letters of R. A. F. Penrose, Jr.* (New York, 1952), p. 160.

29. Nash, *Life of Herbert Hoover: The Engineer*, p. 572.

30. Payson J. Treat oral history (1967), p. 4, HHPL. See also Treat to Hoover, October 10, 1907, Payson J. Treat Papers, Box 1, HI.

31. Treat oral history, pp. 4–5; Treat to Hoover (plus enclosure), June 7, 1908, "Stanford—Books, Money For," Pre-Commerce Papers.

32. E. D. Adams to Hoover, September 8, 1908, Adams Papers.

33. The gift was originally a loan made in 1912. See W. E. Caldwell (secretary, Stanford University Board of Trustees) to Hoover, February 6, 1912, "Stanford—Book Collection—China," Pre-Commerce Papers; Hoover to E. D. Adams, March 5, 1912, George E. Crothers Papers, Stanford University Archives; E. D. Adams to Hoover, May 8, 1912, Adams Papers, Box 1; Hoover to Vanderlynn Stow, April 23, 1913, and W. E. Caldwell to Hoover, May 27, 1913 both in Board of Trustees Supporting Documents, May 23, 1913 folder, Stanford University Archives.

34. Treat oral history, p. 1.

35. Ibid., p. 2.

36. Branner to Hoover, August 29, 1908, Branner Papers, Box 7.

37. Jordan to George E. Crothers, September 14, 1908, David Starr Jordan Papers, Series I—AA, letter book #50, Stanford University Archives. See also Branner to Hoover, September 17, 1908, Branner Papers, Box 7.

38. Hoover to Branner, October 20, 1908, Branner Papers, Box 40.

39. Branner to Lou Henry Hoover, March 18, 1907, Branner Papers, Box 6.

40. Stanford University Board of Trustees Minutes, September 5, 1908, Stanford University Archives.

41. *Daily Palo Alto*, January 14, 1909; Hoover Calendar, HHPL.

42. On Stanford's early liquor problem and the crisis of 1908 see Orrin Leslie Elliott, *Stanford University: The First Twenty-five Years* (Stanford, Calif., 1937), pp. 379–407.

43. Hoover, nineteen-page handwritten manuscript of a speech on the subject "Stanford 14 years after," February 1909, filed in "Stanford—Academic and Financial Position, 1913–1914," Pre-Commerce Papers. At the top of the first page of this manuscript is the heading, evidently in Hoover's hand: "Notes by HH on University [undecipherable] 1913." I suspect that Hoover dated this (in fact, mistakenly dated it) much later, for the internal evidence is persuasive that this speech was written in 1909, not 1913. "Stanford 14 years after" seems clearly to mean fourteen years after his graduation in 1895. Hoover's discussion of student discontent, disciplinary procedures, etc., seems clearly to refer to the crisis of early 1908. There was no such crisis in 1912–1913, nor was the subject of student-faculty friction a burning one then. Finally, Hoover indicates in the speech that he is leaving in twelve hours after a three-week stay on campus—the approximate length of his stay in 1909. I conclude that this speech was prepared for delivery—probably to a faculty group (the internal evidence suggests this)—around February 9, 1909.

44. Treat oral history, pp. 6–7; "Planning the Stanford Union," *Stanford Alumnus* 10 (May 1909): 339.

45. *Daily Palo Alto*, February 2, 1909, p. 1.

46. Ibid., February 3, 1909, p. 2.

47. "Planning the Stanford Union," pp. 338–42.

48. E. D. Adams to George E. Crothers, February 10, 1909, Ray Lyman Wilbur Personal Papers, Box 78, Stanford University Archives.

49. Adams to Hoover, May 17, 1910, Adams Papers, Box 1.

50. *Daily Palo Alto*, February 2, 1909, p. 1; Hoover to Adams, June 3, 1910, Adams Papers; Hoover to R. W. Barrett, October 6, 1910, George E. Crothers Papers; *Stanford Alumnus* 12 (November 1910): 79–81.

51. *Stanford Alumnus* 14 (September 1912): 17.

52. Stanford Union brochure, n.d. (ca. August 1909), enclosed with R. W. Barrett to John C. Branner, September 1, 1909, Branner Papers, Box 41.

53. Hoover to Adams, October 19, 1909, Adams Papers. Hoover said that he and his friends had not yet determined their respective proportions of the $10,000 pledge.

54. See R. W. Barrett to Hoover, October 19, 1910, "Stanford—Union, 1910," Pre-Commerce Papers; Hoover to E. D. Adams, May 1, 1912, Adams Papers, Box 1; and Hoover's correspondence with Everett W. Smith, 1913–1914, "Stanford—Union," Pre-Commerce Papers.

55. [Hoover], "The Stanford Union" (typescript, January 28, 1956); [Hoover], "The Stanford Union" (typescript, n.d.). Both in "Stanford University—Stanford Union and Women's Clubhouse," Post-Presidential Subject File, Hoover Papers, HHPL.

56. *Stanford Alumnus* 14 (September 1912): 17–18, and 14 (October 1912): 41–42; Hoover to Everett W. Smith, September 27, 1912, "Stanford—Union, 1912," Pre-Commerce Papers.

57. *Daily Palo Alto*, September 11, 1912, p. 1.

58. Elliott, *Stanford University*, pp. 142–43.

59. This at least was the view of Hoover's good friend on the faculty, Professor E. D. Adams. See Adams to Hoover, November 19, 1912, Adams Papers.

60. Henry Rolfe to Guido Marx, August 14, 1912, quoted in Professor Guido Marx's unpublished autobiography (ca. 1941), Stanford University section, pp. 86–87, Marx Papers, Box 2.

61. Hoover Calendar, HHPL.

62. *Stanford Alumnus* 14 (December 1912): 125.

63. John Barneson to Hoover, October 29, 1912, "Mining—Correspondence: Barneson, John," Pre-Commerce Papers.

64. Stanford University Board of Trustees Minutes, November 29, 1912. Hoover remained a trustee until 1961, when he became a trustee emeritus.

65. *Stanford Alumnus* 14 (December 1912): 126.

66. Ibid., p. 127.

67. Hoover Calendar, HHPL.

68. Hoover to Adams, n.d. (late 1912), Adams Papers.

69. Jordan to Hoover, December 3, 1912, Jordan Papers, Series I-A, Box 84.

70. Hoover to W. Mayo Newhall, January 2, 1913, "Stanford—Academic and Financial Position, 1913–1914," Pre-Commerce Papers.

71. Hoover, "Memorandum Prepared for Trustees on General Position and Circulated January 2, 1913," in "Stanford—Academic and Financial Position, 1913–1914," Pre-Commerce Papers. A copy of the part of the memorandum labeled "The Present Position" is in the John C. Branner Presidential Papers, Box 5, Stanford University Archives.

72. Hoover to Frank B. Anderson, January 2, 1913, "Stanford—Academic and Financial Position, 1913–1914," Pre-Commerce Papers.

73. Stanford University Board of Trustees Minutes, January 3, 1913.

74. See Hoover to Leon Sloss, May 20, 1913, Board of Trustees Supporting Documents, May 23, 1913 folder.

75. Stanford University Board of Trustees Minutes, April 25, 1913.

76. Jordan to Hoover, December 3, 1912.

77. After the 1908 disturbances there were demands that Jordan leave. Elliott, *Stanford University*, p. 404. In 1910 at least one trustee considered him a negative influence and wished that he would give up executive work. George E. Crothers to Nathan Abbott, July 6, 1910, copy in Orrin Leslie Elliott Papers, Box 3, Stanford University Archives.

78. Elliott, *Stanford University*, pp. 557–58.

79. Hoover to Jordan, April 30, 1913, Jordan Papers, Series I-A, Box 88.

80. Hoover to Jordan, May 9, 1913, Jordan Papers, Series I-A, Box 89; copy in Board of Trustees Supporting Documents, May 23, 1913 folder.

81. Jordan to Hoover, May 11, 1913, Board of Trustees Supporting Documents, May 23, 1913 folder.

82. Jordan to Edith M. Jordan, May 15, 1913, Jordan Papers, Series I-A, Box 89; Jordan, *Days of a Man*, 2:455. In this latter source, his autobiography, Jordan stated that it was at Hoover's "instance" that the change in Jordan's position came about. The contemporary documents convey the same impression: that Hoover took the initiative.

83. Jordan to Edith Jordan, May 15, 1913.

84. Hoover to Jordan, May 9, 1913.

85. Jordan to Hoover, May 12, 1913, Board of Trustees Supporting Documents, May 23, 1913 folder.

86. Branner to Hoover, May 16, 1913; Branner telegram to Hoover, May 17, 1913; both in Branner Papers, Box 10.

87. A copy of some of Hoover's resolutions, in the form of a memorandum dated by Hoover May 13, 1913, is in the Board of Trustees Supporting Documents, May 23, 1913 folder. See also Hoover to the trustees' University Committee, n.d. (ca. May 19–21, 1913), ibid. For the resolutions as passed, see Stanford University Board of Trustees Minutes, May 23, 1913.

Jordan did not get all he initially desired. He wanted the chancellor, when present, to outrank the president at public functions. In their formal statement of the chancellor's duties, the trustees said nothing about his rank. Jordan also asked that the chancellor be a member of the faculty's Academic Council and a member of the executive committee of the council. The trustees' resolution was silent on this point. The trustees did grant Jordan's wish to be entitled to attend board meetings. In short, Jordan initially seemed to desire a continuing role in academic policy; the trustees moved to deprive him of it. He could only "advise and cooperate" on subjects determined by the trustees or the president.

88. Jordan to Branner, May 18, 1913, Branner Papers, Box 48.

89. Jordan to Lou Henry Hoover, March 7, 1916, David Starr Jordan Papers, HI.

90. Hoover to Jordan, May 9, 1913; Jordan to Hoover, May 11, 1913.

91. *San Francisco Bulletin*, May 19, 1913, pp. 1, 2.

92. Jordan, *Days of a Man*, 2:456–58.

93. Jordan to Branner, May 18, 1913.

94. Ibid., May 23, 1913, Jordan Papers, Series I-A, Box 89.

95. See "Resolutions Drafted by H. C. Hoover and Carried at Meeting of the Trustees, May 23rd 1913" (typescript), in "Stanford—Academic and Financial Position, 1913–1914," Pre-Commerce Papers.

96. For example, regarding the committee on the gymnasium, see Hoover to Leon Sloss, May 20, 1913.

97. "Resolutions Drafted by H. C. Hoover . . . May 23rd 1913"; Stanford University Board of Trustees Minutes, May 23, 1913.

98. "Resolutions Drafted by H. C. Hoover . . . May 23rd 1913."

99. Trustees' press release, n.d. (ca. May 24, 1913), Board of Trustees Supporting Documents, May 23, 1913 folder. The trustees authorized the issuance of a press release on May 23 in a resolution drawn up by Hoover. See "Resolutions Drafted . . ." and Elliott, *Stanford University*, p. 561.

100. Jordan to Branner, May 24, 1913, Branner Papers, Box 48.

101. Ray Lyman Wilbur to Hoover, May 26, 1913, Wilbur Personal Papers, Box 31; Adams to Hoover, June 2, 1913, and Adams to Dr. J. M. Stillman, June 2, 1913, Adams Papers.

102. Jordan to Branner, May 18 and 23, 1913.

103. Hoover Calendar, HHPL.

104. Hoover to Timothy Hopkins, February 24, 1914, Board of Trustees Supporting Documents, March 27, 1914 folder; Stanford University Board of Trustees Minutes, February 27, 1914; "Resolutions prepared by H. C. Hoover and adopted by Trustees Feb 27 1914" (typescript), in "Stanford—Academic and Financial Position, 1913–1914," Pre-Commerce Papers.

105. Stanford University Board of Trustees Minutes, January 30, 1914. Hoover was energetically involved in this, too. See Hoover to Joseph Donohoe Grant, December 29, 1913, Board of Trustees Supporting Documents, January 30, 1914 (2) folder.

106. Hoover to Timothy Hopkins, February 24, 1914.

107. Hoover to Branner, August 6, 1913, "Stanford—Salaries," Pre-Commerce Papers.

108. Hoover's report on faculty salaries is in the form of a letter to Horace Davis (a fellow trustee), January 27, 1914, filed in Board of Trustees Supporting Documents, January 30, 1914 (1) folder.

109. Stanford University Board of Trustees Minutes, January 30, 1914. Elliott, *Stanford University*, pp. 565–66, credits President Branner with devising the new pay structure that the trustees adopted on January 30, 1914. The structure that he ascribes to Branner, however, is included in Hoover's report of January 27, 1914.

110. Hoover's faculty salary report, January 27, 1914.

111. Hoover, "Memorandum Prepared for Trustees on General Position and Circulated January 2, 1913."

112. Adams to Hoover, June 2, 1913, Adams Papers; Adams, "Snap Shots of Herbert Hoover," pp. 9–10.

113. Hoover to Adams, June 3, 1913, Adams Papers.

114. Adams, "Snap Shots," p. 11.

115. Hoover's faculty salary report, January 27, 1914.

116. Professor Guido Marx, unpublished autobiography (ca. 1941), p. 59, in Guido Marx Papers, Box 2.

117. Richard M. Atwater interview, ca. 1931, Walter W. Liggett Papers, New York Public Library.

118. Marx, unpublished autobiography, p. 58.

119. Stanford University Board of Trustees Minutes, August 29, 1913.

120. Elliott, *Stanford University*, p. 548.

121. Ibid., pp. 541, 546, 548.

122. Branner to Hoover, November 11, 1913, and Branner to Thomas Welton Stanford, January 8, 1914; both in Branner Papers, Box 11.

123. Branner to Hoover, November 11, 1913.

124. Branner to Dr. Henry S. Pritchett, December 6, 1913, Branner Papers, Box 11.

125. Branner to the Board of Trustees, December 20, 1913, Branner Papers, Box 47.

126. Fernando Sanford to Branner, December 26, 1913, copy in Board of Trustees Supporting Documents, February 27, 1914 folder; Branner to Thomas Welton Stanford, January 8, 1914.

127. Branner to Pritchett, December 27, 1913, Branner Papers, Box 11.

128. Branner to Stanford, January 8, 1914.

129. Stanford University Board of Trustees Minutes, January 30, 1914.

130. Branner to Pritchett, February 20, 1914, Branner Papers, Box 11. See also Branner to E. D. Adams, February 2, 1914, Branner Papers Box 11.

131. Hoover to Branner, February 16, 1914, Branner Presidential Papers, Box 5.

132. Branner to Hoover, February 19, 1914, Branner Presidential Papers, Box 5.

133. Hoover to Timothy Hopkins, February 23, 1914, Board of Trustees Supporting Documents, February 27, 1914 folder.

134. Stanford University Board of Trustees Minutes, February 27, 1914; "Resolutions prepared by H. C. Hoover and adopted by Trustees Feb 27 1914," in "Stanford—Academic and Financial Position, 1913–1914," Pre-Commerce Papers. The resolution that Hoover prepared and the trustees adopted (with certain modifications) was first adopted by the trustees' University Committee on February 24. See minutes of University Committee, February 24, 1914, in "Stanford Minutes," Pre-Commerce Papers.

135. Branner to Adams, February 28, 1914, and Branner to Stanford, March 3, 1914, Branner Papers, Box 11.

136. Branner to Adams, February 26 and 28, 1914, Branner Papers, Box 11; Elliott, *Stanford University*, pp. 551, 565.

137. Hoover Calendar, HHPL.

138. Branner to Stanford, March 3, 1914.

139. Branner to Adams, March 12, 1914, Adams Papers.

140. Various items in the Board of Trustees Supporting Documents, April 24, 1914 folder, illuminate the negotiations for a merger. See also Stanford University Board of Trustees Minutes, April 24 and May 29, 1914.

141. Branner to the Board of Trustees, December 20, 1913.

142. Branner to Adams, March 12, 1914; Timothy Hopkins to Hoover, March 26, 1914, "Stanford—Medical School, 1914," Pre-Commerce Papers; Adams to F. C. Woodward, March 26, 1914, Adams Papers.

143. Board of Trustees Minutes, March 27, 1914; Branner to Adams, March 30, 1914, and Branner to Pritchett, April 6, 1914, Branner Papers, Box 11.

144. Branner to Adams, March 30, 1914.

145. Hoover to Timothy Hopkins, April 7, 1914, "Stanford—Medical School, 1914," Pre-Commerce Papers.

146. Hoover to Wilbur, April 14, 1914, Wilbur Personal Papers, Box 31.

147. Branner to Adams, June 2, 1914, Branner Papers, Box 11; Elliott, *Stanford University*, p. 554.

148. Branner to Adams, June 2, 1914.

149. Dr. Victor C. Vaughan to Branner, June 9, 1914, copy in Stanford University Board of Trustees Minutes, June 26, 1914.

150. For a lengthy account of the medical school controversy see Elliott, *Stanford University*, pp. 534–56.

151. Branner to David Starr Jordan, June 4, 1914, and Branner to Stanford, July 8, 1914, Branner Papers, Box 11.

152. Branner to Jordan, June 4, 1914.

153. Hoover to Wilbur, June 16, 1914, Wilbur Personal Papers, Box 31.

154. Hoover to Jordan, June 12, 1914, "Jordan, David Starr," Pre-Commerce Papers.

155. Hoover to Timothy Hopkins, October 7, 1914, Commission for Relief in Belgium Papers, HI.

156. Hoover to Jordan, June 8, 1914, "Jordan, David Starr," Pre-Commerce Papers.

157. Hoover to Wilbur, June 16, 1914.

158. Wilbur to Edgar Rickard, October 1, 1919, Ray Lyman Wilbur Papers, Box 47, HI.

CHAPTER 4

1. Ray Lyman Wilbur, *The Memoirs of Ray Lyman Wilbur* (Stanford, Calif., 1960), pp. 228–31.

2. Herbert Hoover, *The Memoirs of Herbert Hoover*, vol. 1: *Years of Adventure* (New York, 1931), p. vi.

3. Andrew D. White, *The Autobiography of Andrew Dickson White*, vol. 2 (New York, 1905), pp. 489–90.

4. Hoover, *Years of Adventure*, pp. 184–85; Hoover, *An American Epic*, vol. 2 (Chicago, 1960), p. 389; typescript interviews of Herbert Hoover, June 13 and 29, 1961, in "Hoover Institution Book: Source Materials—Interviews with Herbert Hoover," Kenneth Colegrove Papers, Herbert Hoover Presidential Library (hereinafter HHPL); Colegrove, draft of chapter 1 of proposed book about the Hoover Institution on War, Revolution and Peace, in "Hoover Institution Book—Drafts," Colegrove Papers.

5. E. D. Adams to Hoover, July 10, 1914; Hoover cable to Adams, July 21, 1914; Adams to Hoover, July 23, 1914. All in E. D. Adams Papers, Hoover Institution (hereinafter HI). For more on the two men's friendship, see Adams, "Snap Shots of Herbert Hoover" (typescript, 1929), Adams Papers, Stanford University Archives.

6. Adams to Hoover, February 16, 1915, Adams Papers, HI.

7. Hoover to Adams, March 7, 1915, ibid.

8. Adams to Hoover, May 29 and September 3, 1915, and February 27, 1918, Adams Papers, Stanford University Archives; Adams to Hoover, August 14, 1916, copy in "Hoover Institution Book—Source Material, Documents, 1914–16," Colegrove Papers.

9. Edward M. House diary, February 16, 1915, Yale University Library.

10. Joseph C. Kiger, ed., *Research Institutions and Learned Societies* (Westport, Conn., 1982), p. 271.

11. Hoover to W. Mayo Newhall, October 25, 1914, "Stanford, re Presidency," Pre-Commerce Papers, Herbert Hoover Papers, HHPL. See also Hoover to W. Mayo Newhall and Timothy Hopkins, December 7, 1914 (separate letters), ibid.

12. Hoover to Newhall, October 25, 1914.

13. Timothy Hopkins to Hoover, January 29, 1915, "Stanford, re Presidency," Pre-Commerce Papers.

14. Ralph Arnold to Hoover, May 13 and June 28, 1915, Ralph Arnold Collection, Box 38, Huntington Library; E. D. Adams to Hoover, May 19, 1915, E. D. Adams Papers, Stanford University Archives.

15. Hoover to Newhall, October 25, 1914; Timothy Hopkins to Hoover, November 12, 1914, and January 8, 1915, "Stanford re Presidency," Pre-Commerce Papers.

16. Hoover to Newhall, October 25, 1914.

17. Ibid.; Hoover to Newhall and Hopkins, December 7, 1914 (separate letters).

18. Hoover to Newhall, December 7, 1914.

19. Arnold to Hoover, March 3 and 18, 1915, Arnold Collection, Box 38.

20. Hoover to Arnold, March 25, 1915, ibid.

21. Arnold to Hoover, January 18, 1915, ibid.

22. Hoover to Arnold, February 21, 1915.

23. Arnold to Hoover, March 18, 1915.

24. Arnold to Hoover, March 13, 18, and May 31, 1915; Adams to Hoover, May 19, 1915.

25. Arnold to Hoover, May 13, 1915.

26. Hoover to Arnold, June 6, 1915, Arnold Collection, Box 38.

27. Arnold to Hoover, June 28, 1915, ibid.

28. Arnold cable to Hoover, June 28, 1915, ibid.

29. Arnold to Hoover, June 28, 1915.

30. Hoover cable to his wife, July 12, 1915, "Hoover, Herbert, 1915," Personal Correspondence: 1874–1920, Lou Henry Hoover Papers, HHPL; slightly edited copy, dated July 16, 1915, addressed from Mrs. Hoover to Arnold, in Arnold Collection, Box 38.

31. Charles P. Eells to Arnold, July 21, 1915; Arnold to Hoover, July 23, 1915; both in Arnold Collection, Box 38.

32. David Starr Jordan to Hoover, July 29, 1915, "Stanford—Jordan, Dr. David S.," Pre-Commerce Papers.

33. Ibid.

34. Arnold to Hoover, August 9, 1915, Arnold Collection, Box 38.

35. Lou Henry Hoover cable to her husband, August 8, 1915, "Hoover, Herbert, 1915," Personal Correspondence: 1874–1920, Lou Henry Hoover Papers.

36. Arnold to Hoover, September 30, 1915, Arnold Collection, Box 38; Joseph D. Grant to Hoover, October 7, 1915, "Grant, Joseph D.," Pre-Commerce Papers.

37. Wilbur, *Memoirs*, pp. 178–79.

38. Hoover to Ray Lyman Wilbur, November 11, 1915, copy in Adams Papers.

39. Brand Whitlock to Hoover, January 24, 1916, in American Legation, Brussels, Correspondence, 1916, vol. 71, file 848, RG 84, National Archives, Washington, D.C.

40. Hoover to Whitlock, January 28, 1916, in ibid., vol. 72.

41. Hoover to Wilbur, November 11, 1915.

42. Hoover to W. Mayo Newhall, May 30, 1916, Board of Trustees Supporting Documents, August 1, 1916 folder, Stanford University Archives.

43. Wilbur to Hoover, June 29, 1916, "Stanford University, 1914–1921," Pre-Commerce Papers.

44. Stanford University Board of Trustees Minutes, August 1, 1916, Stanford University Archives; W. Mayo Newhall to Hoover, August 10, 1916, Board of Trustees Supporting Documents, August 1, 1916 folder; Joseph D. Grant to Hoover, August 16, 1916, "Grant, Joseph D.," Pre-Commerce Papers.

45. Newhall to Hoover, August 10, 1916.

46. Wilbur, *Memoirs*, pp. 244, 253–77.

47. William C. Mullendore, *History of the United States Food Administration* (Stanford, Calif., 1941), p. 358.

48. For a list of homes that Hoover and/or his wife leased on the Stanford campus before 1917, see Lou Henry Hoover telegram to Herbert Hoover, May 11, 1920, Herbert Hoover Collection, Box 3, HI.

49. Ibid.

50. For a time before the war the Hoovers had planned to build their "dream house" in San Francisco and had even purchased a lot in the city at the corner of Baker Street and Broadway. At some point in the war they abandoned the idea. See George H. Nash, *The Life of Herbert Hoover: The Engineer, 1874–1914* (New York, 1983), pp. 503–4; Curtis H. Lindley to Hoover, January 1, 1914, "Lindley, Curtis H.," Pre-Commerce Papers.

51. Lou Henry Hoover telegram to Hoover, May 14, 1917, "Hoover, Lou Henry," Pre-Commerce Papers.

52. Hoover telegram to Lou Henry Hoover, May 15, 1917, ibid.

53. Wilbur, *Memoirs*, pp. 210–11. The structure was authorized in 1915 but not completed and occupied until mid-1918.

54. *San Francisco Examiner*, October 13, 1917; copy in Clippings File, HHPL.

55. Birge M. Clark, *Memoirs about Mr. and Mrs. Herbert Hoover, with Particular Emphasis on the Planning and Building of Their Home on San Juan Hill* (Palo Alto, Calif., privately printed, 1969), p. 4; Birge M. Clark, "The Hoovers wanted a house that was livable, unostentatious, unconventional—and fireproof," *Stanford Historical Society Newsletter* 2 (Spring/Summer 1978): 4; National Register of Historic Places Inventory—Nomination Form for Lou Henry Hoover House, July 23, 1984, copy in the possession of the author.

56. Lou Henry Hoover telegram to Hoover, May 11, 1920; Lou Henry Hoover to Edgar Rickard, March 3, 1925, "Taxes for: 1924," Subject File, Lou Henry Hoover Papers, HHPL. In the first of these sources, Mrs. Hoover indicated that she bought Professor Whittaker's house around July 1918; in the second, she gave the date as 1915. I believe that the former source is correct.

The address of the Whittaker house was then 7 Cabrillo Street; today it is 746 Santa Ynez Street. See Birge Clark memorandum, August 23, 1968, Hoover Collection, Box 3. (Many street names and numbers on the campus have been changed since 1919.)

57. See volumes 2 and 3 of Hoover's four-volume series on his relief work, *An American Epic* (Chicago, 1959–1964).

58. Hoover cable to his wife, enclosed in Edgar Rickard telegram to Lou Henry Hoover, January 6, 1919, "Hoover, Lou Henry," Pre-Commerce Papers.

59. Carol Green Wilson notes of interview with Birge M. Clark, January 30, 1950, Carol Green Wilson Papers, Box 5, HI; Clark, *Memoirs*, p. 15; Clark, "The Hoovers wanted . . . ," p. 5. In his 1950 interview, Clark recalled that Hoover had two other requirements: the house must have a view, and the roofs must be useful.

60. Clark, *Memoirs*, p. 4; Clark, "The Hoovers wanted . . . ," p. 4.

61. Hoover cable to Lou Henry Hoover, contained in Hoover cable no. "Food 665" from Paris to ARA, New York office, April 22, 1919, in Hoover Institution Records, Series F-02, HI. Copy in "Hoover Institution Book—Source Material," Kenneth Colegrove Papers, Box 23, HHPL.

62. Allan Hoover to Herbert Hoover, June 17, 1919, "Hoover, Allan, 1919," Personal Correspondence, 1874–1920, Lou Henry Hoover Papers.

63. Birge M. Clark, "Memo on Planning and Construction of the Hoover Home on the Stanford Campus," cited in National Register of Historic Places Inventory—Nomination Form for the Lou Henry Hoover House.

64. Clark, *Memoirs*, p. 7; Clark, "The Hoovers wanted . . . ," p. 5.

65. Clark, "The Hoovers wanted . . . ," p. 5.

66. National Register of Historic Places Inventory—Nomination Form for the Lou Henry Hoover House.

67. The $137,000 figure was Hoover's in 1944; the $170,000 figure was his wife's in 1925. See: Hoover to W. Parmer Fuller, December 27, 1944, Post-Presidential Individual File, Hoover Papers, HHPL; Lou Henry Hoover to Edgar Rickard, March 3, 1925 (cited in note 56).

68. National Register of Historic Places Inventory—Nomination Form for the Lou Henry Hoover House.

69. Clark, *Memoirs*, p. 9; Clark, "The Hoovers wanted . . . ," p. 6.

70. "The Hoovers did not want the house to be related to any historical style" (Clark, *Memoirs*, p. 14). Clark stated that the home's resemblance to Algerian or Pueblo Indian dwellings was "purely coincidental" (p. 15).

71. Hoover, quoted by Clark in 1950 (see note 59).

72. Quoted in Clark, *Memoirs*, p. 15.

73. Hoover press release, September 27, 1919, Public Statements File, HHPL; Clark, *Memoirs*, pp. 25–26.

74. Clark, *Memoirs*, p. 26; Clark, "The Hoovers wanted . . . ," p. 5.

75. Telephone interview with Edgar McDowell (son of J. E. McDowell), November 12, 1986.

76. Edgar McDowell was so informed by his parents. Ibid.

77. Clark, *Memoirs*, p. 14; Lou Henry Hoover to Edgar Rickard, March 3, 1925. (In this letter Mrs. Hoover mistakenly recalled purchasing the McDowell house in 1918.)

78. McDowell interview.

79. Lou Henry Hoover to Edgar Rickard, March 3, 1925

80. Edgar Eugene Robinson to Hoover, January 14, 1919, Edgar Eugene Robinson Papers, Box 2, Stanford University Archives.

81. Charles B. Burdick, *Ralph H. Lutz and the Hoover Institution* (Stanford, Calif., 1974), p. 9.

82. No reply by Hoover has been found.

83. Hoover, cable no. "Food 665," April 22, 1919 (cited in note 61).

84. Ray Lyman Wilbur and Edgar Rickard, telegram to Lou Henry Hoover, April 30, 1919, Hoover Institution Records, Series F-02, HI; Edgar Rickard cable no. "Food 689" to Hoover, May 13, 1919, ibid.; Witold S. Sworakowski, unpublished typescript history of Hoover Institution, chap. 3, p. 3, Hoover Institution Records, Series T-16, Box 241C.

85. Hoover cable no. "Food 789" to Edgar Rickard, May 15, 1919, American Relief Administration Papers, New York—Paris Cable File, Box 13, HI; Edgar Rickard telegram to Ray Lyman Wilbur, May 15, 1919, Hoover Institution Records, Series F-02 (copy in "Documents Relating to the Founding and Establishment of the Hoover Institution" [typescript, n.d.], in Hoover Institution Records, Series F-03).

86. E. D. Adams, *The Hoover War Collection at Stanford University, California: A Report and an Analysis* (Stanford, Calif., 1921), p. 9.

87. Burdick, *Ralph H. Lutz*, p. 10.

88. E. D. Adams to Ray Lyman Wilbur, June 16, 1919, Hoover Institution Records, Series D-03, Box 156.

89. E. D. Adams to Ray Lyman Wilbur, February 4, 1920, Hoover Institution Records, Series F-03.

90. Adams to Wilbur, August 9, 1921, Hoover Institution Records, Series F-01.

91. Hoover to E. D. Adams, June 20, 1919, "Adams, E. D.," Pre-Commerce Papers.

92. Adams to Wilbur, August 20, 1919, Hoover Institution Records, Series D-03, Box 156.

93. Hoover to whom it may concern, July 29, 1919, Hoover Institution Records, Series D-01, Box 189.

94. Hoover to ARA personnel, July 29, 1919, Hoover Institution Records, Series F-01, Box 1.

95. Lewis Strauss to E. D. Adams, June 21, 1919; Hoover to Major General J. C. Harbord, August 7, 1919. Both in Hoover Institution Records, Series D-03, Box 156.

96. Hoover to Harbord, August 7, 1919.

97. Binkley's salary came out of Hoover's $50,000 fund, Lutz's evidently from the ARA, which became a private organization (headed by Hoover) in July 1919. See E. D. Adams's itemized statement of expenses for the "Hoover History Fund," January 1, 1920, enclosed with Ray Lyman Wilbur to the Stanford University board of trustees, January 30, 1920, in Board of Trustees Supporting Documents, January 30, 1920 folder, Stanford University Archives.

98. Adams to Wilbur, February 4, 1920.

99. The phrase was General John J. Pershing's.

100. Adams to Wilbur, February 4, 1920.

101. Adams, *Hoover War Collection*, p. 9.

102. Ray Lyman Wilbur, quoted in *Stanford Observer*, April 1985, sec. 2: *Hoover Today*, p. 6.

103. Adams to Wilbur, February 4, 1920.

104. Hoover to whom it may concern (in behalf of Lutz), September 2, 1919, Hoover Institution Records, Series D-03, Box 156; Burdick, *Ralph H. Lutz*, pp. 17–34.

105. "Herbert Hoover" (actually E. D. Adams) cable to Henry Suzzallo, August 30, 1919, Hoover Institution Records, Series D-03, Box 156; Adams to Wilbur, September 18, 1919, Hoover Institution Records, Series D-03, Box 156.

106. Adams to Wilbur, February 4, 1920.

107. *New York Times*, September 14, 1919, p. 17.

108. "A Man and the Game," *Stanford Illustrated Review* 21 (November 1919): 90.

109. Memorial resolution for Theodore J. Hoover, 1955, Faculty File, Stanford University Archives.

110. Wilbur, *Memoirs*, p. 299.

111. Report by Hoover and two other trustees to the Stanford board of trustees, n.d. but ca. October 11, 1919, in Board of Trustees Supporting Documents, October 11, 1919 folder, Stanford University Archives.

112. Ibid.

113. Hoover press release, September 27, 1919, Public Statements File, HHPL.

114. Report by Hoover et al., n.d.; Hoover, letter, October 16, 1919, to the editor of the *Daily Palo Alto*. This letter was printed in part in the *Daily Palo Alto,* October 17, 1919, and in entirety in the *Stanford Illustrated Review* 21 (November 1919): 88–89, 104–5. A copy is in "Stanford—Tuition, 1919," Pre-Commerce Papers. Quotations are drawn from the version published in the *Stanford Illustrated Review*.

115. Stanford University Board of Trustees Minutes, September 26, 1919, Stanford University Archives.

116. Ibid., October 11, 1919.

117. The university had heretofore charged certain incidental and special fees but no general tuition.

118. Report by Hoover et al., n.d.; Stanford University Board of Trustees Minutes, October 11, 1919.

119. Stanford University Board of Trustees Minutes, October 11, 1919; Ray Lyman Wilbur to the Board of Trustees, October 11, 1919, in Board of Trustees Supporting Documents, October 11, 1919 folder.

120. David Starr Jordan, for one, greatly regretted the change but added that it "had to be." David Starr Jordan to Anna G. Lyle, October 18, 1919, David Starr Jordan Papers, Box 25, HI.

121. Jane Stanford, address of October 3, 1902, quoted in Stanford University,

The Founding Grant with Amendments, Legislation, and Court Decrees (Stanford, Calif., 1971), p. 24.

122. "Tuition as the Students See It," *Stanford Illustrated Review* 21 (November 1919): 90, 110.

123. In her address on October 3, 1902, in which she amended the Founding Grant, Mrs. Stanford had also decreed: "The Board of Trustees shall determine whether or not any charge for tuition, or registration fee, shall be levied in any department of the University, and the amount of such charge or fee; and it may exempt residents of California from the payment of any such charge or fee." It is not clear from this text whether or not Mrs. Stanford contemplated the eventual imposition of a *general* tuition fee, but the trustees in 1919 construed this passage as legal warrant to do so. See Trustee Charles P. Eells's memorandum, "As to the Power and right of the Stanford Trustees to collect Tuition Fees from students under existing law" (n.d., but ca. October 11, 1919), in Board of Trustees Supporting Documents, October 11, 1919 folder.

124. Hoover letter of October 16, 1919, as printed in *Stanford Illustrated Review*.

125. Wilbur, *Memoirs*, p. 299.

126. *New York Times*, November 14, 1919, p. 17.

127. Ray Lyman Wilbur to Hoover, January 3, 1920, "Wilbur, Ray Lyman and Marguerite," Personal Correspondence, 1874–1920, Lou Henry Hoover Papers.

128. Hoover to Dr. Wallace Buttrick, January 21, 1920, "Stanford—General Education Board," Pre-Commerce Papers.

129. Hoover telegram to his wife, November 13, 1919, "Stanford—Home for Convalescent Children," Pre-Commerce Papers; Ray Lyman Wilbur to Edgar Rickard, February 21, 1920, Ray Lyman Wilbur Personal Papers, Box 36, Stanford University Archives.

130. Edgar Rickard telegram to Lou Henry Hoover, June 13, 1919, "Stanford—War Memorial," Pre-Commerce Papers. Hoover made the payment in 1922. Receipt, dated October 3, 1922, in Wilbur Personal Papers, Box 36.

131. Hoover to Wilbur, February 28, 1920, in Wilbur Personal Papers, Box 36.

132. Ibid.

133. Stanford University Board of Trustees Minutes, April 30, 1920, August 27, 1920, and February 25, 1921; Wilbur to Hoover, August 28, 1920, "Stanford—Union," Pre-Commerce Papers; J. Pearce Mitchell, *Stanford University, 1916–1941* (Stanford, Calif., 1958), p. 9. The precise sum appropriated by the trustees to the Stanford Union expansion project is uncertain. The trustees' minutes indicate an initial commitment of $100,000 (April 1920), raised to $126,000 (August) and supplemented by $50,000 more (February 1921). However, a trustees' resolution on November 5, 1920 referred to an authorized expenditure of $130,000 to date, which with the $50,000 added the following February would make a total of $180,000. And Mitchell, the university's historian, reported the total loan as $200,000. Hoover's own contribution of $100,000, of course, was an outright gift.

134. Board of Trustees Minutes, April 30, 1920.

135. According to Hoover's fellow trustee Leland Cutler, it was primarily Hoover who secured Bakewell and Brown's first Stanford assignment: design of the Thomas Welton Stanford Art Gallery (completed in 1917). On one occasion in later years, said Cutler, Hoover "made a particularly strong battle" to retain Bakewell and Brown as the university's architects. Leland W. Cutler, *America Is Good to a Country Boy* (Stanford, Calif., 1954), pp. 68–69.

136. Hoover reviewed, and commented upon, the plans. Hoover to Wilbur, June 4, 1920; Wilbur to Hoover, August 28, 1920. Both in Ray Lyman Wilbur Papers, Box 120, HI.

137. *Annual Report of the President of Stanford University for the Twenty-ninth Academic Year Ending August 31, 1920* (Stanford, Calif., 1920), p. 26.

138. Stanford University Board of Trustees Minutes, August 27, 1920. See also report by Hoover et al., n.d. (ca. October 11, 1919).

139. Aileen Sinclair to Hoover, September 22, 1921, "Stanford University: 1921–1923," Commerce Papers, Herbert Hoover Papers, HHPL.

140. Stanford University Board of Trustees Minutes, August 2, 1920.

141. Ray Lyman Wilbur to the Board of Trustees, November 4, 1920, Board of Trustees Supporting Documents, November 5, 1920 folder.

142. Hoover letter, October 16, 1919. According to Hoover, this was the sum available after "necessary depreciation."

143. Stanford University Board of Trustees Minutes, November 5, 1920; *Annual Report of the President of Stanford University for the Thirtieth Academic Year Ending August 31, 1921* (Stanford, Calif., 1921), pp. 22–27.

144. Stanford University Board of Trustees Minutes, November 5, 1920.

145. The trustee was William B. Bourn. See Ray Lyman Wilbur to Hoover, January 17 and February 14, 1921; Wilbur telegram to Hoover, February 25, 1921. All in Wilbur Personal Papers, Box 31.

146. Wilbur to Hoover, January 17, 1921.

147. Mitchell, *Stanford University, 1916–1941*, p. 12; Peter C. Allen, *Stanford: From the Foothills to the Bay* (Stanford, Calif., 1980), p. 223; *Annual Report of the President of Stanford University for the Thirty-sixth Academic Year Ending August 31, 1927* (Stanford, 1927), p. 13.

148. Ray Lyman Wilbur to the Board of Trustees, January 6, 1920, Board of Trustees Supporting Documents, January 30, 1920 folder.

149. Stanford University Board of Trustees Minutes, January 30, 1920; Leon Sloss to Hoover, February 10, 1920, in Board of Trustees Supporting Documents, January 30, 1920 folder.

150. Hoover to Frank L. Polk, April 7, 1920, Hoover Institution Records, Series D-01, Box 189.

151. Burdick, *Ralph H. Lutz*, pp. 34–37.

152. Wilbur to the Board of Trustees, January 6, 1920.

153. Burdick, *Ralph H. Lutz*, pp. 37–40; Peter Duignan, *The Library of the*

Hoover Institution on War, Revolution and Peace (Stanford, Calif., 1985), p. 5; Allen Glen Wachhold, "Frank A. Golder: An Adventure in Russian History" (Ph.D. dissertation, University of California at Santa Barbara, 1984).

154. *Annual Report of the President of Stanford University for the Thirty-first Academic Year Ending August 31, 1922* (Stanford, Calif., 1922), p. 6; Hoover, memorandum entitled "The Stanford Food Research Institute" (May 16, 1942), and Hoover memorandum entitled "Food Research Institute" (January 25, 1956), in "Stanford University—Food Research Institute," Post-Presidential Subject File, Herbert Hoover Papers, HHPL.

155. *Stanford Illustrated Review* 22 (May 1921): 305.

156. Ray Lyman Wilbur to Dr. Alonzo E. Taylor, July 30, 1920, Wilbur Personal Papers, Box 82.

157. Stanford University Board of Trustees Minutes, August 2, 1920; Hoover to James R. Angell, November 19, 1920, Food Research Institute Papers, Box 1, HI.

158. Hoover to James R. Angell, November 29, 1920, Food Research Institute Papers, Box 1.

159. *Annual Report of the President of Stanford University . . . August 31, 1921*, pp. 7–9.

160. *Daily Palo Alto*, February 28, 1921, p. 1; *Stanford Illustrated Review* 22 (May 1921): 305.

161. Ernest Barbour O'Byrne, "The Research Institutes of Stanford University" (Ph.D. dissertation, Stanford University, 1951), p. 54.

162. *Daily Palo Alto*, February 28, 1921, p. 1; *Stanford Illustrated Review* 22 (May 1921): 305.

163. Hoover, "Food Research Institute" (1956).

164. *Daily Palo Alto*, February 28, 1921, p. 2.

165. Wilbur, *Memoirs*, p. 278.

166. *Annual Report of the President of Stanford University . . . August 31, 1921*, p. 9.

167. John Maynard Keynes, *The Economic Consequences of the Peace* (London, 1920), p. 257n.

CHAPTER 5

1. Lou Henry Hoover to Ray Lyman Wilbur, October 3, 1923, Ray Lyman Wilbur Personal Papers, Box 31, Stanford University Archives; Wilbur to Lou Henry Hoover, October 3, 1923, ibid.; Wilbur to Stanford University Board of Trustees, October 24, 1923, in Board of Trustees Supporting Documents, Box 15, Stanford University Archives.

2. Memorial resolution for Theodore J. Hoover, 1955, Faculty Files, Stanford University Archives.

3. Hoover's speech is in the Public Statements File, Herbert Hoover Presidential Library (hereinafter HHPL).

4. *Annual Report of the President of Stanford University for the Thirtieth Academic Year Ending August 31, 1921* (Stanford, Calif., 1921), p. 27; Ray Lyman Wilbur to the men and women of Stanford, January 23, 1922, Hoover Institution Records, Series D-03, Box 156, Hoover Institution on War, Revolution and Peace (hereinafter HI); J. Pearce Mitchell, *Stanford University, 1916–1941* (Stanford, Calif., 1958), p. 35.

5. Hoover to Ray Lyman Wilbur, January 31, 1922, Hoover Institution Records, Series D-03, Box 156.

6. Mitchell, *Stanford University*, pp. 35–36; J. E. McDowell to Herbert Hoover, October 3, 1927, "Stanford University—Stanford Alumni," Commerce Papers, Herbert Hoover Papers, HHPL. In 1927 Hoover gave $500 to the "First Million for Stanford" campaign. It is not known how much he may have contributed earlier.

7. Ray Lyman Wilbur to the parents of Stanford University students, August 5, 1916. Quoted in Ray Lyman Wilbur, *The Memoirs of Ray Lyman Wilbur* (Stanford, Calif., 1960), pp. 217, 221–22.

8. Associated Students of Stanford University, *The Centennial Newsletter, 1985–1991: 1986 Edition*, pp. 19–20, copy in Stanford University Archives.

9. Herbert Hoover to Ray Lyman Wilbur, n.d. [November 1924], in Wilbur Personal Papers, Box 106; typed copy (with a few alterations) in appendix to Ray Lyman Wilbur, Jr. oral history (1971), HHPL.

10. [Unknown author] to William H. Crocker, July 30, 1924, "Stanford University," Commerce Papers; *San Francisco Examiner*, August 6, 1924.

11. *San Francisco Examiner*, September 19, 1924; "A School of Business Administration," *Stanford Illustrated Review* 26 (October 1924): 18; *Annual Report of the President of Stanford University for the Thirty-fourth Academic Year Ending August 31, 1925* (Stanford, Calif., 1926), p. 39; Warren H. McBryde, "Stanford Graduate School of Business: Its Conception, Inception, and Beginnings," Graduate School of Business, Stanford University, *Alumni Bulletin* 21 (November 1951): 1–3. McBryde's article is a valuable one, but it mistakenly dates Hoover's Bohemian Club speech as occurring in July 1921. The correct date is August 2, 1924.

12. Hoover to Wallace Alexander, n.d. (but ca. August 15, 1924), Herbert Hoover Papers, Box 343, HI.

13. Stanford University Board of Trustees Minutes, June 18, 1925, Stanford University Archives; *Annual Report of the President of Stanford University . . . August 31, 1925*, p. 39.

14. Mitchell, *Stanford University*, p. 80. Harvard's, of course, was the other.

15. McBryde, "Stanford Graduate School of Business," p. 3.

16. Weldon B. Gibson, *SRI: The Founding Years* (Los Altos, Calif., 1980), pp. 1–15.

17. Charles B. Burdick, *Ralph H. Lutz and the Hoover Institution* (Stanford, Calif., 1974), p. 46.

18. "The Hoover War Library," *Concerning Stanford* 1 (June 1925): 4.

19. Hoover interview in the *Morning Oregonian* (Portland), August 23, 1926; copy in "Oregon Collections," HHPL.

20. For example, Hoover to Tasker H. Bliss, June 24, 1924, Hoover Institution Records, Series F-01, Box 1A.

21. For information on Hoover's use of Department of Commerce attachés to secure material abroad for his war library, see Hoover Institution Records, Series F-01, Box 2.

22. Julius Klein memo to Lawrence Richey, n.d. but ca. September 19, 1927; Klein to E. D. Adams, September 19, 1927; Klein to C. E. Herring, September 19, 1927. All in ibid.

23. E. D. Adams to Ray Lyman Wilbur, October 19, 1922, in Wilbur Personal Papers, Box 1.

24. Adams to Frank A. Golder, January 8, 1923, copy in Hoover Institution Records, Series D-03, Box 156.

25. Adams to Hoover, January 10, 1924, Hoover Institution Records, Series D-01, Box 1; copy in E. D. Adams Papers, Box 2, Stanford University Archives.

26. Ibid.

27. Adams to Wilbur, August 27, 1919, Hoover Institution Records, Series F-02; quoted in Gary Norman Paul, "The Development of the Hoover Institution on War, Revolution and Peace Library, 1919–1944" (Ph.D. dissertation, University of California at Berkeley, 1974), p. 7.

28. *Daily Palo Alto Times*, March 7, 1941, 50th anniversary of Stanford University supplement, p. 7; Witold S. Sworakowski, unpublished history of the Hoover Institution, chapter completed March 3, 1970, pp. 2–3, copy in Hoover Institution Records, Series T-16, Box 242A.

29. Burdick, *Ralph H. Lutz*, pp. 41–42.

30. Hoover interview in *Morning Oregonian* (Portland), August 23, 1926.

31. Adams's word. Adams to Frank A. Golder, January 23, 1923, Hoover Institution Records, Series D-03, Box 156.

32. Burdick, *Ralph H. Lutz*, p. 42.

33. Ibid., pp. 40, 42.

34. For example, see George T. Clark to Frank A. Golder, August 18, 1924, copy in Hoover Institution Records, Series D-03, Box 19.

35. Hoover to Wilbur, January 16, 1924, Hoover Institution Records, Series D-03, Box 156.

36. Alonzo E. Taylor to Hoover, August 9, 1921, ibid.

37. Hoover to Taylor, August 17, 1921, ibid., Series F-01, Box 1.

38. Adams to Christian Herter, August 9, 1921, ibid.

39. Adams to Wilbur, November 18, 1921, ibid., Series D-01, Box 1; Wilbur to George T. Clark, November 22, 1921, ibid., Series D-03, Box 156. Wilbur's letter was also printed in the *Annual Report of the President of Stanford University for*

the Thirty-first Academic Year Ending August 31, 1922 (Stanford, Calif., 1922), pp. 218–19.

40. Hoover to Adams, December 14, 1921, Hoover Institution Records, Series F-01, Box 1.

41. *Annual Report of the President of Stanford University . . . August 31, 1922,* p. 219.

42. Burdick, *Ralph H. Lutz,* pp. 49, 52.

43. Ibid., p. 55.

44. George I. Gay and H. H. Fisher, *Public Relations of the Commission for Relief in Belgium,* vol. 2 (Stanford, Calif., 1929), pp. 212, 485.

45. CRB memorandum of discussion on liquidation, June 14, 1922, Commission for Relief in Belgium Liquidation Records, Box 5, HI; Hoover to the CRB directors, August 7, 1922, ibid.; Ray Lyman Wilbur to the Stanford University Board of Trustees, September 12, 1922, Board of Trustees Supporting Documents, Box 15.

46. Hoover to the CRB directors, August 7, 1922.

47. Memorandum of agreement between the Board of Trustees of Stanford University and the Commission for Relief in Belgium, enclosed with Wilbur to the Board of Trustees, September 12, 1922. See also CRB memorandum of discussion on liquidation, June 14, 1922.

48. Hoover to Wilbur (plus enclosure), August 16, 1922, Wilbur Personal Papers, Box 32.

49. Hoover to the Belgian ambassador to the United States, August 19, 1922, Commission for Relief in Belgium Liquidation Records, Box 5.

50. Stanford University Board of Trustees Minutes, September 29, 1922; Wilbur to Edgar Rickard and William B. Poland, September 29, 1922, Wilbur Personal Papers, Box 32.

51. Wilbur to the Board of Trustees, January 10, 1923, Board of Trustees Supporting Documents, Box 15.

52. Adams to Golder, January 23, 1923.

53. Ibid.

54. See Adams to Edgar Rickard, January 29, 1923, Hoover Institution Records, Series F-01, Box 1.

55. Wilbur to Adams, January 27, 1923, ibid., Series D-03, Box 156.

56. Burdick, *Ralph H. Lutz,* pp. 54–55.

57. Note Wilbur's announced "inclination" (January 27, 1923) to give Clark control of acquisitions for the Hoover War Library

58. Adams to Ralph Lutz, June 25, 1923, Hoover Institution Records, Series D-03, Box 156.

59. Ibid.

60. Hoover to Wilbur, September 1, 1923, "Wilbur, Ray Lyman," Commerce Papers.

61. Adams to Hoover, August 17, 1923, Hoover Institution Records, Series F-01, Box 1.

62. Hoover to the Trustees of the ARA, August 31, 1923, copy in Board of Trustees Supporting Documents, Box 15.

63. Memorandum of agreement between the ARA and Stanford University, November 1923, Board of Trustees Supporting Documents, Box 16; Hoover to Wilbur, September 14, 1923, Hoover Institution Records, Series F-02. See also Wilbur to the Board of Trustees, September 20, 1923, Board of Trustees Supporting Documents, Box 15.

64. Hoover to Wilbur, September 1, 1923.

65. Hoover to the ARA trustees, August 31, 1923.

66. Memorandum of agreement, November 1923.

67. Hoover to Wilbur, September 1, 1923.

68. Wilbur to Hoover, October 2, 1923, Hoover Institution Records, Series F-01, Box 1.

69. E. D. Adams et al., "Report requested by President Wilbur on plan of organization of Hoover War Library" (n.d. but probably late 1923 or very early 1924), Hoover Institution Records, Series D-03, Box 156. This typewritten report includes a summary of a conference with President Wilbur on October 2, 1923.

70. Wilbur to Hoover, October 2, 1923.

71. Adams et al., "Report"; Wilbur to Hoover, October 2, 1923.

72. Adams et al., "Report."

73. Ray Lyman Wilbur to the Board of Trustees (plus enclosure: "Plan of Organization of the Hoover War Library"), February 1, 1924, Board of Trustees Supporting Documents, Box 16.

74. "Plan of Organization of the Hoover War Library."

75. Ibid.; Hoover to Wilbur, January 16, 1924.

76. Hoover to Wilbur, February 6, 1924, Hoover Institution Records, Series D-03, Box 156.

77. Wilbur to Hoover, February 12, 1924, Hoover Institution Records, Series F-01, Box 1.

78. Hoover to Wilbur, February 20, 1924, ibid.

79. Wilbur to D. P. Blodgett, March 21, 1924, Board of Trustees Supporting Documents, Box 16.

80. In 1919, 1920, and 1921 Hoover's fund was the sole source of income for his library. In 1922 the University began to help defray the cost of its operation. For a list of the university's contributions from 1922 to 1945, see D. I. McFadden to Alvin C. Eurich, August 29, 1946, in Donald B. Tresidder Papers, Box 11, Stanford University Archives.

81. Wilbur to the Board of Trustees, September 18, 1924, in Board of Trustees Supporting Documents, Box 16.

82. Edgar Rickard to Ralph Lutz, April 28, 1937, Hoover Institution Records, Series T-02, Box 71, HI.

83. Hoover to Bliss, June 24, 1924.

84. Rickard to Lutz, April 28, 1937.

85. Ibid. This author is unable to verify Hoover's recollection. In 1937, when Hoover made his statement, evidently no one asked him for corroboration. Hoover was known to have an excellent memory, and for Rickard (who handled his financial records) this was enough.

86. Lutz to Rickard, May 5, 1937, Hoover Institution Records, Series T-02, Box 71; account sheet entitled "Hoover Institute and Library: Funds Received and Expenditures from 1919 to August 31, 1947," in Tresidder Papers, Box 12.

87. Hoover to Donald B. Tresidder, March 15, 1946, Tresidder Papers, Box 11.

88. Hoover to Wilbur, January 16, 1924.

89. Ibid.

90. Adams et al., "Report."

91. Frank A. Golder and Harold H. Fisher, "Memorandum for Mr. Hoover" (August 6, 1924), Hoover Institution Records, Series D-03, Box 156.

92. Hoover to Wilbur, August 8, 1924, Hoover Institution Records, Series F-02; copy in "Wilbur, Ray Lyman," Commerce Papers.

93. Hoover, draft letter to the Board of Trustees, n.d., attached to ibid.

94. Hoover to Wilbur, August 8, 1924.

95. Ralph H. Lutz, "The Hoover War Library Grows Yearly in Importance as a Great Field for Historical Research," *Stanford Illustrated Review* 24 (June 1923): 464–65.

96. Hoover to Wilbur, August 8, 1924.

97. Wilbur to the Board of Trustees, September 18, 1924.

98. Stanford University Board of Trustees Minutes, September 26, 1924; Golder/Fisher memorandum, August 6, 1924.

99. George T. Clark to Frank A. Golder, August 18, 1924 (cited in note 34).

100. *Annual Report of the President of Stanford University . . . August 31, 1925*, pp. 277–78.

101. Ibid., pp. 277–92. For an account of the academic politics involved in preparing this report, see Burdick, *Ralph H. Lutz*, pp. 63–66.

102. Adams to Edgar Rickard, January 9, 1925, Hoover Institution Records, Series D-03, Box 18.

103. Burdick, *Ralph H. Lutz*, p. 41.

104. Ibid., p. 49.

105. Adams to Lutz, June 25, 1923; Adams to Rickard, January 9, 1925.

106. Adams to Rickard, January 9, 1925.

107. Ibid.

108. Rickard to Adams, January 23, 1925, Hoover Institution Records, Series D-03, Box 18.

109. *Annual Report of the President of Stanford University . . . August 31, 1925*, pp. 20, 277.

110. This letter has not been found, but Rickard referred to it in a second letter to members of the CRB, ARA, and U.S. Food Administration on March 27, 1926. A copy of this second letter is in the Hoover Institution Records, Series T-16, Box 241C.

111. Ibid.; Adams to Rickard, January 9, 1925.

112. Burdick, *Ralph H. Lutz*, pp. 62–63.

113. Rickard letter to members of the CRB, ARA, and U.S. Food Administration, March 27, 1926.

114. Lutz to Wilbur, August 22, 1941, quoted in Paul, "Development of the Hoover Institution Library," p. 34; Lutz, draft plan of reorganization of Hoover War Library, July 1927, quoted in ibid., pp. 199–200. (See also p. 195.)

115. Lutz, draft plan of reorganization, July 1927.

116. Lutz memorandum, June 25, 1925, quoted in Paul, "Development of the Hoover Institution Library," pp. 195–96.

117. Burdick, *Ralph H. Lutz*, p. 88.

118. Ibid., p. 86; Paul, "Development of the Hoover Institution Library," p. 199.

119. Lutz to Wilbur, July 25, 1927, copy in Hoover Institution Records, Series D-03, Box 156.

120. Adams to Lutz, August 8, 1927, ibid.

121. Ibid.

122. Wilbur to Lutz, September 15, 1927, ibid.

123. Herbert Hoover, *The Memoirs of Herbert Hoover*, vol. 2: *The Cabinet and the Presidency* (New York, 1952), p. 190.

124. Wilbur, *Memoirs*, pp. 386–87.

125. Will Irwin, *Herbert Hoover: A Reminiscent Biography* (New York, 1928).

126. Wilbur, *Memoirs*, pp. 387–89.

127. Leland W. Cutler to the men and women of Stanford, March 20, 1928, copy in Wilbur Personal Papers, Box 32.

128. Leland W. Cutler to Wilbur, March 26, 1928, ibid.

129. Wilbur, *Memoirs*, p. 387.

130. Stanford University faculty telegram to Hoover, June 16, 1928, "Congratulations on Nomination," Subject File, Campaign and Transition Papers, Hoover Papers, HHPL.

131. Wilbur, *Memoirs*, p. 395.

132. Ibid., pp. 395–98.

133. Ibid., pp. 393−94; Wilbur telegram to Hoover, June 27, 1928, Wilbur Personal Papers, Box 32.

134. Wilbur, *Memoirs*, pp. 398−99; *New York Times*, August 12, 1928, pp. 1, 2.

135. *Stanford Daily*, November 1, 1928, p. 1.

136. Ibid., November 6, 1928, p. 1.

137. Ibid., November 7, 1928, pp. 1, 2, 3; Wilbur, *Memoirs*, p. 401.

138. Francis W. Hirst to E. D. Adams, November 9, 1928, Adams Papers, Box 2.

CHAPTER 6

1. Leland W. Cutler, *America Is Good to a Country Boy* (Stanford, Calif., 1954), p. 246.

2. Stanford University Board of Trustees Minutes, December 19, 1929, Stanford University Archives; Ray Lyman Wilbur, *The Memoirs of Ray Lyman Wilbur* (Stanford, Calif., 1960), p. 403.

3. Wilbur, *Memoirs*, p. 403.

4. *Stanford Daily*, May 15, 1930, p. 2.

5. *New York Times*, May 16, 1930, p. 2; Robert E. Swain to Ray Lyman Wilbur, May 22, 1930, Ray Lyman Wilbur Personal Papers, Box 36, Stanford University Archives.

6. Ray Lyman Wilbur telegram to Robert E. Swain, May 15, 1930, Wilbur Personal Papers, Box 36.

7. Swain to Wilbur, May 22, 1930.

8. Swain statement published in *Stanford Daily*, May 16, 1930, p. 2.

9. [Robert Speers], editorial in *Stanford Daily*, May 16, 1930, p. 2.

10. Swain to Wilbur, May 22, 1930.

11. Wilbur to Swain, May 28, 1930, Wilbur Personal Papers, Box 36.

12. Swain to Wilbur, May 22, 1930; Duncan Aikman, "Hoover-Conscious Stanford," *Outlook and Independent* 156 (November 26, 1930): 498.

13. Aikman, "Hoover-Conscious Stanford," pp. 496−98, 516.

14. Ibid., pp. 497−98; Stanford University Board of Trustees Minutes, December 19, 1929. The trustees initially voted in August 1929 to grant Wilbur a year of sabbatical leave (at reduced salary). In December 1929 they rescinded this resolution and instead granted him a leave of absence with full pay.

15. T. T. C. Gregory to Lawrence Richey, August 27, 1930, Wilbur Personal Papers, Box 77.

16. Ibid.

17. Herbert Hoover telegram to Harry Chandler, August 29, 1930, copy in Wilbur Personal Papers, Box 77.

18. *New York Times*, October 14, 1930, p. 32.

19. *Stanford Daily*, October 13, 1930, p. 1; *New York Times*, October 14, 1930, p. 32, and October 15, 1932, p. 1; *New York Herald Tribune*, October 14, 1930, p. 11.

20. *New York Herald Tribune*, October 15, 1930, p. 14; *Public Papers of the Presidents: Herbert Hoover . . . 1930* (Washington, 1976), pp. 432–33.

21. Ira S. Lillick to Wilbur, October 24, 1930 (two letters), Wilbur Personal Papers, Box 77.

22. *Stanford Chaparral*, October 1930, p. 10.

23. Alonzo E. Taylor to Wilbur, February 28 [1931], Wilbur Personal Papers, Box 82.

24. Thomas P. Pike, *Memoirs of Thomas P. Pike* (San Marino, Calif., 1979), pp. 46–47.

25. A photograph, dated November 12, 1931, of Hoover with Stanford's 1894 football team is in the audiovisual collection at the Herbert Hoover Presidential Library (hereinafter HHPL).

26. For information on Professor Augustus T. Murray's service to President Hoover as a Quaker minister in Washington, see: the August T. Murray Collection, HHPL; the Murray letters in Personal Correspondence, 1929–1933, Lou Henry Hoover Papers, HHPL; and the Lydia Murray Huneke oral history (1967), pp. 1–4, HHPL.

27. Henry M. Robinson to Hoover, April 13, 1931; L. A. Finch to Lawrence Richey, April 17, 1931. Both in Ray Lyman Wilbur Papers, Box 120, Hoover Institution on War, Revolution and Peace (hereinafter HI).

28. Cutler, *America Is Good to a Country Boy*, p. 245.

29. Paul Shoup to Leland W. Cutler, May 23, 1931, Paul Shoup Papers, Box 4, Department of Special Collections, Stanford University Libraries.

30. *New York Times*, June 20, 1931, p. 22; *Stanford Daily*, June 23, 1931, p. 1; Cutler, *America Is Good to a Country Boy*, pp. 246–47.

31. *New York Times*, December 28, 1932, p. 14.

32. Ralph H. Lutz to Edgar Rickard, April 23, 1929, copy in Wilbur Personal Papers, Box 70.

33. Charles B. Burdick, *Ralph H. Lutz and the Hoover Institution* (Stanford, Calif., 1974), pp. 87, 99, 114–17; Gary Norman Paul, "The Development of the Hoover Institution on War, Revolution and Peace Library, 1919–1944" (Ph.D. dissertation, University of California at Berkeley, 1974), p. 201.

34. Edgar Rickard to Swain, March 3, 1932, Hoover Institution Records, Series D-03, Box 156, HI.

35. Rickard to E. D. Adams, January 15, 1930, ibid.

36. Adams to Rickard, January 8, 1930, Hoover Institution Records, Series T-02, Box 71.

37. Adams to Rickard, January 9, 1925, copy in Wilbur Personal Papers, Box

75. For a brief history of the Stanford War Memorial project, see J. Pearce Mitchell, *Stanford University, 1916–1941* (Stanford, Calif., 1958), pp. 5–6.

38. Edgar Rickard to members of the CRB, U.S. Food Administration, and ARA, March 27, 1926, copy in Hoover Institution Records, Series T-16, Box 241C. Another early sketch, cataloged as Map M901, is in the Stanford University Archives.

39. Paul, "Development of the Hoover Institution Library," p. 89.

40. Ralph H. Lutz oral history (1967), pp. 14–15, HHPL.

41. Ibid, p. 15.

42. Lutz to E. D. Adams, May 26, 1930, E. D. Adams Papers, Stanford University Archives; Lutz to Rickard, May 26, 1930, Hoover Institution Records, Series D-03, Box 156; Lutz to Adams, June 2, 1930, ibid., Series D-01, Box 1.

43. Rickard to Lutz, June 2, 1930, Hoover Institution Records, Series D-03, Box 156.

44. Lutz to Rickard, July 27, 1930, ibid.

45. Rickard to Lutz, August 6, 1930, ibid.

46. Mitchell, *Stanford University, 1916–1941*, p. 6.

47. Lutz oral history, p. 16. From the beginning Hoover's friends intended the War Library building to serve (in Rickard's words) as "a memorial to our Chief." Rickard to Hoover War Library Building Fund subscribers, August 17, 1933, Hoover Institution Records, Series D-03, Box 156.

48. Burdick, *Ralph H. Lutz*, p. 98.

49. Rickard to Arthur W. Packard, February 21, 1931, Hoover Institution Records, Series T-02, Box 71.

50. Rickard to Robert E. Swain, March 3, 1932, Hoover Institution Records, Series D-03, Box 156.

51. Burdick, *Ralph H. Lutz*, pp. 114–15.

52. Ibid., p. 117.

53. Rickard to Swain, March 3, 1932.

54. This letter has not been found, but its contents are discussed in Edgar Rickard to Ray Lyman Wilbur, December 19, 1932, Hoover Institution Records, Series D-03, Box 156.

55. Rickard to Wilbur, December 19, 1932.

56. Wilbur to Rickard, December 20, 1932, Hoover Institution Records, Series D-03, Box 156.

57. *Stanford Daily*, October 27, 1932, p. 1.

58. *Stanford Daily*, November 7, 1932, p. 1, November 8, 1932, p. 1, and November 9, 1932, p. 1; *New York Times*, November 9, 1932, p. 14.

59. *San Francisco News*, July 22, 1935, copy in Wilbur Personal Papers, Box 34.

60. I. Harvielle, letter to the editor, *Daily Palo Alto Times*, June 18, 1935, p. 4.

61. Ira S. Lillick to Hoover, March 4, 1937, "Stanford University—Board of Trustees, Correspondence, 1933–37," Post-Presidential Subject File, Herbert Hoover Papers, HHPL; Wilbur to Herbert and Lou Henry Hoover, January 12, 1938, Wilbur Personal Papers, Box 34.

62. Susan Dyer, "The Friends of Music at Stanford" (1959), copy in Stanford University Archives; Elise Kirk, *Music at the White House* (Urbana and Chicago, Ill., 1986), pp. 208–9.

63. Among them: Bernice Miller, Dare Stark McMullin, and Paul Sexson.

64. Wilbur to Hoover, September 20, 1937, Wilbur Personal Papers, Box 34.

65. Weldon B. Gibson, *SRI: The Founding Years* (Los Altos, Calif., 1980), p. 15.

66. Ray Lyman Wilbur to members of the academic staff, March 17, 1933, Hoover Institution Records, Series D-03, Box 156.

67. Hoover address to Stanford University alumni, New York City, October 10, 1935, Public Statements File, HHPL.

68. A. F. Manspeaker to Hoover, July 7, 1961 (plus enclosure), "Stanford University Board of Trustees," Post-Presidential Subject File, Hoover Papers.

69. Ibid.; Hoover statement before San Jose Superior Court, February 10, 1936, "Stanford University Board of Trustees," Post-Presidential Subject File; *New York Times*, February 11, 1936, p. 14; Ray Lyman Wilbur to Arthur Hill Daniels, February 11, 1936, Wilbur Personal Papers, Box 34; Wilbur to Edgar Rickard, February 11, 1936, Wilbur Personal Papers, Box 36.

70. Judge William F. James, memorandum opinion, February 25, 1936, copy in "Stanford University Board of Trustees," Post-Presidential Subject File.

71. Manspeaker to Hoover, July 7, 1961.

72. Wilbur to Hoover, March 20, 1943, Wilbur Personal Papers, Box 35.

73. Manspeaker to Hoover, July 7, 1961.

74. Hoover to Wilbur, October 6, 1933, Hoover Institution Records, Series D-03, Box 156; [Ralph H. Lutz?], "Collecting Program for the Hoover War Library" (October 1933), Hoover Institution Records, Series D-03, Box 156.

75. Joseph S. Davis to Lutz, October 14, 1933, ibid.

76. Hoover to Wilbur, November 14, 1938, Hoover Institution Records, Series F-01, Box 1A. The suggestion for a change of name evidently came from Hoover's friend Harvey Mudd. See Ralph H. Lutz memorandum to Ray Lyman Wilbur, May 14, 1938, Hoover Institution Records, Series D-03, Box 156.

77. Wilbur to Hoover, November 18, 1938, Hoover Institution Records, Series F-01, Box 1A.

78. Ernest Barbour O'Byrne, "The Research Institutes of Stanford University" (Ph.D. dissertation, Stanford University, 1951), p. 94.

79. *Annual Report of the President of Stanford University for the Forty-fourth Academic Year Ending August 31, 1925* (Stanford, Calif., 1935), p. 405. Of the seven

volumes published in 1934–1935, four were new and three were reissues of studies that had appeared before the publication series was begun.

80. Ibid.; minutes of meeting of the publications committee of the Hoover Library on War, Revolution and Peace, February 18, 1941, Ray Lyman Wilbur Presidential Papers, Box 113, Stanford University Archives.

81. Paul, "Development of the Hoover Institution Library," p. 231; Wilbur to Hoover, October 21, 1936 (plus enclosure), Hoover Institution Records, Series F-01, Box 1A.

82. Wilbur to Rickard, March 22, 1933, Hoover Institution Records, Series D-03, Box 156.

83. Wilbur to the Stanford University Board of Trustees, March 25, 1933, Board of Trustees Supporting Documents, Box 20, Stanford University Archives; Stanford University Board of Trustees Minutes, April 20, 1933; Wilbur to Hoover, May 3, 1934 (plus enclosure), Hoover Institution Records, Series F-01, Box 1A.

84. *Annual Report of the President of Stanford University, August 31, 1925,* p. 405; Paul, "Development of the Hoover Institution Library," p. 77.

85. Hoover to Frederick P. Keppel, October 2, 1937, Hoover Institution Records, Series F-01, Box 1A.

86. Stanford University Board of Trustees Minutes, April 20, 1933; financial sheet entitled "Payments to Leland Stanford Junior University" (October 27, 1938), Hoover Institution Records, Series F-01, Box 1A; Hoover to Wilbur, November 8, 1938, "Hoover Institution on War, Revolution and Peace," Post-Presidential Subject File, Hoover Papers; Hoover to Wilbur, January 22, 1941, Wilbur Presidential Papers, Box 113. By later 1938 the ARA had contributed $65,000 toward the Hoover Library's Washington office.

87. Hoover to Wilbur, January 22, 1941.

88. Lutz oral history, p. 16.

89. *New York Times*, December 9, 1938, p. 52; Burdick, *Ralph H. Lutz*, p. 132; Paul, "Development of the Hoover Institution Library," pp. 93–94.

90. Stanford University Board of Trustees Minutes, January 21, 1937; Edgar Rickard to the members of the ARA, April 19, 1937; Rickard to Wilbur, May 12, 1937, Hoover Institution Records, Series F-01, Box 1A.

91. Rickard to Wilbur, November 2, 1938, Hoover Institution Records, Series F-01, Box 1A; Stanford University Board of Trustees Minutes, November 17, 1938; Wilbur to Rickard, November 23, 1938 (two letters), Hoover Institution Records, Series F-01, Box 1A; Rickard to Wilbur, December 13, 1938, Wilbur Presidential Papers, Box 102.

92. Hoover to Keppel, October 2, 1937.

93. Hoover to Arthur W. Packard, October 9, 1937, Hoover Institution Records, Series F-01, Box 1A.

94. Hoover to Wilbur, October 28, 1937, ibid.

95. In addition to the sources cited in note 47, see Rickard to Wilbur, November 2, 1938. In this letter Rickard stated that the Belgian American Educational

Foundation "would like to look upon the Library as a permanent memorial to Herbert Hoover and the organization he created during the war and developed during the post-war period."

96. Arthur Brown, Jr. to Ray Lyman Wilbur, July 27, 1937, quoted in Paul, "Development of the Hoover Institution Library," p. 96; Hoover to Keppel, October 2, 1937.

97. *New York Times*, December 9, 1938, p. 52.

98. See the architect's drawing printed in ibid.

99. Architect's drawing of the Hoover Library tower, April 19, 1939, Hoover Institution Records. See also the drawing printed in *Stanford Illustrated Review* 41 (September 1939): 11.

100. *Stanford Illustrated Review* 41 (September 1939): 11; undated newspaper clipping (ca. 1945), in Hoover Institution Records, Series F-01, Box 4; Hoover, "The Library on War, Revolution and Peace at Stanford University" (typescript, January 8, 1956), in "Hoover Institution on War, Revolution and Peace—Correspondence," Post-Presidential Subject File, Hoover Papers; Hoover to Lloyd Dinkelspiel, August 31, 1957, "Hoover Institution—Dinkelspiel Correspondence," ibid. Wrote Hoover in this last document: "The War Library Tower is an enlargement of one of the two towers of the classic Romanesque Cathedral at Salamanca." The first two sources cited in this note state that the tower design was also drawn from the cathedral in Mexico City, but Hoover himself did not confirm this claim.

101. Hoover, "The Library" (January 8, 1956).

102. *Stanford Illustrated Review* 41 (September 1939): 11.

103. Wilbur, remarks at the dedication of the Hoover Library building in 1941; printed in *Dedication of the Hoover Library on War, Revolution and Peace, Stanford University, June 20, 1941* (Stanford, Calif., 1941), p. 41.

104. *Stanford Daily*, January 4, 1939, pp. 1, 2; *Stanford Illustrated Review* 41 (September 1939): 11.

105. *Stanford Daily*, January 4, 1939, p. 2.

106. Letters to the editor in ibid., January 6, 1939, p. 4, and January 11, 1939, p. 4.

107. Burdick, *Ralph H. Lutz*, p. 166.

108. Wilbur to Hoover, November 15, 1939, Hoover Institution Records, Series F-01, Box 1A.

109. *Stanford Daily*, September 22, 1939, p. 1.

110. Wilbur to Hoover, November 15, 1939.

111. Extracts of minutes of the directors' meeting of the American Children's Fund, March 9, 1939; Rickard to Wilbur, June 8, 1939; Lutz to Wilbur, June 8, 1939; Wilbur to Raymond Sawtelle, June 24, 1939. All in Wilbur Presidential Papers, Box 102. See also Lutz to Rickard, March 27, 1939, quoted in Paul, "Development of the Hoover Institution Library," pp. 78—79.

112. For an account of Lutz's 1939 trip to Europe, see Burdick, *Ralph H. Lutz*, pp. 140–64.

113. Hoover Library cost estimate sheet, January 22, 1940, Hoover Institution Records, Series D-03, Box 156; Donald B. Tresidder to Hoover, August 6, 1946, Donald B. Tresidder Papers, Box 11, Stanford University Archives; D. I. McFadden to Alvin C. Eurich, August 29, 1946, ibid.; "Hoover Institute and Library: Funds Received and Expenditures from 1919 to August 31, 1947," in ibid., Box 12.

As of August 31, 1946, nearly $635,000 had been spent on constructing the Hoover Library. The university's portion of this amount was a little over $96,000. The bulk of the funds came from the Belgian American Educational Foundation ($300,000), the ARA (more than $142,000), and John D. Rockefeller, Jr. ($50,000). Miscellaneous contributors supplied the rest.

114. Burdick, *Ralph H. Lutz*, p. 170.

115. Mitchell, *Stanford University, 1916–1941*, pp. 155–56. See also Templeton Peck, *When We Were Fifty: The Story of Stanford's Golden Jubilee* (Stanford, Calif., 1985).

116. Hoover, address at the symposium of the 50th anniversary of Stanford University, June 19, 1941; printed in Herbert Hoover, *Addresses Upon the American Road, 1940–1941* (New York, 1941), pp. 188–95.

117. *Time* 37 (June 30, 1941): 85.

118. Sidney Fay's address, June 20, 1941, printed in *Dedication of the Hoover Library*, pp. 11–14.

119. Charles Seymour's remarks, ibid., pp. 34–35.

120. Edgar Rickard's remarks, ibid., p. 33; Perrin C. Galpin to Ralph H. Lutz, July 18, 1940, "Hoover Institution—Correspondence and Printed Matter, Carillon," Post-Presidential Subject File, Hoover Papers; James B. Angell oral history (1971), pp. 7–8, HHPL.

121. Hoover's dedicatory address, June 20, 1941, printed in *Dedication of the Hoover Library*, pp. 36–39, and in his *Addresses, 1940–1941*, pp. 196–98.

122. Hoover remarks at Stanford University commemorative exercises, October 1, 1941, Public Statements File, Hoover Papers.

123. Wilbur, *Memoirs*, p. 584n. Wilbur was scheduled to leave the presidency and become chancellor on January 1, 1942.

CHAPTER 7

1. Herbert Hoover, *An American Epic*, vol. 4 (Chicago, 1964), pp. 17–73; Hoover, *Addresses Upon the American Road, 1940–1941* (New York, 1941), pp. 117–61.

2. Hoover to Ray Lyman Wilbur, October 19, 1940, "Stanford University—Food Research Institute," Post-Presidential Subject File, Herbert Hoover Papers,

Herbert Hoover Presidential Library (hereinafter HHPL); Hoover, "The Stanford Food Research Institute" (typescript, May 16, 1942), ibid.

3. Hoover to Wilbur, October 19, 1940.

4. Hoover to Wilbur, December 20, 1940, "Stanford University—Food Research Institute," Post-Presidential Subject File.

5. Karl Brandt, "How Europe Is Fighting Famine," *Foreign Affairs* 19 (July 1941): 806–17.

6. Hoover press release, ca. July 1941, quoted in Hoover, "Food Research Institute" (typescript, January 25, 1956), in "Stanford University—Food Research Institute," Post-Presidential Subject File.

7. Karl Brandt to Hoover, March 28, 1940, quoted in Hoover, "Food Research Institute."

8. Joseph Davis statement, July 19, 1941, quoted in Hoover, "Food Research Institute."

9. Hoover, "Stanford Food Research Institute."

10. Ibid.

11. Hoover, "Food Research Institute."

12. Ibid.

13. Hoover to Karl Brandt, October 10, 1945, "Stanford University—Food Research Institute," Post-Presidential Subject File. I have found no evidence that Brandt apologized.

14. *New York Times*, August 6, 1941, p. 6.

15. Ibid. The British alliance with the Soviet Union, Hoover and his associates argued, "had dissipated that illusion."

16. Frederick E. Terman memorandum entitled "'Hoover' Poll of Stanford Faculty," February 22, 1980, Frederick E. Terman Papers, Box 1, Stanford University Archives.

17. Stanford faculty petition on "Our Nation's Foreign Policy," August 21, 1941, copy in "Stanford University—HH Poll of Faculty," Post-Presidential Subject File.

18. *Daily Palo Alto Times*, September 17, 1941.

19. Hoover to Ralph H. Lutz, August 29, 1941, Hoover Institution Records, Series F-01, Box 6, Hoover Institution on War, Revolution and Peace (hereinafter HI).

20. *Daily Palo Alto Times*, September 17, 1941. See also *Stanford Daily*, September 25, 1941, pp. 1, 2.

21. *Stanford Daily*, September 25, 1941, p. 1; Hoover to Leonard Ely, September 25, 1941 (plus enclosure: Hoover to the 176 signatories of the petition, September 22, 1941), in Ray Lyman Wilbur Papers, Box 120, HI; *Stanford Daily*, October 2, 1941, p. 1; *San Francisco Chronicle*, October 24, 1941 clipping, in "Stanford University—HH Poll of Faculty, September and October 1941," Post-Presidential Subject File.

22. *Stanford Daily*, October 2, 1941, pp. 1, 2; *New York Times*, October 3, 1941, p. 5.

23. Frederick E. Terman memorandum, February 22, 1980.

24. Lewis M. Terman to his colleagues, September 24, 1941, "Stanford University—HH Poll of Faculty," Post-Presidential Subject File.

25. *New York Times*, October 3, 1941, p. 5.

26. Frederick E. Terman memorandum, February 22, 1980.

27. Ralph H. Lutz to Hoover (plus enclosure), October 13, 1941, Hoover Institution Records, Series F-01, Box 6; "Results of Stanford Faculty Poll on U.S. Foreign Policy" (typed report, October 22, 1941), in "Stanford University—HH Poll of Faculty," Post-Presidential Subject File.

28. Hoover to Max Savelle, October 21, 1941, "Stanford University—HH Poll of Faculty, September and October 1941," Post-Presidential Subject File.

29. "Results of Stanford Faculty Poll on U.S. Foreign Policy"; *San Francisco Chronicle*, October 24, 1941; *Stanford Daily*, October 24, 1941, pp. 1, 2.

30. Among those who gave unqualified responses to the faculty interventionists' survey, the ratio approving Roosevelt's foreign policy measures was 9.53 to 1.

31. Hoover to Lewis M. Terman, October 30, 1941, "Stanford University—HH Poll of Faculty," Post-Presidential Subject File.

32. Hoover to the "Stanford Family," February 26, 1942, Ray Lyman Wilbur Personal Papers, Box 75, Stanford University Archives. In 1940–1941 Hoover had launched a pilot fund drive called "Stanford Refunders." Its success encouraged him to expand the project under the name "Stanford Futures." Ibid.; Hoover to Clarence Lloyd Addleman, [November 9?] 1940, Wilbur Personal Papers, Box 75.

33. Hoover to Mr. and Mrs. Paul C. Edwards, September 8, 1942, Paul C. Edwards Papers, Box 1, Stanford University Archives; L. H. Roseberry to Hoover, September 23, 1942, "Stanford University—Correspondence, 1941–42," Post-Presidential Subject File.

34. Hoover to Vannevar Bush, July 11, 1942, copy in Ray Lyman Wilbur Presidential Papers, Box 118, Stanford University Archives.

35. Donald B. Tresidder to Hoover, December 23, 1941, Donald B. Tresidder Papers, Box 38, Stanford University Archives.

36. Hoover to Tresidder, January 27, 1942, ibid.

37. Tresidder to W. Parmer Fuller, Jr., March 3 and 31, 1942, ibid.; Tresidder to Hoover, March 31, 1942, ibid.; Stanford University Board of Trustees Minutes, June 18, 1942, Stanford University Archives; Peter C. Allen, *Stanford: From the Foothills to the Bay* (Stanford, Calif., 1980), p. 57.

38. M. C. Sloss to Vannevar Bush, December 5, 1941; Leland W. Cutler to Hoover, December 6, 1941. Both in "Cutler, Leland W.," Post-Presidential Individual File, Hoover Papers.

39. Ray Lyman Wilbur, *The Memoirs of Ray Lyman Wilbur* (Stanford, Calif., 1960), p. 584n.

40. Stanford University Board of Trustees Minutes, June 18, 1942.

41. W. Parmer Fuller, Jr. to Hoover, December 18, 1942, "Tresidder, Donald," Post-Presidential Individual File; Hoover telegram to Tresidder, December 21, 1942, ibid. In his telegram urging Tresidder to accept, Hoover told him that he possessed "a combination of administrative experience, of understanding of academic ideals, knowledge of physical sciences, and devotion to Stanford that makes you the one man" to be its president.

42. Donald B. Tresidder to Hoover, January 15, 1943; Hoover to Tresidder, January 19, 1943. Both in "Tresidder, Donald," Post-Presidential Individual File.

43. Tresidder to Hoover, September 20, 1943, Hoover Institution Records, Series F-03; Ralph H. Lutz oral history (1967), p. 29n, HHPL.

44. Hoover to Ray Lyman Wilbur, February 15 and April 25, 1943. Both in Wilbur Personal Papers, Box 35.

45. Hoover to Wilbur, April 25, 1943.

46. Ray Lyman Wilbur remarks at Stanford University memorial services for Lou Henry Hoover, January 14, 1944. Copy in Reprint File, HHPL.

47. Hoover to W. Parmer Fuller, Jr., December 27, 1944, "Fuller, W. Parmer, Jr.," Post-Presidential Individual File.

48. Stanford University Board of Trustees Minutes, February 15, 1945; Donald B. Tresidder to Hoover, February 21, 1945, Hoover Institution Records, Series F-03.

49. Hoover to Ray Lyman Wilbur, December 17, 1941, Hoover Institution Records, Series D-03, Box 156; Hoover to Ralph H. Lutz, December 27, 1941, ibid., Series F-01, Box 6.

50. Hoover to Robert E. Wood, December 17, 1941, Hoover Institution Records, Series D-03, Box 156; Peter Duignan, *The Library of the Hoover Institution on War, Revolution and Peace* (Stanford, Calif., 1985), p. 115.

51. Hoover to Wilbur, December 17, 1941.

52. Ernest Barbour O'Byrne, "The Research Institutes of Stanford University" (Ph.D. dissertation, Stanford University, 1951), p. 95.

53. Duignan, *Library of the Hoover Institution on War, Revolution and Peace*, p. 6; *Annual Report of the President of Stanford University for the Fifty-fourth Academic Year Ending August 31, 1945* (Stanford, Calif., 1945), p. 343.

54. Hoover to Donald B. Tresidder, December 29, 1944, Hoover Institution Records, Series T-16, Box 242A; "Financial Statement—War Library—as of August 15, 1945," ibid., Series F-01, Box 1A. Milbank had contributed to the Hoover Library's collection activities. See "Suggested List of Names for Wall" (typescript, n.d., but ca. May 1945), in Tresidder Papers, Box 11.

55. Duignan, *Library of the Hoover Institution on War, Revolution and Peace*, pp. 6–7.

56. Hoover to Douglas MacArthur, August 27, 1945, Hoover Institution Records, Series F-01, Box 6.

57. Hoover to Howard C. Petersen, September 25, 1946; Petersen to Hoover, October 3, 1946. Both in Hoover Institution Records, Series F-01, Box 2.

58. Duignan, *Library of the Hoover Institution on War, Revolution and Peace*, p. 7.

59. Mrs. Hans von Kaltenborn oral history (1968), p. 16, HHPL.

60. Ray Lyman Wilbur to Hoover, May 8, 1945, "Wilbur, Ray Lyman," Post-Presidential Individual File.

61. Charles B. Burdick, *Ralph H. Lutz and the Hoover Institution* (Stanford, Calif., 1974), p. 176; memorial resolutions for Ralph H. Lutz (1968) and Harold H. Fisher (1976), Faculty File, Stanford University Archives.

62. Hoover to Donald B. Tresidder, September 2, 1944, Hoover Institution Records, Series T-16, Box 242A.

63. Hoover to Tresidder, December 29, 1944, ibid.

64. Ibid.

65. *Annual Report of the President of Stanford University . . . 1945*, p. 343.

66. Hoover memorandum on Harold H. Fisher's report on organization of the Hoover Library, September 1, 1945, Wilbur Personal Papers, Box 35.

67. Ibid.; Fisher to Tresidder, July 1, 1944 (plus two memoranda), Tresidder Papers, Box 11.

68. Fisher memorandum to Tresidder, July 1, 1944.

69. Harold H. Fisher to Tresidder, April 8, 1946, Tresidder Papers, Box 31.

70. Edgar Rickard to Tresidder, March 15, 1946, ibid.

71. Fisher to Tresidder, April 8, 1946.

72. Tresidder to Hoover, August 6, 1946, Tresidder Papers, Box 31; Hoover to Tresidder, September 1, 1946, ibid.; Tresidder to the Stanford University board of trustees, September 5, 1946, ibid.; Stanford University Board of Trustees Minutes, September 19, 1946.

73. Stanford University Board of Trustees Minutes, September 19, 1946.

74. Hoover to Tresidder, September 1, 1946.

75. Tresidder to Edgar Rickard, September 2, 1946, Tresidder Papers, Box 31.

76. Ibid.

77. Harold H. Fisher memorandum to Tresidder, October 3, 1946, Tresidder Papers, Box 11; *Annual Report of the President of Stanford University for the Fifty-sixth Academic Year Ending August 31, 1947* (Stanford, Calif., 1947), p. 382.

78. Hoover to Tresidder, April 17, 1943, "Tresidder, Donald," Post-Presidential Individual File.

79. Hoover telegram to Tresidder, October 9, 1946; Bernice Miller to Tresidder, October 9, 1946; Tresidder to Hoover, October 12, 1946. All in "Tresidder, Donald," Post-Presidential Individual File.

80. Tresidder to Hoover, September 3 and October 1, 1947, both in "Tresidder, Donald," Post-Presidential Individual File.

81. *Stanford Alumni Review* 49 (April 1948): 2.

82. Hoover to Wilbur, February 19 and March 2, 1948, "Wilbur, Ray Lyman," Post-Presidential Individual File; Frederick E. Terman oral history (1970), pp. 16–17, 20–21, HHPL.

83. Paul H. Davis to Hoover, July 8, 1948, "Stanford University—Fund Development," Post-Presidential Subject File.

84. Hoover to Davis, July 10, 1948, ibid.

85. Seelye G. Mudd to Hoover, August 25, 1948, "Stanford University Board of Trustees," Post-Presidential Subject File.

86. Hoover to Ira Lillick, August 27, 1948.

87. Witold S. Sworakowski oral history (1967), p. 22, HHPL.

88. Wilbur to J. E. Wallace Sterling, April 28, 1949, Wilbur Personal Papers, Box 80.

89. *New York Times*, August 6, 1949, p. 15, and August 11, 1949, pp. 1, 3; *Daily Palo Alto Times*, August 11, 1949.

CHAPTER 8

1. *New York Times*, August 11, 1949, p. 3.

2. *Stanford Review* 53 (February 1952): 4.

3. Stanford University press release, February 13, 1961, copy in the appendix to David Packard oral history (1967), Herbert Hoover Presidential Library (hereinafter HHPL).

4. *San Francisco Chronicle*, August 4, 1956, p. 1.

5. Hoover to Eugene C. Eppley, September 19, 1956, "Stanford University, Medical Center," Post-Presidential Subject File, Herbert Hoover Papers, HHPL.

6. Hoover to Lloyd Dinkelspiel, September 7, 1956, ibid.

7. Dinkelspiel to Hoover, October 1, 1956, ibid.

8. Hoover to Dinkelspiel, August 30, 1957, "Hoover Institution—Dinkelspiel Correspondence," Post-Presidential Subject File; Hoover to Dinkelspiel, September 28, 1957, "Stanford University Board of Trustees," ibid.

9. Hoover to Dinkelspiel, September 28, 1957.

10. Hoover to Dinkelspiel, August 30, 1957.

11. Leland W. Cutler to Hoover, September 12, 1957, "Cutler, Leland W.," Post-Presidential Individual File, Hoover Papers; Cutler to Dinkelspiel, October 7, 1957, "Stanford University Board of Trustees," Post-Presidential Subject File; Stanford University Board of Trustees Minutes, September 19, 1957, Stanford University Archives.

12. Stanford University Board of Trustees Minutes, November 11, 1957.

13. Hoover to Dinkelspiel, August 31, 1957, "Hoover Institution—

Dinkelspiel Correspondence," Post-Presidential Subject File; Packard oral history, p. 5. Hoover indicated that a second tower should not be allocated to the Hoover Institution but for some other university purpose.

14. Hoover to Dinkelspiel, August 31, 1957.

15. Harold H. Fisher memorandum to Ray Lyman Wilbur, March 29, 1948, Ray Lyman Wilbur Personal Papers, Box 75, Stanford University Archives; memorial resolution for Harold H. Fisher (1976), Faculty File, Stanford University Archives.

16. Fisher memorial resolution.

17. California, Legislature, *Fourth Report of the Senate Fact-finding Committee on Un-American Activities, 1948: Communist Front Organizations* (Sacramento, Calif., 1948), pp. 328, 351–52.

18. Harold H. Fisher, *America and Russia in the World Community* (Claremont, Calif., 1946). The quotations appear in chapter 8.

19. Ibid., p. 139.

20. S. M. Levitas to George Sokolsky, September 14, 1945, copy in "Sokolsky, George," Post-Presidential Individual File.

21. Harold H. Fisher to Perrin C. Galpin, September 29, 1945, ibid.

22. *New York Times*, December 19, 1946, pp. 1, 24.

23. Alfred Kohlberg to Hoover, December 19, 1946; Hoover to Kohlberg, December 21, 1946. Both in Hoover Institution Records, Series F-01, Box 5, Hoover Institution on War, Revolution and Peace (hereinafter HI).

24. Alfred Kohlberg to Harold H. Fisher, January 27, 1947, enclosed with Kohlberg to Hoover, January 28, 1947, in Hoover Institution Records, Series F-01, Box 5.

25. Easton Rothwell memorandum to Ray Lyman Wilbur, March 31, 1948, Wilbur Personal Papers, Box 75; *Annual Report of the President of Stanford University for the Fifty-sixth Academic Year Ending August 31, 1947* (Stanford, Calif., 1947), p. 396; Witold S. Sworakowski oral history (1967), pp. 11–13, HHPL. For example, Hiss was the executive secretary of the Dumbarton Oaks conference in 1944; Rothwell was the assistant executive secretary.

26. Harold H. Fisher memorandum to Donald B. Tresidder, July 2, 1947, Donald B. Tresidder Papers, Box 11, Stanford University Archives; *Annual Report of the President of Stanford University for the Fifty-seventh Academic Year Ending August 31, 1948* (Stanford, Calif., 1948), p. 499.

27. *Annual Report of the President of Stanford University . . . 1948*, p. 498; Harold D. Lasswell, *The World Revolution of Our Time* (Stanford, Calif., 1951), pp. II–III.

28. This was an acronym for: Revolution and the Development of International Relations.

29. *Annual Report of the President of Stanford University . . . 1948*, p. 499; Harold H. Fisher to Herbert Hoover, October 6, 1948 (plus enclosures), Hoover Institution Records, Series T-02, Box 72, HI; Kenneth Colegrove, "Confidential

Report to Frank Mason Regarding the Hoover Institution" (August 29, 1960), in "Hoover Institution Book—Proposals, Outlines, Notes," Kenneth Colegrove Papers, HHPL; United States Congress, Senate, Committee on the Judiciary, Eighty-second Congress, Second Session, Report No. 2050: *Institute of Pacific Relations* (Washington, D.C., 1952), p. 148 (hereinafter cited as the *McCarran Committee Report*).

30. Fisher memorandum to Wilbur, March 29, 1948; *Annual Report of the President of Stanford University . . . 1948*, p. 498.

31. Fisher memorandum to Wilbur, March 29, 1948; Sworakowski oral history, p. 11.

32. Peter Duignan, *The Library of the Hoover Institution on War, Revolution and Peace* (Stanford, Calif., 1985), p. 8.

33. *Annual Report of the President of Stanford University . . . 1948*, p. 501; Sworakowski oral history, p. 6; interview with Thomas T. Thalken, Iowa City, Iowa, December 15, 1986.

34. Sworakowski oral history, p. 10; *Annual Report of the President of Stanford University . . . 1948*, p. 502; Duignan, *Library of the Hoover Institution on War, Revolution and Peace*, p. 32.

35. Sworakowski oral history, pp. 10–13.

36. Fisher memorandum to Wilbur, March 29, 1948.

37. Rothwell memorandum to Wilbur, March 31, 1948.

38. Edgar Rickard to Ray Lyman Wilbur, April 6, 1948 (plus attachment: a draft letter—prepared by Wilbur?—from Hoover to Fisher); Harold H. Fisher to Wilbur, April 20, 1948. Both in Wilbur Personal Papers, Box 75.

39. Hoover to Fisher, April 10, 1948, Hoover Institution Records, Series T-02, Box 72. Hoover's letter closely resembled the draft (cited in note 38) in the Wilbur Papers.

40. Fisher to Wilbur, April 20, 1948.

41. See Allen Weinstein, *Perjury: The Hiss-Chambers Case* (New York, 1978).

42. Sworakowski oral history, pp. 14–15.

43. Ibid., pp. 21–22.

44. Morris M. Doyle oral history (1970), p. 8, HHPL. The quoted words may be a paraphrase (by Doyle) of Sterling's remark.

45. *New York Times*, June 18, 1950, sec. IV, p. 8.

46. Harold H. Fisher to J. E. Wallace Sterling, February 26, 1951, J. E. Wallace Sterling Papers, Box 42, Stanford University Archives.

47. *McCarran Committee Report*, pp. 223–25.

48. Ibid., p. 223.

49. Robert Conquest, *Kolyma: The Arctic Death Camps* (New York, 1978), p. 212. See generally chapter 8.

For Hoover this controversy had a personal dimension: one of the active noncommunist members of the Institute for Pacific Relations was Ray Lyman Wilbur. When the IPR's hidden dominance by the far left began to be revealed in the late 1940s,

Hoover (he later told a friend) persuaded Wilbur to withdraw—only to have Fisher talk Wilbur back in, and Hoover talk him back out. Thalken interview, December 15, 1986.

Ray Lyman Wilbur's posthumously published *Memoirs* (1960) contain a strong defense of the IPR against its critics. It should be added, however, that Wilbur died in 1949, before the congressional hearings that established the communist/procommunist control of the IPR.

50. Thalken interview, December 15, 1986.

51. Witold S. Sworakowski, typescript chapter (entitled "The Dark Years, 1949–1955") of an unpublished and apparently unfinished history of the Hoover Institution. Copy in Hoover Institution Records, Series T-16, Box 241B, HI. See also a statement by Thomas T. Thalken in chapter 34 of a manuscript by Frank Nye that is to be published by the Herbert Hoover Presidential Library Association.

52. J. E. Wallace Sterling to Fred Wickett, February 5, 1952, copy in "Wickett, Mr. and Mrs. Fred," Post-Presidential Individual File.

53. Wickett, marginal note on ibid.

54. Wickett to Hoover, February 21, 1952, "Wickett, Mr. and Mrs. Fred," Post-Presidential Individual File.

55. Hoover to Wickett, February 21, 1952, ibid.

56. Ralph H. Lutz oral history (1967), pp. 21–23; Lasswell, *World Revolution of Our Time*, p. ii. In the preface to this book (the first in the RADIR series), Harold H. Fisher stated that "neither the Carnegie Corporation nor the Hoover Institute commits itself to the views whose publication they made possible." However, this disclaimer was not included on the page bearing the heading "The Hoover Institute Studies."

57. C. Easton Rothwell to J. E. Wallace Sterling, May 20, 1951, Sterling Papers, Box 42; Sworakowski oral history, p. 21.

58. Hoover to J. E. Wallace Sterling, August 19, 1952, Sterling Papers, Box 42; C. Easton Rothwell, "Some Proposals Concerning the Hoover Institution, Its National Position, and Its Relation to Stanford University" (typescript, n.d. but ca. March 1958), p. 12, Hoover Institution Records, Series T-16, Box 234C, HI.

59. Sworakowski, "The Dark Years"; "Report to the Provost on the Relations of the Hoover Institute and Library and the University; From the Committee on Research and Teaching in International Affairs" (typescript, June 1, 1953), p. 25, copy in Sterling Papers, Box 42; Herbert Hoover, "Memorandum on the Hoover Library for the Advisory Board" (typescript, September 1, 1955), Hoover Institution Records, Series F-01, Box 3, HI.

60. Fisher to Sterling, February 26, 1951, Sterling Papers, Box 42.

61. Sterling, handwritten memorandum attached to ibid.; Sterling to Rothwell, June 14, 1951, Sterling Papers, Box 42.

62. Minutes of the Advisory Board of the Hoover Institute and Library, July 30, 1951, "Hoover Institution on War, Revolution and Peace—Minutes of the Advisory Board, Correspondence 1949–56," Post-Presidential Subject File.

63. Ibid.

64. Ibid.

65. Rothwell to Sterling, May 20, 1951.

66. Inez G. Richardson to Sterling, August 23, 1951, Sterling Papers, Box 42; Rothwell to Sterling, September 22, 1951, ibid.; Fisher to Sterling, March 6, 1952, ibid.

67. Hoover to Sterling, March 9, 1953, Sterling Papers, Box 43.

68. Hoover to Sterling, December 1, 1955, Hoover Institution Records, Series F-01, Box 2.

69. Sterling to Hoover, November 28, 1955, ibid. In 1954 Fisher told Sterling that he would not be upset if Sterling abolished Fisher's title of "chairman" if Sterling thought that this would alter Hoover's critical attitude toward the Hoover Institute and Library. Fisher to Sterling, October 4, 1954, Sterling Papers, Box 42. Sterling evidently declined this offer.

70. Sterling to Fisher, March 19, 1952, Sterling Papers, Box 42; undated note concerning Rothwell's appointment by the Stanford University trustees, April 17, 1952, ibid.; Sworakowski oral history, pp. 28–29.

71. Sworakowski oral history, pp. 21–22.

72. Rothwell to Hoover, n.d. (but sometime in 1953), copy in Sterling Papers, Box 42.

73. See Paul R. Farnsworth to Sterling, June 11, 1952, ibid.

74. Paul R. Farnsworth et al., "Preliminary Report to President Sterling on the Hoover Institute and Library" (typescript, n.d. but June 1952), attached to ibid.

75. Sworakowski, "The Dark Years."

76. Ralph H. Lutz to Hoover, April 12, 1952, Hoover Institution Records, Series F-01, Box 6.

77. Robert C. North, *Moscow and Chinese Communists* (Stanford, Calif., 1953); Colegrove, "Confidential Report to Frank Mason."

78. North, *Moscow and Chinese Communists*, chap. 11.

79. Hoover telegram to Senator Joseph McCarthy, November 5, 1952, "McCarthy, Joseph," Post-Presidential Individual File.

80. North, *Moscow and Chinese Communists*, p. 285.

81. The conservative political scientist Kenneth Colegrove later informed one of Hoover's confidants that North's book was a biased one that minimized the brutality and deceit with which the Communists conquered China and repeatedly disparaged Chiang Kai-shek. Colegrove, "Confidential Report to Frank Mason."

82. North, *Moscow and Chinese Communists*, pp. vii–viii.

83. Rothwell to Sterling, n.d. (but 1953), filed with Rothwell to Hoover, n.d., cited in note 72.

84. Expenditure chart attached to the minutes of the annual meeting of the Advisory Board of the Hoover Institute and Library, August 4, 1952, "Hoover Institution on War, Revolution and Peace—Minutes of the Advisory Board, Correspon-

dence, 1949–56," Post-Presidential Subject File; Hoover Institute and Library statement of funds received and expenditures from 1919 to August 31, 1954, copy in Sterling Papers, Box 42.

85. Excerpt from the will of William Robertson Coe; copy in the possession of the author.

86. Ibid.; interview with W. Glenn Campbell, Hoover Institution, Stanford University, August 1, 1986. For Coe's obituary, see *New York Times*, May 16, 1955, p. 33.

87. Hoover, "Memorandum on the Hoover Library for the Advisory Board" (September 1, 1955).

88. Report on the meeting of the Advisory Board of the Hoover Institute and Library, August 1, 1955, "Hoover Institution on War, Revolution and Peace—Minutes of the Advisory Board, Correspondence, 1949–56"; "Hoover Institute and Library Program Report, August 1, 1955 to March 1, 1956," ibid.; Sworakowski, "The Dark Years."

89. Hoover, "Memorandum on the Hoover Library for the Advisory Board" (September 1, 1955); Rothwell, "Some Proposals Concerning the Hoover Institution."

90. Hoover to Sterling, September 13, 1955, Sterling Papers, Box 42.

91. Sterling telegram to Hoover, September 16, 1955, ibid.

92. Hoover to Sterling, September 23, 1955, Hoover Institution Records, Series F-01, Box 2.

93. Ibid.; Hoover to Sterling, November 28, 1952, Sterling Papers, Box 43; Hoover, "Memorandum on the Hoover Library for the Advisory Board"; Hoover to Lloyd Dinkelspiel, November 21, 1957, "Dinkelspiel, Lloyd," Post-Presidential Individual File.

94. Hoover, "Memorandum on the Hoover Library for the Advisory Board"; Thalken interview.

95. Sterling to Hoover, October 17, 1955, Sterling Papers, Box 42.

96. Hoover to Arch W. Shaw, September 29, 1955; Hoover to Sterling, October 19, 1955; Hoover to A. C. Mattei, December 5, 1955; Mattei to Hoover, January 6, 1956. All in Hoover Institution Records, Series F-01, Box 2.

97. Hoover to Sterling, October 19, 1955.

98. Draft in Hoover Institution Records, Series F-01, Box 2. Hoover's first installment was in the form of 250 shares of stock in a company in which he had investments. Hoover to the Stanford University Board of Trustees, October 18, 1955, Hoover Institution Records, Series F-01, Box 2.

99. Hoover to Sterling, December 12, 1955; Joseph Pew, Jr. to Sterling, December 21, 1955. Both in Hoover Institution Records, Series F-01, Box 2.

100. Sworakowski, "The Dark Years."

101. "Hoover Institute and Library Program Report, August 1, 1955 to March 1, 1956."

102. Ibid.; Rothwell, report to the meeting of the Advisory Board of the Hoover Institute and Library, July 30, 1956, "Hoover Institution on War, Revolution and Peace—Minutes of the Advisory Board, 1956–57," Post-Presidential Subject File; Hoover Institution press release, March 6, 1957, Hoover Institution Records, Series T-16, Box 234C; Sworakowski oral history, pp. 5–6, 8–9.

103. Sworakowski oral history, p. 13.

104. Report on the meeting of the Hoover Library and Institute Advisory Board, July 30, 1956, "Hoover Institution on War, Revolution and Peace—Minutes of the Advisory Board, Correspondence, 1949–56," Post-Presidential Subject File. See also: Rothwell to Hoover, October 18, 1956, Hoover Institution Records, Series T-16, Box 241B. Also: [Hoover], "The Basis for Presentation of History by the Hoover Institution" (typescript, n.d. but ca. 1958), Sterling Papers, Box 42.

105. *Palo Alto Times*, September 16, 1955.

106. Hoover to Lloyd Dinkelspiel, September 21, 1955 (plus enclosure), "Hoover Institution—Dinkelspiel Correspondence," Post-Presidential Subject File. For other conservative critiques of the Fund for the Republic, see various clippings in "Fund for the Republic," Post-Presidential Subject File, Hoover Papers.

107. Dinkelspiel merely acknowledged receiving Hoover's material about the fund. Dinkelspiel to Hoover, October 17, 1955, "Hoover Institution—Dinkelspiel Correspondence," Post-Presidential Subject File, Hoover Papers.

108. Hoover telegram to Sterling, July 1, 1957, Sterling Papers, Box 42; Stanford University Board of Trustees Minutes, July 18, 1957.

109. Hoover telegram to Sterling, July 1, 1957; report of the annual meeting of the Advisory Board of the Hoover Institution on War, Revolution and Peace, July 29, 1957, "Hoover Institution on War, Revolution and Peace—Minutes of the Advisory Board, 1957–58," Post-Presidential Subject File.

110. Hoover telegram to Sterling, July 1, 1957.

111. Hoover Institution press release, July 18, 1957, Hoover Institution Records, Series T-16, Box 242A.

112. Hoover statement about the Hoover Institution, October 31, 1957, in Hoover Institution Records, Series F-01, Box 4.

113. Hoover to William K. Whiteford, November 30, 1957, "Hoover Institution on War, Revolution and Peace—Correspondence," Post-Presidential Subject File, Hoover Papers; copy also in Hoover Institution Records, Series F-01, Box 4.

114. Rothwell to Hoover, October 18, 1956.

115. Witold S. Sworakowski to Allan Hoover, June 14, 1958, Hoover Institution Records, Series T-16, Box 234C.

116. Rothwell to Hoover, October 18, 1956.

117. Report of the meeting of the Hoover Institute and Library Advisory Board, July 30, 1956.

118. Report of the annual meeting of the Advisory Board of the Hoover Institution, July 29, 1957.

119. Sworakowski to Allan Hoover, June 14, 1958; Sworakowski, "Remarks to Some Proposals Concerning the Hoover Institution" (n.d. but ca. July 4, 1958), in Hoover Institution Records, Series T-16, Box 234C; Sworakowski, "Note on the Project 'The Soviet Union as a Treaty Partner' " (January 20, 1959), ibid.; Sworakowski, "Note on the Project 'The Soviet Union as a Treaty Partner' " (October 20, 1959), ibid.

120. List of members of the Advisory Board of the Hoover Institute and Library on War, Revolution and Peace, March 2, 1956, "Hoover Institution on War, Revolution and Peace—Minutes of the Advisory Board, 1955–56"; Rothwell report to the Advisory Board, July 30, 1956; report on the meeting of Hoover Institute and Library Advisory Board, July 30, 1956; Rothwell, report to the Hoover Institute and Library Advisory Board, January 23, 1957, "Hoover Institution on War, Revolution and Peace—Minutes of the Advisory Board, 1956–57," Post-Presidential Subject File.

121. Hoover to Ralph H. Lutz, March 17, 1958, Hoover Institution Records, Series F-01, Box 6; Rothwell, "Some Proposals Concerning the Hoover Institution" (1958).

122. Hoover to Lutz, March 17, 1958.

123. Sworakowski oral history, pp. 16–18; Thalken interview; Rothwell to Sterling, October 10, 1958, Sterling Papers, Box 43. Expenditures on the library of the Hoover Institution had increased from $180,122 in 1955–1956 to $237,372 in 1957–1958, only to fall to $217,040 in 1958–1959. See list of library expenditures of the Hoover Institution, 1950–1951 to 1967–1968, Hoover Institution Records, Series T-16.

124. Thalken interview. According to Thalken, Fisher and Rothwell "had filled the Hoover Institution staff with left-wing liberals."

125. Rothwell to Hoover, n.d. (1953).

126. Rothwell to Sterling, October 10, 1958. Rothwell strongly disputed Hoover's claim.

127. Report on the meeting of the Hoover Institute and Library Advisory Board, July 30, 1956; report of the annual meeting of the Advisory Board of the Hoover Institution, July 29, 1957. See also Felix Morley to Arthur Kemp, October 12, 1958, and Kemp's undated reply, both in "Morley, Felix," Post-Presidential Individual File.

128. Hoover to Lawrence Richey, June 3, 1957, "McCarthy, Joseph R.," Post-Presidential Individual File. For other correspondence concerning Hoover's solicitation effort, see various items in this folder.

129. Hoover to Lloyd Dinkelspiel, November 21, 1957, "Stanford University Board of Trustees," Post-Presidential Subject File. The content of Hoover's remarks was not new (see his letter to Sterling, November 28, 1952, cited in note 93), but its timing was significant.

130. Bernice Miller, *What Herbert Hoover has done for Stanford University* (booklet, November 1957), copy in "Stanford University," Post-Presidential Subject File.

131. *New York Times*, October 30, 1957, p. 10.

132. Ralph H. Lutz to Hoover, November 28, 1957, Hoover Institution Records, Series F-01, Box 6.

133. Hoover to Lutz, November 29, 1957, ibid.

134. Rothwell to Hoover, October 18, 1956.

135. Sworakowski oral history, p. 26.

136. Hoover to Sterling, August 30, 1957, Sterling Papers, Box 43.

137. Sterling to Hoover, September 24, 1957, ibid.

138. Hoover telegram to Sterling, November 10, 1957, ibid.

139. Sterling to Hoover, November 27, 1957 and May 14, 1958, ibid.

140. Hoover to Sterling, February 23, 1958, ibid.

141. Hoover to Sterling, April 14, 1958, ibid.

142. Hoover to Sterling, May 4, 1958, ibid.

143. Hoover to Sterling, May 23, 1958, ibid.

144. Hoover to Sterling, February 23, 1958; Lloyd Dinkelspiel to Hoover, March 20, 1958, "Stanford University—Board of Trustees, Correspondence, 1958–63," Post-Presidential Subject File; [Hoover], "The Basis for Presentation of History by the Hoover Institution."

145. Sworakowski memorandum, May 20, 1958; Sworakowski to Allan Hoover, June 14, 1958 and July 5, 1958. All in Hoover Institution Records, Series T-16, Box 234C.

146. Hoover, "Mr. Hoover's Recommendations as to the Management and Policies of the Hoover Institution" (typescript, April 9, 1959), enclosed with Hoover to David Packard, April 10, 1959, Hoover Institution Records, Series F-03, HI.

147. Rothwell, "Some Proposals Concerning the Hoover Institution" (cited in note 58).

148. Sworakowski, "Remarks to Some Proposals Concerning the Hoover Institution" (cited in note 119); Sworakowski oral history, pp. 27–28.

149. Sworakowski, "Remarks to Some Proposals Concerning the Hoover Institution"; Sworakowski to Allan Hoover, July 5, 1958.

150. *New York Times*, April 19, 1958, p. 9, April 20, 1958, p. 12, and May 4, 1958, p. 1.

151. Fred A. Wickett to Hoover, September 26, 1958, "Wickett, Mr. and Mrs. Fred," Post-Presidential Individual File.

152. Hoover to Wickett, October 2, 1958, ibid.

153. Hoover to James B. Black, August 25, 1958, excerpt quoted in [Hoover], "The Relation of the Hoover Institution to Stanford University" (typescript, n.d., but ca. October 1960), in Hoover Institution Records, Series F-01, Box 4.

154. Hoover, "The Basis for Presentation of History by the Hoover Institution" (cited in note 104).

155. Sworakowski oral history, pp. 17, 18, 21.

156. Nye, unpublished manuscript (cited in note 51), chapter 33.

157. Thalken interview.

158. Clippings from *San Francisco Examiner*, April 5, 1959, and *San Francisco Chronicle*, April 6, 1959, in Sterling Papers, Box 43.

159. Thalken interview; Sterling to Hoover, July 24, 1958, Sterling Papers, Box 43. Sterling told Hoover that the donation of some of the memorabilia to Iowa was "wonderful."

160. Rothwell to Sterling, October 10, 1958.

161. Hoover to Sterling, October 27 and 30, 1958 (two letters), Sterling Papers, Box 43.

162. Hoover to Sterling, October 27, 1958.

163. Ibid.; Hoover to Sterling, October 30, 1958.

164. [Hoover], "The Relation of the Hoover Institution to Stanford University"; Fred A. Wickett to Bernice Miller, October 15, 1958, "Wickett, Mr. and Mrs. Fred," Post-Presidential Individual File.

165. [Hoover], "The Relation of the Hoover Institution to Stanford University."

166. Stanford University Board of Trustees Minutes, November 20, 1958.

167. Hoover to William C. Mullendore, November 28, 1958, "Mullendore, William C.," Post-Presidential Individual File; Hoover to Jeremiah Milbank, December 6, 1958, "Milbank, Jeremiah," ibid.

168. Hoover to Sterling, January 2, 1959, Sterling Papers, Box 43.

169. Sworakowski oral history, pp. 25–26; Sworakowski, report ("Summary of Operations") to the Advisory Board of the Hoover Institution, August 3, 1959, "Hoover Institution on War, Revolution and Peace—Minutes of the Advisory Board, 1958–59," Post-Presidential Subject File.

170. Hoover to Sterling, January 2, 1959.

CHAPTER 9

1. Herbert Hoover to J. E. Wallace Sterling, October 27, 1958, J. E. Wallace Sterling Papers, Box 43, Stanford University Archives.

2. Hoover to Sterling, January 3, 1959, ibid.; Hoover, "Appendix no. 4" enclosed with Hoover to David Packard, April 12, 1959, Hoover Institution Records, Series F-03, Hoover Institution on War, Revolution and Peace (hereinafter HI).

3. Hoover to Sterling, January 3, 1959.

4. David Packard to Hoover, January 23, 1959, copy in Sterling Papers, Box 42.

5. Sterling to Hoover, January 13, 1959, ibid., Box 43.

6. Witold S. Sworakowski to Allan Hoover, February 28, 1959 and March 7, 1959; Allan Hoover to Sworakowski, March 17, 1959. All in Hoover Institution Records, Series T-16, Box 234C, HI.

7. Sworakowski to Allan Hoover, February 28, 1959; C. Easton Rothwell to Sterling, March 19, 1959, Sterling Papers, Box 42. Rothwell's resignation was effective May 31, 1959, but he left active duty on April 1.

8. Sterling to Hoover, April 1, 1959, Sterling Papers, Box 43; *Stanford Daily*, April 7, 1959.

9. Hoover to Sterling, April 4, 1959, Sterling Papers, Box 43.

10. Sterling to Hoover, April 11, 1959, ibid.

11. Ibid.

12. Interview with Thomas T. Thalken, Iowa City, Iowa, December 15, 1986.

13. *New York Times*, April 5, 1959, p. 78; clipping from *San Francisco Examiner*, April 5, 1959, in Sterling Papers, Box 43.

14. Clipping from *San Francisco Examiner*, April 6, 1959, in Sterling Papers, Box 43.

15. See chapter 34, p. 6, of an unpublished manuscript by Frank Nye to be published by the Herbert Hoover Presidential Library Association.

16. Arnold G. Stifel, April 13, 1959, "Stifel, Arnold G.," Post-Presidential Individual File, Herbert Hoover Papers, Herbert Hoover Presidential Library (hereinafter HHPL).

17. Hoover to Arnold G. Stifel, April 16, 1959, Hoover Institution Records, Steries T-16, Box 242A.

18. Hoover to David Packard, April 8, 1959, ibid., Series F-03; Hoover to Sterling, April 15, 1959, Sterling Papers, Box 43; David Packard to Hoover, April 17, 1959, copy in Sterling Papers, Box 43; David Packard oral history (1967), pp. 1–3, HHPL.

19. In the opinion of one staunch Hoover man, Sterling "was certainly counteracting and trying to eliminate whatever Hoover was doing." Witold S. Sworakowski oral history (1967), p. 23, HHPL.

20. See [Hoover], "General Comment and Summary" (typescript, n.d., but probably May 1959), Hoover Institution Records, Series F-03. Hoover's document was an analysis of a letter by President Sterling of April 29, 1959 containing Sterling's proposals for the reorganization of the Hoover Institution.

21. Hoover to Fred A. Wickett, May 11, 1959, "Wickett, Mr. and Mrs. Fred," Post-Presidential Individual File.

22. Stanford University Board of Trustees Minutes, May 21, 1959, Stanford University Archives; copy in "Hoover Institution on War, Revolution and Peace— Minutes of the Advisory Board, 1958–59," Post-Presidential Subject File, Hoover Papers.

23. Packard oral history, p. 22; Thomas P. Pike oral history (1968), p. 14, HHPL.

24. George G. Montgomery oral history (1971), p. 6. Montgomery noted that the Hoover Institution was not comparable to such university facilities as the medical school or the school of engineering. "The university hadn't financed it and the univer-

sity didn't establish it and the buildings were not built by the university—it was an organization Mr. Hoover put here because of his affection for the University and because he thought this was the proper location for it."

25. Arthur Kemp oral history (1968), p. 81, HHPL.

26. Pike oral history, pp. 14, 15.

27. "Resolutions Prepared by Mr. Herbert Hoover and Submitted to David Packard on May 3, 1959 in New York City" (typescript), in Hoover Institution Records, Series F-03.

28. Trustees' resolution of May 21, 1959, in Stanford University Board of Trustees Minutes, May 21, 1959.

29. Hoover to Arnold G. Stifel, June 11, 1959, "Stifel, Arnold G.," Post-Presidential Individual File.

30. [Hoover], "Proposals as to the Hoover Institution" (July 22, 1959), in "Hoover Institution on War, Revolution and Peace—Minutes of the Advisory Board, 1957—59," Post-Presidential Subject File.

31. Stanford University Board of Trustees Minutes, September 17, 1959; Hoover to his fellow trustees, June 2, 1960, copy in Paul C. Edwards Papers, Stanford University Archives.

32. Northcutt Ely to Hoover, April 11, 1961, Hoover Papers.

33. For a clue to Hoover's attitude see: Fred A. Wickett to Hoover, May 3, 1959, and Hoover to Wickett, May 11, 1959. Both in "Wickett, Mr. and Mrs. Fred," Post-Presidential Individual File.

34. Peter S. Stern, "Cold War Scholarship," *The Nation* 209 (September 1, 1969): 177. See also Philip Rhinelander memorandum to Sterling, October 28, 1959, Sterling Papers, Box 42.

35. Raymond Moley oral history (1967), pp. 24—25, HHPL.

36. Minutes of the trustees' special committee on the Hoover Institution, October 15, 1959, incorporated in the Stanford University Board of Trustees Minutes, October 15, 1959.

37. Stanford University Board of Trustees Minutes, November 19, 1959; interview with W. Glenn Campbell at the Hoover Institution, Stanford University, August 1, 1986. Campbell recalled that Sterling's welcome to him upon his arrival was a distinctly unenthusiastic one. But the next day Sterling indicated that he did want Campbell to come to the Hoover Institution. (Sterling, of course, was under a virtual order from the trustees to offer Campbell the directorship.)

38. Campbell interview; Otis Pease memorandum to Philip Rhinelander and Albert Bowker, June 13, 1961, Sterling Papers, Box 42.

39. Arnold J. Zurcher to Hoover, October 13, 1959, copy in Sterling Papers, Box 52. The grant was in five annual installments of $50,000 each.

40. Hoover to Jeremiah Milbank, November 21, 1959, "Milbank, Jeremiah," Post-Presidential Individual File.

41. Hoover to Sterling, March 20, 1960, Hoover Institution Records, Series F-01, Box 2, HI.

42. *The Hoover Institution on War, Revolution and Peace, Stanford, California* (booklet, n.d.), copy in Hoover Institution Records, Series F-01, Box 3.

43. *Stanford Daily*, March 30, 1960, p. 2; Sterling to Hoover, April 14, 1960, Hoover Institution Records, Series T-16, Box 241C.

44. Stanford University Board of Trustees Minutes, March 17, 1960. The trustees' resolution was printed in the *Stanford Daily*, March 30, 1960, p. 2.

45. Curiously, the trustees' resolution of March 17, 1960 claimed that Hoover's 1959 statement of purpose was prefatory to "the resolutions on operating policies." In fact, the trustees' May 21, 1959 document was a *single* resolution, and Hoover's statement appeared in Paragraph One. Formally, at least, Hoover's statement was on par with the subsequent paragraphs that formulated the institution's operating policies.

46. *Stanford Daily*, March 29, 1960, p. 1.

47. Ibid., March 30, 1960, p. 2.

48. For comments by various Stanford professors, see *Stanford Daily*, March 30, April 1, 4, 1960.

49. *Palo Alto Times*, March 30, 1960, p. 17; *San Francisco Examiner*, March 31, 1960.

50. "Mr. Hoover Leaves His Mark," *New Republic* 142 (May 2, 1960): 5.

51. Ralph H. Lutz to Thomas T. Thalken, April 3, 1960; copy supplied to the author by Mr. Thalken.

52. John K. Stewart oral history (1967), p. 27, HHPL.

53. Sworakowski oral history, pp. 23–24.

54. Sterling statement to the Academic Council, April 1, 1960, in Minutes of the Stanford University Academic Council, Stanford University Archives.

55. Sterling remarks to Witold S. Sworakowski, March 31, 1960, recalled in Sworakowski oral history, pp. 24–25.

56. Sterling statement to the Academic Council, April 1, 1960.

57. Thalken interview; memoranda by Thalken supplied to the author.

58. Minutes of the Stanford University Academic Council, April 1, 1960.

59. Hoover to Ben C. Moreell, April 2, 1960, quoted in Ben C. Moreell oral history (ca. 1967), p. 53, HHPL; Moreell oral history, pp. 52–53.

60. Hoover to Sterling, April 18, 1960, Sterling Papers, Box A15.

61. Sworakowski oral history, p. 25.

62. Hoover to his fellow trustees, June 2, 1960, copy in Paul C. Edwards Papers, Box 1, Stanford University Archives.

63. Professor Gordon Wright et al. to Professor E. R. Hilgard, chairman, Advisory Board, Stanford University, May 6, 1960, in the Minutes of the Stanford University Academic Council.

64. Stanford University Board of Trustees Minutes, May 19, 1960; "Report to the Academic Council from the Advisory Board" (n.d. but ca. July 5, 1960), in the Minutes of the Stanford University Academic Council.

65. Hoover to his fellow trustees, June 2, 1960.

66. Hoover to Ralph H. Lutz, June 14, 1960, Hoover Institution Records, Series F-01, Box 6.

67. Stanford University Board of Trustees Minutes, June 16, 1960.

68. Ibid.

69. "Report to the Academic Council from the Advisory Board" (n.d. but ca. July 5, 1960); Minutes of the Stanford University Academic Council, January 6, 1961.

70. Hoover to W. Glenn Campbell, February 6, 1961, Hoover Papers.

71. Thalken interview; Sworakowski oral history, p. 23. See also Kenneth Colegrove, "Confidential Report to Frank Mason Regarding the Hoover Institution" (August 29, 1960), in "Hoover Institution Book—Proposals, Outlines, Notes," Kenneth Colegrove Papers, HHPL.

72. Hoover to Frederick E. Terman, November 10, 1960, Frederick E. Terman Papers, Box 1, Stanford University Archives.

73. Hoover to Lewis L. Strauss, March 15, 1961 ("Letter No. 2"), Hoover Papers.

74. Hoover to W. Glenn Campbell, February 6, 1961.

75. Frank Nye manuscript, chapter 3 (cited in note 15).

76. Hoover to Franklin Floete (Administrator, General Services Administration), December 15, 1960, "Deed of Gift," Hoover Papers. Hoover's offer was subject to a number of conditions and restrictions upon access to his papers.

77. Franklin Floete to Hoover, December 30, 1960, ibid.

78. Hoover himself had acknowledged this in his June 2, 1960 letter to his fellow trustees (cited in note 62).

79. Hoover's attorney later argued that because of subsequent unresolved differences between Hoover and Sterling over the terms of this gift (as noted earlier in the text), the transfer could be regarded as never having been completed. Northcutt Ely to Hoover, April 11, 1961, Hoover Papers.

80. Campbell interview.

81. Hoover to Strauss, March 15, 1961 ("Letter No. 2").

82. Ibid., Hoover to Strauss, March 15, 1961 (a separate letter), Hoover Papers; Hoover to Strauss, June 20, 1961, ibid.

83. W. Glenn Campbell to Hoover, March 30, 1961, Hoover Papers.

84. Hoover to Thomas P. Pike, March 24, 1961 (plus enclosure: "Memorandum No. 2"); Hoover to Northcutt Ely, May 5, 1961; Hoover to Strauss, June 20, 1961; Ely to Hoover, August 22, 1961. All in Hoover Papers.

85. Hoover to Pike, March 24, 1961 (plus enclosure).

86. Stanford University Board of Trustees Minutes, April 20, 1961; Thomas P. Pike to Hoover, April 25, 1961, Hoover Papers.

87. Hoover to Ely, May 5, 1961; Stanford University Board of Trustees Minutes, May 18, 1961.

88. Stanford University Board of Trustees Minutes, May 18, 1961; Robert Minge Brown to Northcutt Ely, May 19, 1961, Hoover Papers; Thomas P. Pike to Hoover, May 22, 1961, ibid.

89. Brown to Ely, May 19, 1961.

90. PACE was an acronym for "Plan of Action for a Challenging Era."

91. Hoover telegram to the announcement luncheon for Stanford's PACE campaign, April 18, 1961, "PACE Program," Post-Presidential Subject File.

92. *New York Times*, July 23, 1961, p. 39.

93. Stewart oral history, pp. 17–25.

94. Dudley Swim to Hoover, July 10, 1961, "Swim, Dudley," Post-Presidential Individual File.

95. Hoover to Dudley Swim, July 20, 1961, ibid.

96. Hoover remarks at the Stanford PACE dinner, July 20, 1961, copy in "Stanford University—Fund Development," Post-Presidential Subject File.

97. Thalken interview. Thalken said: "Hoover had a love for Stanford University that defied logic."

98. Stewart oral history, p. 25.

99. Dwight L. Wilbur oral history (1967), p. 17, HHPL. At the PACE dinner on July 20, 1961, after describing how he had been able to obtain a Stanford education, Hoover said, "With that background, can any of you wonder at my devotion to Stanford, with its Founders and its traditions for its unending kindness?"

100. Campbell interview.

101. Hoover to Thomas P. Pike, May 1, 1962, Hoover Papers.

102. Stanford University Board of Trustees Minutes, May 17, 1962; Thomas P. Pike to Hoover, May 23, 1962, Hoover Papers.

103. Packard oral history, p. 18.

104. Hoover tape recording to the "Friends of Stanford," May 15, 1962, Public Statements File, Hoover Papers.

105. Telephone conversation with W. Glenn Campbell, February 13, 1987.

106. Campbell interview; Stanford University press release, 1986, concerning the Keck Science Building (copy in the possession of the author).

107. Stanford University Board of Trustees Minutes, January 19, 1961.

108. Ibid., November 15, 1962.

109. Ibid., April 18, 1963; *Palo Alto Times*, March 6, 1963; Hoover to Morris Doyle, March 8, 1963, Board of Trustees Supporting Documents, Box 30, Stanford University Archives.

110. Packard oral history, p. 15.

111. Sworakowski oral history, p. 32.

112. Ibid., p. 30; *Stanford Daily*, October 10, 1967, p. 1.

113. Stanford University press release, July 23, 1964, Sterling Papers, Box 42.

114. David Packard to Hoover, April 28, 1964, "Packard, David," Post-Presidential Individual File.

115. Stanford University News Service press release, April 29, 1964 (for release on May 1, 1964), copy in "Hoover Institution on War, Revolution and Peace," Post-Presidential Subject File.

CHAPTER 10

1. Stanford University News Service press release, April 29, 1964 (for release on May 1, 1964), copy in "Hoover Institution on War, Revolution and Peace," Post-Presidential Subject File, Herbert Hoover Papers, Herbert Hoover Presidential Library (hereinafter HHPL).

2. "He probably did more for Stanford University than anyone else, with the exception of the founders." Dwight L. Wilbur oral history (1967), p. 17, HHPL. See also Morris M. Doyle oral history (1970), p. 7, HHPL.

3. Duncan Aikman, "Hoover-Conscious Stanford," *Outlook and Independent* 156 (November 26, 1930): 496–98, 516.

4. Herbert Hoover, undated autobiographical fragment. This source was once at HHPL but has not recently been located. I have relied on a partial verbatim transcript of the document courteously provided to me by Professor Craig Lloyd, a researcher who did see the document and made notes on it several years ago.

Index